Williams-Ford Texas A&M Military History Series

A SEARCH FOR STRATEGY

BRITISH-AMERICAN MILITARY
COLLABORATION IN 1942

JOHN F. SHORTAL

Texas A&M University Press
College Station

Copyright © 2025 by John F. Shortal
All rights reserved
First edition

∞ This paper meets the requirements of ANSI/NISO Z39.48-1992 (Permanence of Paper).
Binding materials have been chosen for durability.

Library of Congress Cataloging-in-Publication Data

Names: Shortal, John F., 1951– author
Title: A search for strategy : British-American military collaboration in 1942 / John F. Shortal.
Other titles: British-American military collaboration in 1942
Description: College Station : Texas A&M University Press, [2025] | Series: Williams-Ford Texas A&M University military history series | Includes bibliographical references and index.
Identifiers: LCCN 2025000037 (print) | LCCN 2025000038 (ebook) | ISBN 9781648433054 hardcover | ISBN 9781648433061 ebook
Subjects: LCSH: Combined Chiefs of Staff (U.S. and Great Britain) | World War, 1939-1945—United States | World War, 1939-1945—Great Britain | Military planning—United States—History—20th century | Military Planning—Great Britain—History—20th century | United States—Military Relations—Great Britain | Great Britain—Military relations—United States | Combined operations (Military science)—History—20th century | Strategy—History—20th century | BISAC: HISTORY / Wars & Conflicts / World War II / European Theater | HISTORY / Wars & Conflicts / World War II / General
Classification: LCC D769.25 .S64 2025 (print) | LCC D769.25 (ebook) | DDC 940.54/012—dc23/eng/20250311
LC record available at https://lccn.loc.gov/2025000037
LC ebook record available at https://lccn.loc.gov/2025000038

Cover: Meeting of Allied leaders, 1943. Front row: Mackenzie King, Franklin Roosevelt, and Winston Churchill. Back row: Gen. Henry Arnold, Air Marshal Charles Portal, Gen. Alan Brooke, Adm. Ernest King, Field Marshal John Dill, Gen. George Marshall, Adm. Dudley Pound, and Adm. William Leahy (courtesy of the George C. Marshall Foundation, Lexington, Virginia, USA)

For Pam, my best friend and greatest supporter

CONTENTS

List of Illustrations ix

Key Players xiii

Acknowledgments... xvii

Introduction I

Chapter 1.
Allies Meet after Pearl Harbor:
      December–January 1942 15

Chapter 2.
Two Colonies:
      Malaya and the Philippines, January and February 1942 .. 34

Chapter 3.
Dispersion Unchecked:
      March 1942 62

Chapter 4.
A Tentative Agreement on an Offensive against Germany:
      April 1942 89

Chapter 5.
Second Thoughts on a Second Front:
      May 1942 112

Chapter 6.
Sledgehammer, Gymnast, and the Second Washington Conference:
      June 1942 126

Chapter 7.
Churchill and Roosevelt Give Guidance:
    July 1942 154
Chapter 8.
Aftermath 186
Notes 209
Select Bibliography 241
Index   249

ILLUSTRATIONS

Figures

Figure 1.
President Roosevelt signing the Lend-Lease bill, March 1941 8

Figure 2.
Battleship Row, 7 December 1941, after Japanese attack 15

Figure 3.
Ford Island and ships offshore 16

Figure 4.
British military chiefs with Winston Churchill 18

Figure 5.
Admiral Stark's luncheon at the Arcadia Conference 21

Figure 6.
Gen. George Catlett Marshall, US Army chief of staff 23

Figure 7.
Lt. Gen. Henry H. "Hap" Arnold at War Department Munitions
    Building 26

Figure 8.
Surrender table at the Ford Motor Factory 43

Figure 9.
Gen. Douglas MacArthur and Manuel Quezon 51

Figure 10.
Gen. Douglas MacArthur with Maj. Gen. Jonathan Wainwright .. 53

LIST OF ILLUSTRATIONS

Figure 11.
Adm. Ernest King 59

Figure 12.
General Stilwell marches out of Burma 65

Figure 13.
Gen. Alan Brooke 73

Figure 14.
Combined Chiefs of Staff meet in the Public Health Building in
    Washington, DC 78

Figure 15.
Gen. George Marshall; John G. Winant, US ambassador to Great
    Britain; and Harry Hopkins 105

Figure 16.
Doolittle raid on Japan 110

Figure 17.
Gen. Jonathan Wainwright broadcasts his surrender message ... 113

Figure 18.
Pres. Franklin Roosevelt, Field Marshal John Dill, Gen. George
    Marshall, Capt. John McCrea, and Adm. Ernest King
    reviewing parade 119

Figure 19.
V. M. Molotov in Washington, DC 121

Figure 20.
Pres. Franklin Roosevelt, Gen. George Marshall, and Adm. Ernest
    King review Memorial Day Parade 127

Figure 21.
Japanese aircraft carrier *Hiryu* burning 128

Figure 22.
Gen. Albert Wedemeyer and Gen. Hastings Ismay 146

Figure 23.
Winston Churchill at Fort Jackson, SC 150

Figure 24.
Harry Hopkins confers with Gen. George C. Marshall and Adm.
   Ernest J. King 169

Figure 25.
Gen. Dwight D. Eisenhower, Allied commander in North Africa . 182

Figure 26.
Adm. William D. Leahy, USN 183

Figure 27.
US Marine Corps M2A4 Stuart light tank, hoisted from USS
   Alchiba into an LCM landing craft 191

Figure 28.
North Africa Invasion 202

Figure 29.
Meeting of Allied leaders 207

Maps

Map 1.
South Pacific lines of communication to Australia 31

Map 2.
Japanese invasion of Malaya, 1941–42 41

Map 3.
The Philippines, 8 December 1941–8 January 1942 50

Map 4.
Bataan, January–April 1942 54

Map 5.
Burma, 1942 63

Map 6.
Japanese conquest of Burma, April–May 1942 67

Map 7.
Japanese advance into the Solomons–New Guinea Area,
    January–July 1942 77

Map 8.
Pacific and adjacent theaters, May 1942 115

Map 9.
Lines of communication in French North Africa 178–179

Map 10.
Operation Torch, November 1942 196–197

KEY PLAYERS

British and American Leaders, 1942

The British

Gen. Sir Harold Alexander:
    Initially general officer commading British forces in Burma. After the fall of Rangoon, appointed commander in chief, Allied Land Forces in Burma. In August, appointed commander in chief, Middle East Command.

Gen. Claude Auchinleck:
    Commander in chief, Middle East theater, until relieved in August.

Gen. Sir Alan Brooke:
    Chief of the Imperial General Staff. In March, succeeded Admiral of the Fleet Dudley Pound as chairman of the British Chiefs of Staff Committee.

Field Marshal Sir John Dill:
    Replaced as chief of the Imperial General Staff in December 1941. Represented the British Army at the Arcadia Conference. Throughout 1942 served as the chief of the British mission in Washington. Respected by both Marshall and Brooke; served as an honest broker on the Combined Chiefs of Staff.

Brig. Vivian Dykes:
    Lead British Army planner at the Arcadia Conference and subsequently selected as the chief of the Combined Secretary, British Joint Staff Mission in Washington.

Lt. Gen. Sir Hastings Ismay:
: Principal assistant to Winston Churchill in his capacity as minister of defence, also deputy secretary of the War Cabinet and secretary of the Imperial Defence Chiefs of Staff Committee. Close confidante of the prime minister.

Brig. Edward Ian Claud Jacob:
: Military assistant secretary to the British War Cabinet. Attended the Arcadia Conference as the principal British secretary and notetaker.

Maj. Gen. Sir John Kennedy:
: Director of military operations at the War Office. Close advisor to both Dill and Brooke.

Gen. Bernard Montgomery:
: Selected as the commander of the Eighth Army in August, defeated Field Marshal Rommel at the second battle at El Alamein.

Vice Adm. Lord Louis Mountbatten:
: Chief of Combined Operations and a member of the Chiefs of Staff Committee.

Chief of the Air Staff, Air Chief Marshal Sir Charles Portal:
: Head of the Royal Air Force. The Americans viewed him as the smartest and most reasonable British member of the Combined Chiefs of Staff.

First Sea Lord Adm. Sir Alfred Dudley Pound:
: Head of the Royal Navy and chairman of the British Chiefs of Staff Committee until replaced by Brooke in March. Tired after two years and seriously ill.

Cmdr. Charles Thompson:
: Churchill's personal aide.

Gen. Sir Archibald Wavell:
: Commander in chief, India.

The Americans

Lt. Gen. Henry "Hap" Arnold:
: Commanding general Army Air Forces. Member of the Joint Chiefs of Staff.

Lt. Gen. Mark Clark:
: Deputy commander of Allied forces in North Africa.

Lt. Gen. Dwight Eisenhower:
: Chief of the War Plans Division, later assistant chief of staff of the Operations Division. Selected as the commanding general, European theater of operations, and subsequently supreme commander, Allied Expeditionary Force for Operation Torch.

Maj. Gen. Thomas Handy:
: War planner who succeeded Eisenhower as assistant chief of staff in charge of the Operations Division.

Harry Hopkins:
: Trusted confidante and advisor to President Roosevelt.

Adm. Ernest King:
: Chief of Naval Operations. Succeeded Admiral Stark. Member of the Joint Chiefs of Staff.

Henry Knox:
: Secretary of the Navy.

Adm. William Leahy:
: Former chief of Naval Operations and US ambassador to Vichy France. Selected as chief of staff to the commander in chief in July. Member and titular head of the Joint Chiefs of Staff. Close friend of President Roosevelt.

Gen. George Marshall:
: Chief of staff of the US Army. The most dominant personality among the Joint Chiefs of Staff.

Capt. John McCrea:
: Naval aide to President Roosevelt.

Lt. Gen. Joseph McNarney:
: The US Army deputy chief of staff.

Maj. Gen. Walter Bedell Smith:
: American secretary to the Combined Chiefs of Staff in Washington. Selected by Eisenhower to serve as his chief of staff at Allied Forces Headquarters in September.

Lt. Gen. Joseph Stilwell:
: Chief of staff to Generalissimo Chiang Kai-Shek and commander of US Forces in China, Burma, and India.

Adm. Harold Stark:
: Chief of Naval Operations at the Arcadia Conference. Replaced by Admiral King in March. Appointed commander US Naval Forces Europe.

Henry Stimson:
: Secretary of war.

Brig. Gen. Albert Wedemeyer:
: War planner who accompanied Marshall to London in April.

ACKNOWLEDGMENTS

During my research and writing, I benefitted from the advice and assistance of many individuals. It is a pleasure for me to acknowledge the friends and colleagues who helped throughout this project. I owe a special debt of gratitude to Dr. Edward Drea, who made time in his busy schedule to read and comment on my entire manuscript. He not only improved my scholarship but encouraged me throughout my research and writing. I would also like to thank Dr. Steve Rearden for his cogent insights and advice on my manuscript. Both historians helped make this book a reality.

In writing this book I have been fortunate in the assistance I have received, and I would like to express my gratitude to the following: the Library of Congress, Washington, DC; the Franklin Delano Roosevelt Library, Hyde Park, New York; Dr. David Crist at the Joint History Office; Dr. Timothy Nenninger at the National Archives and Records Administration, College Park, Maryland; the British National Archives at Kew, Richmond; Melissa Davis, the director of Library and Archives at the George C. Marshall Foundation, Lexington, Virginia; Col. Kenneth Foulks and Dr. Jon Hoffman, at the US Army Center of Military History, Fort McNair, Washington, DC; Jennifer King at the Australian War Memorial, Campbell, Australia; Andrew Webb, at the Imperial War Museum, London; Col. (Ret) Michael Perry and Molly Bompane at the US Army Heritage and Education Center, Carlisle, Pennsylvania; Lisa Crunk at the US Navy History and Heritage Command, Washington, DC.

I would like to thank Jay Dew and Marguerite Avery of Texas A&M University Press for their support and enthusiasm. I appreciate their unwavering sponsorship for this project. I also want to thank Abagail

Chartier and Katie Smith for their superb editorial skill in improving the quality of my book.

The maps in this book are reproduced with the permission of the United States Army Center of Military History. They are from the Green Book Series, *The U.S. Army in World War II.*

While I have benefitted from the assistance of those mentioned above, I alone am responsible for any errors contained within this manuscript. The opinions expressed in this book do not represent the official views of the Department of Defense or the Joint Chiefs of Staff.

I am most grateful to my wife, Pamela. No one could ever hope for a better partner, advocate, and friend. This book is for her.

JOHN SHORTAL
Washington, DC

A SEARCH FOR STRATEGY

INTRODUCTION

During his 5 March 1946 address at tiny Westminster College in Fulton, Missouri, Winston Churchill used the catchphrase "iron curtain" to describe the Soviet Union's creation of a communist sphere of influence in Eastern Europe. Reporters covering the event seized upon Churchill's remark, and it remained perhaps the most memorable metaphor of the Cold War era.

Churchill coined another term that day that also quickly gained popularity. The United States and the British Commonwealth enjoyed a "special relationship" because of the military, political, social, and cultural connections between them. "Neither the sure prevention of war, nor the continuous rise of world organization will be gained without what I have called the fraternal association of English-speaking peoples. This means a special relationship between the British Commonwealth and Empire and the United States." For all his rhetorical flourishes, Churchill was emphasizing that Great Britain and the United States had to build upon the "intimate relationship" that they had developed in World War II to prevent future wars and to support the fledgling United Nations.[1]

Churchill's concept of a special relationship between the United States and the United Kingdom espoused at Westminster College evolved over the next several years into a major theme in his six-volume *History of the Second World War*. He repeatedly underscored his close bond with Pres. Franklin D. Roosevelt and insisted that their relationship was the key to the British-American partnership that had "saved the world."[2]

Churchill the politician, and Churchill the historian, was concerned with history's verdict. The historian Churchill sought to ensure his reputation and legacy by writing that history as his own story. In the 1930s, he told Prime Minister Stanley Baldwin that "history will say that the Right Honorable Gentleman was wrong in this matter. I know because I shall write that history." He made a similar remark to Joseph Stalin, leader of the USSR, in January 1944. "I agree that we should leave the past to history, but remember if I live long enough I may be one of the historians." He reiterated it again in January 1948, this time to the House of Commons. "For my part, I consider that it will be found much better by all parties to leave the past to history, especially as I propose to write that history."[3]

Churchill reveled in his accomplishments as prime minister during the Second World War. As he lived it and wrote it, he had led Great Britain back from the verge of defeat to total victory over his adversaries. Overcoming countless obstacles, he shone as a beacon of hope in Britain's darkest hours. He pugnaciously defended his reputation and, being exceptionally thin-skinned, deeply resented the criticism of his leadership that appeared in the late 1940s, particularly in Ralph Ingersoll's and Elliott Roosevelt's books that evaluated him poorly for interfering with Allied strategy to accomplish imperial ends. Two other important books published around the same time, Robert Sherwood's biography of Harry Hopkins, Pres. Franklin D. Roosevelt's key advisor, and the Supreme Allied Commander Gen. Dwight Eisenhower's memoir, while complimentary of the former prime minister, questioned Churchill's strategic motives for delaying the cross-channel invasion in France—the so-called second front.[4]

In 1948 Churchill commenced to set the record straight by keeping his promise and writing the history of the Second World War. He succeeded beyond all expectations. His work has dominated the historiography of the war for seventy years. In the 1950s, when the State Department prepared its official history of the Washington and Casablanca conferences, it relied heavily on Churchill's memoirs as the official record of secret conversations because Roosevelt had not allowed note takers at the sessions. British historian Sir John Harold Plumb commented that "Churchill the historian lies at the very heart of all historiographies of the Second World War and will always remain there." David Reynolds was more succinct: Churchill "remains in command of history."[5]

Churchill took great pains to portray the close working relationship he enjoyed with President Roosevelt and American military leaders. Stressing the intimate collaboration between the American and British military advisors on the Combined Chiefs of Staff (CCS), Churchill recalled policy consensus and downplayed any dissension or disagreements in Allied war councils.

"There is one thing worse than fighting with allies and that is fighting without them," quipped Churchill. Field Marshal Sir William Slim, perhaps the most successful field commander in the war, did him one better in April 1952 when he explained the challenges of working with allies to students at the US Army Command and General Staff College. Slim spoke from his vast personal experience operating with allies in Burma (Myanmar) and China and used irony to make his point.

> Allies, altogether, are really very extraordinary people. It is astonishing how obstinate they are, how parochially minded, how ridiculously sensitive to prestige and how wrapped up in obsolete political ideas. It is equally astonishing how they fail to see how broad-minded you are, how clear your picture is, how up-to-date you are and how cooperative and big hearted you are. It is extraordinary. But let me tell you, when you feel like that about allies—and you have even worse allies than the British, believe me—when you feel like that, just remind yourself of two things. First, you are an ally too, and all allies look just the same. If you walk to the other side of the table, you will look just like that to the fellow sitting opposite. Then the next thing to remember is that there is only one thing worse than having allies—that is not having allies.[6]

There was no "special relationship" before Pearl Harbor. Tensions and mistrust characterized the British-American militaries. Some of these ill-feelings dated from the military relationship between Britain and the United States during the First World War. Britain and France had fought Germany for three years at terrible cost before the United States even entered the war. The war-weary British and French wanted the United States to provide combat troops to fill their depleted ranks. That entailed amalgamating American forces into the French and British units serving on the western front, in effect placing American troops under foreign command. For political reasons, Pres. Woodrow Wilson wanted an intact American army to assist in securing the coalition's victory in order to keep his bargaining options open at any postwar conference. The American Expeditionary Force commander, Gen. John J. Pershing, interpreted his instructions from Wilson to mean that he would build an independent American army in France to fight under its own commanders. For military reasons, the general refused to break-up American units to provide replacements for depleted allied units.[7]

The Americans' decision irritated the British and French military leadership who needed immediate military help. The British commander Gen. Sir Douglas Haig was frustrated that Pershing "did not seem to realize the urgency of the situation ... He hankers after a great self-contained American Army but ... it is ridiculous to think such an Army could function unaided in less than two years." Pershing, however, was adamant and refused to be intimidated. As an "associate" power, the United States would use its military power as it best saw fit.[8]

The argument seesawed back-and-forth for eighteen months; the British repeatedly demanding the use of American troops as fillers in British and French units and the Americans repeatedly refusing. British appeals to President Wilson were in vain because the president supported Pershing. In June 1918, at the Allied conference at Versailles, Marshal Ferdinand Foch, the Supreme Allied Commander, bluntly demanded of Pershing, "You are willing to risk our being driven into the Loire River?" Pershing was willing to accept responsibility for that possibility. British Prime Minister Lloyd George ominously interjected, "Well, we will refer it to your President." "Refer it to the President and be damned," Pershing shot back. "I know what the President will do. He will simply refer it back to me for recommendation and I will make the same recommendation as I have made today." The Allies never resolved their major disagreement. Memories long outlived the war and hard feelings lingered. The British resented the Americans' unwillingness to conform with London's strategy. The Americans remembered British bullying and condescension toward their independent force.[9]

The American Navy had similar difficulties with their British counterparts. The British had the most powerful fleet in the world and dominated naval matters among the Allies. They had their specific doctrine and expected the Americans to conform to it. The chief of Naval Operations, Adm. William S. Benson, disagreed. He wanted the US fleet kept in American waters to check the potential German submarine threat to Allied merchant shipping. Once the United States entered the war, Benson sent Adm. William Sims to command US Naval forces in Britain, along with the admonition, "Don't let the British pull the wool over your eyes. It is none of our business pulling their chestnuts out of the fire. We would as soon fight the British as the Germans." Regardless of this counsel, Sims worked well with his counterparts. He realized the British were practically starving because of heavy shipping losses to U-boats in March and April 1917. By July, Sims had successfully deployed the majority of American destroyers to British ports to counter the immediate submarine menace near the British Isles. The British responded by sharing information about U-boat activities but withheld their most important intelligence source, the decryptions obtained from intercepted German radio signals. Still the American Navy resented being the "junior partner" and the British made little attempt to allay this perception.[10]

Adm. Ernest King, who became the chief of Naval Operations in early 1942, had served on the staff of the Atlantic Fleet coordinating with the British during the First World War. King keenly resented British condescension, believing that they had run the war as they saw fit and ignored American advice. "The British have been managing world affairs for well over three hundred years, that is, ever since the defeat of the Spanish Armada in 1588." They were used to having their own way, because they had the most money and the largest fleet. King accepted that the British understood the world situation before 1914 far better than the Americans, but during the 1920s and 1930s Americans grew more sophisticated about international affairs, and the modernized US fleet, not the British navy, ruled the seas. In King's opinion, the British failed to grasp the implications of the changed relationship.[11]

The rivalry between the two navies intensified during the initial interwar period. A navy's size was a yardstick of prestige and national honor. President Wilson was determined to build a fleet "second to none" so the United States could "do what we please." In 1919 the Royal Navy had forty-two capital ships (battleships and cruisers), the United States sixteen, and Japan fourteen. If naval shipbuilding continued at its current pace, by 1924 Britain would have forty-three capital ships, the United States thirty-five, and the Japanese twenty-two. No one, however, could afford a naval race of such proportions. The outcome of the Washington Naval Conference appeared to settle the issue.[12]

The Washington Naval Conference of 1921 and 1922 and subsequent naval arms limitation conferences attempted to redress naval shipbuilding consistent with postwar fiscal constraints. The most famous provision was the February 1922 agreement to establish a 5:5:3 ratio on capital warship tonnage among Britain, America, and Japan, respectively. Another clause paused capital ship construction for ten years. To gain Japanese consent, all parties agreed not to strengthen their military bases in the western Pacific, except for Hawaii, Singapore, and Japan's home islands. No one left happy. The British felt that they should have the largest fleet because their far-flung empire required a two-fleet navy. The Americans had scrapped more naval tonnage than anyone, and believed the British cheated by building cruisers, which were not covered in the agreement. The Japanese resented the second-class status associated with a smaller fleet than either the United States or Britain. The disarmament process had fueled distrust and jealousy.[13]

The British retained their preeminent navy but resented American attempts to build a bigger and more powerful navy. In 1927, the Chancellor of Exchequer, Winston Churchill, told the British cabinet, "No doubt it is quite right in the interests of peace to go on talking about war with the United States being 'unthinkable.'" He then warned, "Everyone knows that this is not true. However foolish and disastrous such a war would be ... we do not wish to put ourselves in the power of the United States. We cannot tell what they might do if at some future date they were in a position to give us orders about our policy, say, in India, or Egypt, or Canada, or on some other great matter behind which their electioneering forces were marshalled." That future date arrived sooner than expected.[14]

On 10 May 1940, the German Army crossed its western frontier into France. Six weeks later 330,000 British troops, carrying only their personal weapons, evacuated the continent from Dunkirk. They abandoned all their artillery, heavy weapons, and ammunition stocks. By the end of June 1940, the land forces in the United Kingdom amounted to twenty-six British and one Canadian division. Available equipment sufficed to arm just two of them. German U-boat attacks on merchant shipping exacerbated the situation by hampering the replenishment of military equipment. Prime Minister Churchill looked to the United States for assistance during the dangerous summer of 1940.[15]

In 1918, the British had 433 destroyers at sea. In 1940 they had only 94 of the essential anti-submarine warships. London asked Washington to supply 50 obsolete destroyers to help counter the U-boat threat. In the absence of a so-called special relationship, the United States drove a very hard bargain for these ships. President Roosevelt faced an isolationist Congress and nation and had to avoid perceptions that the United States was moving toward war. In exchange for the outdated destroyers, he wanted key naval and air bases in British dominions, including Newfoundland, Trinidad, Bermuda, Jamaica, Santa Lucia, British Guiana, and the Bahamas.[16]

The British originally expected to provide these facilities to the Americans without a transfer of sovereignty. The Americans, however, demanded basing rights as a "free gift" in order to build air and naval facilities in Newfoundland, Canada, and Bermuda, as well as a ninety-nine-year lease on the Caribbean and Guiana bases. Washington further requested that no matter what Britain's fate, the British would never surrender their fleet but rather would dispatch it overseas to defend other parts of their vast empire. London deeply resented this hard-nosed bargaining, but in August 1940 with the Battle of Britain still in doubt, they had no choice but to accept.[17]

Churchill put a positive spin on the deal in his 5 September 1940 speech to the House of Commons. "The exchanges which have taken place are simply measures of mutual assistance rendered to one another by two friendly nations, in a spirit of confidence, sympathy, and good will ... I have no doubt that Herr Hitler will not like this transference of destroyers, and I have no doubt that he will pay the United States out, if he ever gets the chance." He went on to say that the Admiralty was "very glad to have these fifty destroyers."[18]

Churchill's history, *Their Finest Hour*, praised the agreement and portrayed it as part of the special relationship and developing British-American Alliance. According to his recollections, "Thus we obtained fifty American destroyers" and "granted ninety-nine-year leases of the air and naval bases in the West Indies and Newfoundland," promising not to surrender the British Fleet. Such transactions were "acts of good will performed on their merits and not as bargains."[19]

In December 1940 the British notified the United States Government that they were bankrupt. In March 1941, Roosevelt reacted with the

President Roosevelt signing the Lend-Lease bill, March 1941 (Library of Congress)

Lend-Lease Bill, which allowed the United States to sell, lend, or lease military equipment to "any country whose defense the President deems vital to the defense of the United States." In return the British abolished their imperial preference system, which opened commercial and economic markets in the British Empire to the United States. Churchill was initially ecstatic and cabled Roosevelt, "The strain has been serious, so I thank God for your news."[20]

Read superficially, the Lend-Lease program was a generous act by the United States. Churchill told the British public that Lend-Lease provided "two successive enactments about 3,000,000,000 (pounds) sterling [that] were dedicated to the cause of world freedom without—mark this, for it is unique—the setting up of any account in money. Never again let us hear the taunt that money is the ruling thought or power in the hearts of American democracy. The Lend and Lease Bill must be regarded without question as the most unsordid act in the whole of recorded history." At the same time, doubts crept in about American generosity. Britain was virtually bankrupt: Its gold reserves dwindled to a mere twelve million US dollars, the lowest level in their history. Churchill privately complained, "We are not only being skinned but flayed to the bone. I would like for them to get hooked a little firmer, but they are pretty well on now. The power of the debtor is in the ascendant, especially when he is doing all the fighting." British leaders especially resented the Americans charging them for weapons that British soldiers were using to fight the war while American civilians sat safely at home.[21]

The British especially resented the provisions on imperial preferences and exchange and other trade controls in the postwar period. The British negotiator, John Maynard Keynes, believed the Americans were making unreasonable demands. He believed that the wording on imperial preferences "permitted all sorts of cunningly devised tariffs, which were in fact discriminatory." Keynes felt they were "wholly impossible" and that after the war Britain would be disadvantaged economically.[22]

Churchill's inner feelings showed through in a close-hold conversation with the British Ambassador to the United States. Told that the Americans were concerned with payments for Lend-Lease,

Churchill responded, "By all means let us have an account if we can get it reasonably accurate, but I shall have my account to put in too, and my account is for holding the baby alone for eighteen months, and it was a very rough brutal baby I had to hold. I don't quite know what I shall have to charge for it."[23]

Churchill's postwar memoirs described the Lend-Lease program in glowing terms, though, as an act of generosity from one ally to another. "There was no provision for repayment. There was not even to be a formal account kept in dollars or sterling. What we had was lent or leased to us because our continued resistance to the Hitler tyranny was deemed to be of vital interest to the great Republic."[24]

As much as Churchill wished and misremembered, there was no "special relationship." President Roosevelt's principal advisor, Harry Hopkins, described the coordination between the United States and Great Britain in this period as a "common law marriage." It was not recognized officially by Congress because Anglophobia and isolationist sentiment were widespread and strong in the United States. British-American cooperation continued, albeit it out of sight of the American public's eyes. Britain and the United States exchanged scientific information on various topics, including atomic energy and radar; enjoyed close cooperation between the FBI and British security offices to counter German espionage and sabotage activities; coordinated between the US Atlantic Fleet and the British Fleet to secure sea lanes in the Atlantic; agreed to repair British warships and merchant ships damaged in the Mediterranean Sea campaigns in American shipyards; trained Royal Air Force pilots and crews in the United States; and commenced initial strategic discussions between the American and British military staffs on combined actions if America entered the war.[25]

Strategic talks, however, yielded mixed results. They were neither as harmonious nor as fruitful as Hopkins and Churchill portrayed them after the war. Senior US and British officials met on two occasions to discuss strategy before the December 1941 Japanese attack on Pearl Harbor, Hawaii. In early 1941, they met in Washington at the American and British Conversations (also known as ABC-1). Later in August of that year, they reassembled during the Atlantic Conference held in Placentia Bay, Newfoundland, Canada. At both, the respective military attendees identified some common ground, but on major issues such as the strategy in the Far East or the best approach to defeating Germany they remained far apart.

Churchill's memoirs emphasized the positive aspects of these secret staff talks held prior to Pearl Harbor. He noted that the "discussions began in Washington covering the whole scene and framing a combined world strategy. The United States war chiefs agreed that should the war spread to America and to the Pacific the Atlantic and European theater should be regarded as decisive. Hitler must be defeated first." Churchill glossed over the numerous disagreements and disparate viewpoints between the two militaries as well as their divergent strategies.[26]

The American and British staffs did agree that in case of a two-front war against Germany and Japan, Germany was the greater threat. Therefore, the United States would dedicate the bulk of its resources to defeating Germany before the Anglo-American allies turned their combined might on Japan. The British would win by exhausting Germany from afar while the Americans would win by directly engaging and destroying the German army. No attempt was made to reconcile the opposing strategies. The British were satisfied with the American decision to make Germany the primary enemy and to devote its resources accordingly.[27]

A major disagreement on strategy in the Pacific almost brought the ABC-1 conference to a premature close. The British argued that Singapore was the key to the defense of the Far East, by which they meant their South Asian colonies and dominions. They had constructed the Singapore naval base during the 1920s and 1930s for that purpose and to allay the fears of Australia and New Zealand about Japan's potential southward expansion. Postwar austerity measures made it impossible to build a second fleet to base at Singapore, so London promised its dominions that in case of war a fleet would deploy from European waters to Singapore within 70 days. The interval increased incrementally to 180 days. By February 1941, the British were fighting for their existence in Europe and incapable of meeting even the extended timetable. To resolve their strategic dilemma, the

British proposed to deploy an American fleet to Singapore, which in any case was more important than the American colony in the Philippines.[28]

The Americans found this logic absurd. The fleet was already at the Pearl Harbor naval base and US strategists regarded the Philippines as the strategic key to the western Pacific. The British representatives appealed to their ambassador, who approached the secretary of state for resolution. The Americans believed that interjecting a purely miliary topic into diplomatic channels violated the spirit of the military staff meetings' charter and suspended further discussions. Churchill accepted that Roosevelt would not support British imperial aspirations and broke the impasse by directing the British side to drop the subject: "I particularly depreciated the raising of this controversy. Our object is to get the Americans into the war, and the proper strategic dispositions will soon emerge when they run up against reality, and not trying to enter into hypothetical paper accords beforehand."[29]

The first face-to-face meeting of the British and American Chiefs of Staff occurred at the Atlantic Conference in August 1941. This brief meeting was another missed opportunity. The British again briefed their peripheral strategy for defeating Germany, but no substantive discussions ensued. Adm. Harold Stark, the chief of Naval Operations, made it very clear at the session's opening that the Americans were not prepared to make any commitments. Following Stark's instructions, the Americans offered no alternative plan for Europe, leading the British to question their counterpart's strategic competence.[30]

Adm. Ernest King, the US commander in chief of the Atlantic Fleet, was critical of the British strategy that "had little idea of setting up matters to cope with Germany on land." Instead of an open exchange of ideas to clarify positions, the military leaders departed with misconceptions about each other.[31]

On the eve of Pearl Harbor, each nation found the other's motives suspect. The British ambassador to the United States, Lord Halifax, regarded Americans as weak, inferior, and not very bright. Americans struck him as very crude and semi-educated and [they] have not begun to appreciate . . . that the essential element of education is not to know things but to know how little you know. And I think also that national life has been pretty easy for them and they shrink from things that are hard. The consequence is that they are tempted . . . to think that everything can be resolved on an emotional level by soft words and fine thoughts, that are not always reflected in action."[32]

Anglophobia was always close to the surface and, combined with anti-imperialism, caused senior US officials to view their British counterparts as manipulators rooted in selfishness, imperial ambition, and lack of morality. Vice Pres. Henry Wallace recalled that the British were constantly "trying to play their customary role of getting more than they are entitled to." Felix Frankfurter, the distinguished Supreme Court justice, lamented "a lack of consciousness of comradeship between the two peoples," which obscured the fact that the "aims of the British people in waging this war are substantially our aims." In short, there was nothing even close to a special relationship between Britain and the United States. Leaders on both sides viewed each other's recommendations through a prism of national prejudices and misconceptions.[33]

Despite this diversity in national perspectives and resources, as the leaders grew to learn each other's strengths and weaknesses over time, British and American military leaders successfully forged a war-winning alliance. Their first meeting after Pearl Harbor, at the Arcadia Conference in Washington in December 1941–January 1942, found the chiefs of both nations determined to cooperate and find common ground. The "Germany First" strategy was reconfirmed.

In the months immediately following the conference the war went very badly for the Allies. In the Pacific, the Japanese juggernaut seemed unstoppable, and despite the Germany First agreement, resources were desperately needed in the Pacific. The Japanese thrust drove the British, Dutch, and Americans from southwest Asia and left Australia and New Zealand defenseless against feared invasion.

What follows is a month-by-month account, from Pearl Harbor through July 1942, of the military chieftains' efforts to find common ground and agree on a strategy to defeat Germany. The special relationship never emerged during this period; it developed later in the war. The first half of 1942 was marred by ups and downs in the military relationship between the American and British military chiefs during a low point in the war. The chiefs of both nations argued fiercely for their national positions, straining trust but never breaking it. The hard debates and frank discussions were the first steps to the special relationship and a formidable alliance.

Churchill correctly extolled the special relationship; it just did not happen as quickly and as smoothly as his historical portrayal. As Slim had pointed out, the allies were "obstinate," "parochially minded," and "ridiculously sensitive to prestige." They each had their own ideas on strategy and resources and were convinced they had the best solution for winning the war. They had not yet learned to listen or to take the time to "walk to the other side of the table" and see the other's perspective. That slow walk occurred during the first months of 1942.[34]

1

Allies Meet after Pearl Harbor

December–January 1942

On Sunday morning, 7 December 1941, Japanese naval airmen neutralized the powerful US Pacific Fleet at Pearl Harbor, Hawaii. Half a world away, Winston Churchill heard the news that evening on the radio at home. After speaking to Pres. Franklin Roosevelt by phone to

View looking up Battleship Row on 7 December 1941, after the Japanese attack. USS Arizona (BB-39) is in the center, burning furiously. To the left are USS Tennessee (BB-43) and the sunken USS West Virginia (BB-48). (Navy History and Heritage Command Photograph, NH 97378)

CHAPTER 1

Photograph of the western side of Ford Island and ships in moorings offshore, taken from a Japanese navy plane during the attack. Ships are (from left to right): USS Detroit (CL-8); USS Raleigh (CL-7), listing to port after being hit by one torpedo; USS Utah (AG-16), capsized after being hit by two torpedoes; and USS Tangier (AV-8). Japanese writing in the lower left states that the photograph's reproduction was authorized by the Navy Ministry. (Navy History and Heritage Command Photograph, NH 50933)

confirm the news, he retired for the night convinced that the mighty American war engine lay at his disposal. He had a rude awakening.

While Churchill slept, the US secretary of war, Henry Stimson, had informed British air marshal Arthur Harris, a member of the British Joint Mission in Washington, that some American-built B-24 bombers previously earmarked for Great Britain under Lend-Lease were being withheld because the United States now needed those bombers to protect the American West Coast.[1]

Stimson next requested the Supply Priorities and Allocation Board (SPAB), chaired by Vice Pres. Henry Wallace, to give top precedence to equipping the American armed forces because the American people "would now insist that our own forces should be responsible for defense much more than in the past when they were willing to depend upon the policy of subsidizing and arming outside nations."

The following day the president approved the withdrawal of aircraft production from delivery to the British until the US Army Air Corps reached fifty-four air groups. Churchill recalled in his memoirs that when he awoke the next morning, he decided to visit President Roosevelt in Washington to coordinate strategic interests.[2]

In fact, Churchill was caught short, unprepared for this unilateral US action and its serious effect on the existing Lend-Lease program, which was designed to provide the British with the American-manufactured military equipment it desperately needed to fight Germany. In November and December 1941, before Pearl Harbor, Lend-Lease turned over every medium tank that US industry manufactured to Great Britain for operations in the Middle East. During its first year (1941), Lend-Lease shipped five out of every six American-manufactured tanks to foreign nations overseas. Earlier Stimson had warned the president of the impossibility of training newly formed American armor units without tanks. With the United States at war, the American military expected a greater share of American-manufactured equipment. But cutbacks to the Lend-Lease program meant Great Britain, among other nations, would receive less American military assistance.[3]

The unanticipated shortage of American arms and equipment immediately affected British operational plans, especially in North Africa. Churchill requested an emergency meeting with Roosevelt and his military advisors to "review the whole war plan in the light of reality and new facts, as well as problems of production and distribution." Roosevelt initially tried to delay the session after his advisors warned that Churchill hoped to gain American support for a strategy suited to British imperial requirements. The president drafted two replies, neither of which was sent, that recommended delaying the "conference until early stages of mobilization are complete here and situation in Pacific more clarified." Roosevelt appreciated Churchill's concerns about Lend-Lease deferments and promised that once the US naval situation in the Pacific and on the American West Coast stabilized, shipments would resume to Britain. He believed everything else, except the delivery of aircraft, could be worked out.[4]

While Roosevelt searched for soothing words to delay a meeting, Churchill was not to be put off. On 10 December, he again pressed for a meeting due to the "great danger in our not having full discussion on the highest level about the extreme gravity of the naval position as well as upon all the production and allocation issues involved." Despite his advisors' misgivings, the president cabled the British prime minister that the Americans would be "delighted to have you at the White House."⁵

Two days later, Churchill boarded the battleship *Duke of York* bound for the United States. The prime minister brought his top military advisors to the conference. Adm. Dudley Pound, the First Sea Lord, represented the Royal Navy; Air Marshal Charles Portal the Royal Air Force; and Field Marshal John Dill, the former chief of the Imperial General Staff, represented the army. Churchill's retinue also included Lord Beaverbrook, the minister of supply. The new Army chief, Gen. Alan Brooke, remained in London to oversee the British war effort.⁶

British military chiefs Air Marshal Charles Portal, Adm. Dudley Pound, Gen. Alan Brooke, and Adm. Louis Mountbatten with Winston Churchill (courtesy of the George C. Marshall Foundation, Lexington, Virginia, USA)

"Arcadia" was the code name for the American-British Joint Chiefs of Staff Conference, held between 24 December 1941 and 14 January 1942. This was a series of twelve meetings between the senior military leaders of both nations to coordinate the combined war effort. The Pearl Harbor attack changed the dynamic of the British-American Alliance. Unlike past meetings, Allied consultation at Arcadia now included commitments. Churchill "wanted to show the President how to run the war." Put differently, the British "welcomed American participation in their war on the assumption that the Americans would help carry through British plans." The problem was that, as Slim had pointed out, allies have ideas of their own. This independent thinking by the American chiefs would prove dismaying to their British counterparts.[7]

Secretary of War Henry Stimson anticipated a "sharp divergence" with the British on several topics, particularly joint strategy, and was concerned that Churchill's outsize personality would make it difficult for President Roosevelt to say "no." It was his responsibility, Stimson felt, to protect the president from undue influence by the prime minister.[8]

In the frenetic days after Pearl Harbor, the US Army and Navy struggled to respond to the numerous wartime requirements. "My impression of Washington," Brig. Gen. Joseph Stilwell wrote, "is a rush of clerks in and out of doors, swing doors always swinging, people with papers rushing after other people with papers, groups in corners whispering in huddles, everybody jumping up just as you start to talk, buzzers ringing, telephones ringing, rooms crowded, with clerks banging away on typewriters."[9]

The British, upon arrival in America, were also surprised by Washington's disorganization that extended all the way to the top. Col. Ian Jacob, the British secretary for the conference, observed that, compared to Churchill, Roosevelt "is a child in military affairs, and evidently has little realization of what can and cannot be done. He does not seem to grasp how backward his country is in its war preparations, and how ill prepared his Army is to get involved in large scale operations." This patronizing British attitude, never far below the surface, annoyed the American staff throughout the conference.[10]

American military planners felt that the British substituted patronizing arrogance to overcompensate for their string of military defeats in Norway, France, Crete, Greece, and Africa. The British staff were similarly dismissive of their American counterparts. According to Jacob, the Americans "do not appear to have thought out and laid the foundations for the vast amount of administrative action which should follow automatically on the outbreak of war." His initial impression of the US Army was that all the generals were "too old." He doubted they had the energy or intellect to match up well with their British counterparts. Jacob reserved special venom for Adm. Harold Stark, chief of Naval Operations, whom he christened "Tugboat Annie," describing him as "a little man, with a perky face, and looks as if he ought to be Captain of a showboat."[11]

There were, of course, more balanced impressions. Brig. Gen. Thomas Handy, a US Army planner, acknowledged that the Americans needed to improve and were "more or less babes in the woods in this planning and joint business with the British. They'd been doing it for years. They were experts at it, and we were just starting. They'd found a way to get along between services, that they had to get along." Capt. John McCrea, the US Navy's conference secretary, concurred that the British "knew their stuff" and "their staff organization was superb."[12]

Churchill's postwar memoir mentions nothing of the disarray in Washington, nor American ineptitude, nor British-American friction. Instead, he emphasized the strong bond that developed between himself and the president, a relationship that he believed was the key to the war effort. "I formed a very strong affection, which grew with our years of comradeship, for this formidable politician who had imposed his will for nearly ten years upon the American scene, and whose heart seemed to respond to many of the impulses that stirred my own."[13]

Churchill's major concern was that the Americans would view Japan as the principal enemy and devote the bulk of their resources to the Pacific. His fears were groundless. At the opening session on the first day of the conference, Admiral Stark pledged a firm American commitment to honor the Germany First strategy. The United States

Admiral Stark's luncheon at the Arcadia Conference (Naval History and Heritage Command, NH 120087)

formally recognized that Germany was the principal threat, and the bulk of the nation's resources should be dedicated to its defeat. America would hold in the Pacific and send only minimal resources to that theater. The British had gained their primary goal at the conference quickly and smoothly.[14]

The prime minister's other overriding worry was the American reaction to a British grand strategy of reprising the peripheral strategy of attrition that relied on air and sea power to weaken Germany at the edges before Allied ground forces could return to the European continent. British strategy would secure essential air and sea lines of communication and wear down Germany by naval blockade, strategic bombing, propaganda, and support to resistance groups designed to close an ever-tightening ring around Germany. They would concentrate resources against Germany and only dedicate minimum resources to Pacific and other areas as needed to maintain vital interests. After Germany was worn down and weakened to the point of collapse, the Allies would launch a final assault on the continent. The strategy minimized the cost of victory in terms of Allied lives but conceded that a large-scale offensive against Germany in western Europe was unlikely until at least 1944. Both sides, however, accepted this basic strategy with little discussion, despite the traditional American strategy that envisaged direct confrontation with and the destruction of the German army in western Europe as rapidly as possible.[15]

When the Joint Chiefs of Staff historian writing the official history of the war with Germany asked Admiral Stark after the war why the United States acquiesced to the British peripheral strategy, Stark replied that in early 1942 a large-scale land invasion of Europe seemed "very far away." Stark pointed out that the United States had limited resources and numerous other urgent issues to deal with, such as sending US troops to Iceland and Northern Ireland, bombers to Britain, and supplies to Australia, and aiding the Philippines. According to Stark, the Americans accepted a defensive strategy "to keep the seas open," while they built up men and material for an offensive against Germany.[16]

General Marshall, the army chief of staff, recognized America's weakness in early 1942, but insisted a direct approach was the best way to defeat Germany. He did not find the two approaches mutually exclusive. If attrition assisted in accomplishing a return to northern France and the destruction of the German army, so much the better. At the time, however, Marshall failed to realize the significant differences of opinion between the allies, which became more manifest during the following months and would be extremely divisive.[17]

President Roosevelt subtly supported the peripheral strategy because he believed that it was important for Allied morale that American troops actively engage Axis forces. Where they fought was less important than the political message it sent to the American people that their soldiers were fighting. Although the full implications of his remarks were not completely understood, they later proved among the most significant of the conference.[18]

Earlier, in mid-November, British forces had launched a major offensive in Libya, Operation Crusader. The campaign was initially successful, pushing back German and Italian forces. Churchill confided to his wife on 21 December that "before the end of the year he

Gen. George Catlett Marshall, US Army chief of staff (Army Heritage and Education Center Photograph)

[General Claude Auchinleck] will be at Benghazi and well on the road further west. . . . It is very important for the Americans that we should have proof that our soldiers can fight a modern war and beat the Germans on even terms, or even at odds, for that is what we have done. This lends weight to our counsels and requests." The prime minister's unfounded optimism convinced him that the British were on the verge of killing or capturing one hundred thousand Italian and fifty thousand German soldiers.[19]

Buoyed by the anticipated victory, Churchill proposed on 23 December (at Arcadia), that the British land 55,000 troops in French North Africa in three weeks. At the same time, the United States would land 25,000 troops to occupy French North Africa, and he expected that this force would be augmented by another 150,000 American troops within six months. The British strategy assumed that the occupation of French North Africa would provide a launching pad for the Allied invasion of Italy, opening a possible route to invade the northwest European continent. The president had reservations, the major one being that an occupation of French colonies might drive the Vichy Government to turn the French fleet over to Germany, but agreed to consider the matter.[20]

The American chiefs of staff were also skeptical of Churchill's North African venture (code-named "Gymnast"), judging it "motivated more largely by political [rather] than sound strategic purposes" and "persuasive rather than rational." They disagreed with British contentions that the occupation of North Africa would open the sea lanes in the Mediterranean and regarded British assertions that North Africa was a good base from which to invade Europe as "fantastic." In brief, Marshall's planners thought the entire proposal, a diversionary operation that would detract from the main effort in western Europe, was "a mistake of the first magnitude." Although the German counteroffensive during the conference wiped out the British gains and dashed many of Churchill's roseate expectations, he refused to give up and continued to advocate for the project while in Washington.[21]

Despite the vagaries of a return to the continent, the Americans still asked for British views on a direct approach to defeat Germany. Field Marshal Dill doubted that a large-scale invasion would be possible "until the Germans showed signs of cracking." Dill estimated that a cross-channel attack required fifty-seven divisions and the transport to move them. Such forces did not exist in the United States in late 1941. Otherwise, there was no discussion of an invasion of Europe because the military chiefs of both nations did not regard it as realistic in late December 1941. Given the limited resources then available, the Arcadia discussions emphasized defensive measures in the Atlantic and Mediterranean, so the North Africa proposal fit with the concept of "closing and tightening the ring" and building up resources before taking on the main German force.[22]

In his memoirs, Churchill makes no mention of this philosophical difference of opinion, and he ignores the discussions on the plan to defeat Germany. His historical focus remained fixed on the Germany First decision, insisting that the staffs agreed that only the minimum forces necessary for the safeguarding of vital interests in other theaters (the Pacific) should be diverted from operations against Germany."[23]

Relations in the planning meetings were strained as the new allies viewed each other through a prism of national prejudices and preconceived notions. With both sides suspicious of their new partner's motives, little attempt was made to see the other's point of view. The lead British army planner, Brig. Vivian Dykes, for example, found the lead US Navy planner, Adm. Richmond Kelly Turner, haughty and arrogant. Col. Ian Jacob, the British secretary, believed Turner's parochial attitude was unsuitable because "'take,' he could understand, but 'give,' was not in his vocabulary." The tension between the British and American planners continued throughout the conference and ran deeper than personalities. It reflected differing cultures, experiences, systems, methodology, and national perspectives and objectives.[24]

During the conference, Churchill was the president's guest at the White House. On Christmas Eve, during a private meeting with Roosevelt, the prime minister received an urgent request from the British commander in chief in the Far East, Lt. Gen. Henry Pownell, for additional troops to defend Singapore. For whatever reason, Roosevelt remarked offhandedly that since there was slim hope that reinforcements now en route from America could break through the Japanese blockade of the Philippines, they could be diverted elsewhere in the Far East in the interest of Allied cooperation. In the absence of any senior to advise the president on the potential political repercussions of his comment, Churchill seized the moment to guide the president on the best strategy for protecting Britain's Far Eastern empire. Churchill immediately told his military advisors to change the following day's agenda to work out the details of diverting military resources intended for the Philippines to Singapore.[25]

Churchill next cabled Australian prime minister John Curtin that while the Americans understood Singapore's importance, they wanted to move troops and aircraft through Australia to relieve the Philippine Islands, if possible. If not, the president was agreeable to troops and aircraft being diverted to Singapore.[26]

Generals Marshall and Arnold (chief of the Army Air Forces) were understandably upset by the memo diverting American assets to Singapore and showed the secretary of war a copy the following morning. It made no sense to Stimson. Gen. Douglas MacArthur's defense in the Philippines was front-page news in every newspaper

Lt. Gen. Henry H. "Hap" Arnold, chief of the Army Air Forces, at War Department Munitions Building (Army Heritage and Education Center Photograph)

in the country. It was a major domestic political error to abandon the islands and to divert US resources to Singapore. The secretary was concerned that one of his worst fears had been realized: Churchill had influenced the president to adopt a position favorable to the British Empire and detrimental to the United States. Stimson told the generals he would handle it, and he immediately contacted the president's special advisor, Harry Hopkins, threatening to resign if the president diverted resources from the Philippines to Singapore. Hopkins confronted the president, who quickly backtracked from the statement.[27]

In hindsight, Churchill's ability to maneuver the president into potentially abandoning the Philippines jarred the American military leaders into action. It forced both sides out of their comfort zones and generated frank discussions on Far East strategy. This led to innovative organizations and figured in future methods of collaboration between the Allies.

Marshall understood that the root issue was neither support to the Philippines or Singapore, but a squabble over limited resources. To end the divisiveness, Marshall introduced the idea of a unified command within a designated theater. Marshall's revolutionary recommendation cut straight to the heart of the issue. The air, land, and sea commanders of the various governments operating in the Far East all believed theirs was the most important location and that they should receive the bulk of the scarce resources. A single theater commander, however, could rise above service and national prerogatives and see the big picture.[28]

Initially Marshall received little support for unity of command, but over the next few days, with President Roosevelt's strong assistance, this changed. The US Navy came around with the president's endorsement, and through a series of exceptional planning papers the British chiefs began to view the proposal favorably. But Churchill remained stridently opposed to a single theater commander concept.[29]

Roosevelt arranged for Marshall to brief the prime minister at the White House, providing Churchill the chance to observe Marshall closely. Churchill had not reckoned with Marshall's iron will and honesty. He quickly learned that no one could browbeat or intimidate Marshall, as Churchill did with his own military advisors.

Churchill immediately criticized Marshall's concept for a single theater commander. He opposed the army controlling the navy and told Marshall that "a ship is a very special thing; difficult to have it under a ground commander." He started to give Marshall a history lesson on Admirals Francis Drake and Martin Frobisher from the sixteenth century. Marshall cut off the prime minister by remarking that he was not interested in ancient history. His concern was with the present threat in the Pacific and in forming "a united front against an enemy which was fighting furiously." Marshall's candor surprised Churchill, but he understood why the army chief had the ear and the confidence of the president. He also realized that Roosevelt looked to Marshall for strategic guidance and that Marshall was someone worth knowing.[30]

Churchill cabled Clement Atlee, "Question of unity of command in the South-West Pacific has assumed urgent form. Last night President urged upon me appointment of a single officer to command Army, Navy and Air Force of Britain, America and Dutch, and this morning General Marshall visited me at my request and pleaded case with great conviction.... It is certain that new far-reaching arrangement will have to be made."[31]

The chiefs turned a major corner after agreeing on unity of command, and they decided to build on the mutually beneficial relationship to develop a system for coordination between themselves and provide strategic guidance to theater commanders. Accordingly, the organization for strategic coordination between the American and British chiefs of staff would be known as the Combined Chiefs of Staff. Likewise, the term "Joint" would be applied to "inter-service collaboration" of one nation." Thus, the organization for coordinating strategic guidance among the US Army, Navy, and Air Force chiefs of staff would be identified as the Joint Chiefs of Staff.[32]

The British also recommended the establishment of three combined committees: a Combined Intelligence Committee to share intelligence; a Combined Allocation and Priorities Committee to link resources with strategy and assist in the distribution of weapons and equipment; and a Combined Movements Committee to supervise the priorities of overseas movements.[33]

Churchill was very proud of the Combined Chiefs of Staff and saw it as a major personal accomplishment. Shortly after the conference ended, he cabled Roosevelt that the new organization "was functioning smoothly and well. I even think we may plume ourselves a little having brought it all into action so soon." After the war he wrote, "It may well be thought by future historians that the most valuable and lasting result of our Washington Conference—'Arcadia,' as it was code named—was the setting up of the now famous Combined Chiefs of Staff.... There never was a more serviceable war machinery established among the allies, and I rejoice that in fact if not in form it continues to this day."[34]

The British had three major objectives for the conference. First, a commitment from the United States on the Germany First strategy. Second, now that America was belligerent, they wanted to ensure that Lend-Lease equipment promised to them would still be delivered to arm and equip their own forces. Third, realizing that as the industrial might of the United States mobilized, the amount of war material produced would increase exponentially, they wanted an increased share of that expanded production.[35]

The British arrived with concerns about the American rearmament program but left astonished. On 6 January, Roosevelt announced the production goals of tanks, planes, ships, and munitions for 1942 and 1943. (The United States would produce 60,000 planes and 45,000 tanks in 1942 and 125,000 planes and 75,000 tanks in 1943.) These numbers impressed Churchill and his chiefs. The British may not have gotten everything they wanted, but the integration of their requirements into America's mobilization and armaments production blueprint (Victory Program) certainly answered most of their needs.[36]

Unlike Churchill, the Germans were incredulous when they heard Roosevelt's production goals. Goebbels believed the production figures were "insane" and accused the Americans of exaggerating. Hitler had scoffed at America as nothing more than a land of "beauty queens, millionaires, stupid records, and Hollywood." Neither he nor Goebbels recognized the United States' great potential for war production. They would soon learn.[37]

Operation Gymnast, the invasion of French North Africa, continued to be an irritation as Churchill incessantly demanded studies on the topic throughout the conference. It was one of the first subjects he broached with Roosevelt on 23 December and the last on 14 January. A major problem was Churchill's assumption that the French would not oppose the Allied occupation of North Africa but would invite the British-Americans to seize their colonial territory in Africa. He understood that the French resented the British after their evacuation from the continent and the fall of France. The resulting British blockade, destruction of the French fleet at anchor at Toulon, and seizure of French merchantmen exacerbated this hostility. The United States had taken a different approach in dealing with the French government, relying on appeasing the Vichy regime in hopes of preventing full collaboration with the Germans. Churchill hoped to leverage the good American relations with Vichy in North Africa.[38]

Marshall was not willing to risk French opposition. He repeatedly advised that the United States must be successful in its first engagement with German forces. He felt this must be an overriding consideration for Gymnast. The United States could not afford to take risks because he believed that failure would hurt the morale of the American people. The Allies must have sufficient force to assure victory. Roosevelt echoed this sentiment, telling Churchill and the chiefs, "We can take no chances on the possibility of our first major expedition being a failure; that if the risk looks great, we must think twice before we go ahead."[39]

In the interval since Churchill had proposed Gymnast in his first meeting with the president, the initial successful Crusader operation in Libya had collapsed under fierce German counterattacks. In London, General Brooke, like Marshall, thought it highly unlikely that the French would invite the British-Americans to occupy their colonies and doubted the Allies possessed the strength to overcome determined opposition. Brooke also recognized that the Crusader offensive was finished, despite the optimistic reports exchanged between Auchinleck and the prime minister. Brooke's estimate was that Auchinleck lacked troops in the desert and would not receive reinforcements because Churchill was diverting air and sea resources to the Pacific. In short, an advance to the Tunis border was now impossible.[40]

The major drawback to Churchill's proposal to move American troops to North Africa was a lack of shipping, mainly in troop transports and escort vessels, which were needed by the United States. Churchill insisted that there was no shipping shortage and demanded that the Americans try harder and find the ships. He unrealistically wanted the Americans to simultaneously ship troops to Iceland, Northern Ireland, Australia, and the Middle East, and he did not want to hear any excuses. He "would be frightfully unhappy if we had to adjust between expeditions."[41]

Brig. Gen. Dwight Eisenhower, the lead planner for the Far East, summed up the British-American dilemma in his diary: "Ships! Ships! All we need is ships! Also, ammunition, anti-aircraft guns, tanks, airplanes, what a headache!"[42]

The shipping situation grew worse in the last days of the conference as the Japanese advance in the Pacific picked up momentum. The Japanese captured Manila on 2 January and were attacking the American and Filipino forces on the Bataan Peninsula. Two days later, the Japanese invaded British North Borneo, and six days after that, the Dutch East Indies. Despite Churchill and his chiefs' optimism that Singapore would hold for six months, by 13 January, the Japanese were within 150 miles of Singapore. After these disasters,

ALLIES MEET AFTER PEARL HARBOR

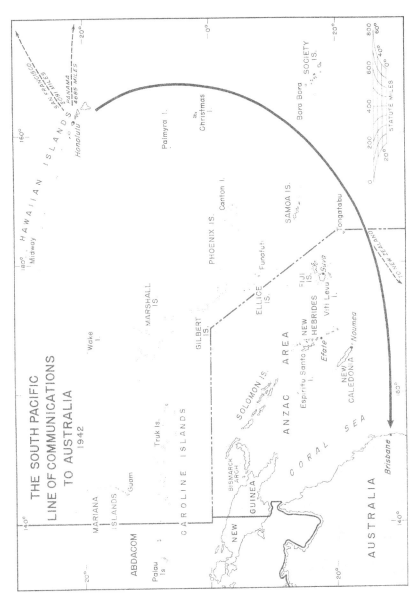

South Pacific lines of communication to Australia (courtesy of US Army Center of Military History)

resources were urgently needed for the Pacific. On 14 January 1942, the Combined Chiefs recommended diverting supplies and equipment from the Atlantic theater to the Pacific. The political leaders agreeing that reinforcing the Pacific was the priority, the prime minister acknowledged the necessity of postponing the operation in North Africa until May.[43]

Both Churchill and Roosevelt were more enamored with a potential occupation of French North Africa (for political reasons) than were their chiefs of staff (for military ones). For Churchill, the operation would provide a base from which to attack Rommel from the rear and end once and for all the long-drawn-out campaign in Libya. It would also provide additional security to the British forces in Gibraltar and relieve the pressure on the beleaguered base in Malta. For Roosevelt, North Africa afforded the opportunity for American troops to engage Axis forces quickly in the Atlantic and reassure the American people that the United States was actively engaged in the fight against Germany. Meanwhile, their respective chiefs of staff were less concerned with political dynamics than they were with the sheer logistical shortcomings that the British-American alliance currently confronted.[44]

Churchill's memoirs do not mention the stress he was under or the disagreements between the American and British staffs. Instead, he wrote of the special bond and cooperation amongst the Allies and simply said of the meeting that "there was complete agreement upon broad principles and targets of the war." Any differences were attributed to "shipping," and Gymnast was "obviously set back by months."[45]

Churchill departed Washington in good spirits. The production numbers of 45,000 tanks and 60,000 planes in 1942 and 125,000 planes and 75,000 tanks in 1943, one advisor observed, left the prime minister "drunk with the figures." In Churchill's mind a special relationship was forming, most importantly with Roosevelt. He believed that he was successful in guiding the president on strategy. At the close of the conference, the president told him, "Trust me to the bitter end." In London, the prime minister confidently told the War Cabinet that "there was little risk of the Americans abandoning the conventional principles of war. They were not above learning from us, providing we do not set out to teach them." He told King George VI that the two nations were now "married" after months of "walking out."[46]

In their private discussions, Roosevelt and Churchill discovered that they shared many similar strategic views as civilian political leaders that had more in common with each other than they did with their military advisors. The British and American chiefs seemed to likewise agree with each other more than they did with their own heads of state on the appropriate short-term strategy. This proved especially true between service chiefs. Portal and Arnold agreed on the importance of air power while Pound and Stark both clearly understood the limitations of shipping and naval escorts in moving resources around the globe. Marshall and Dill formed an important affinity that would energize the Combined Chiefs of Staff in the months ahead. However, serious mistrust and prejudice still existed among staff officers of both nations as they continued to focus on national objectives and goals.[47]

Three major issues remained open when the conference ended on 14 January 1942: a timeline and location for the return to the western European continent had not been established; no decision was made on French North Africa; and no decision was made on how or where to halt the Japanese juggernaut in the Pacific.[48]

These three issues would consume the British-American Alliance in the first eight months of 1942. The crucible of discussions and coordination on these topics would either create a special relationship or shatter the fledgling alliance.

2

Two Colonies

Malaya and the Philippines, January and February 1942

The Arcadia Conference ended on 14 January 1942 on a high note. Just three weeks after the Pearl Harbor attack, the American and British chiefs of staff agreed on the Germany First strategy; a grand strategy or broad blueprint for defeating Germany before Japan; a single theater command in the Far East; and a Combined Chiefs of Staff to give strategic guidance and allocate resources to the theater commands. This last forced the Americans to establish the Joint Chiefs of Staff (JCS) to integrate interservice planning, intelligence, and resources to coordinate with the British.

Arcadia established the basis for a successful British-American coalition. However, this potential was not immediately realized because major near-term issues still remained unresolved. The American chiefs had delayed Churchill's plan for a North Africa campaign, Operation Gymnast, but it remained under consideration. Nor had the British-American military chiefs reconciled an appropriate operational strategy for defeating Germany. There was agreement on a broad strategic principal, but the gap between their respective national strategies and actual execution was left unbridged. The British, for example, believed that a peripheral strategy was the best method, while the Americans insisted on a direct approach. In the words of the official British historian, "A form of words had been found to which both parties could assent; but that did not necessarily mean that they had yet discovered a common strategy." This became the source of divisiveness and strained the fledgling alliance in the months ahead.[1]

Regardless of the strategic agreement on the Germany First strategy at the Arcadia Conference, the United States sent the bulk of its resources to the Pacific in its immediate aftermath. Though long a proponent of a Pacific-first strategy, the US Navy was not attempting to circumvent the Germany First agreement. Great Britain was just as concerned with the threat to their overseas empire, with its most valuable possessions in the Far East. The unprecedented Japanese advance in East Asia appeared invincible in the early months of 1942. In only five weeks, the Japanese had captured Guam, Wake Island, and Hong Kong, and Japanese forces were advancing on Singapore, threatening Burma, and pushing to seize Manilla in the Philippines. With the American Pacific Fleet crippled and Britain's naval resources consumed by fighting in the Atlantic and Mediterranean, Churchill's memoirs acknowledged that the Allies endured "a long period of torturing defeats." In Britain "it seemed everything was growing worse." In first two months of 1942, the British-American alliance could only respond with a piecemeal dispersion of resources scattered across vast oceans to try to stem the tide of the Japanese thrust.[2]

Thus, Churchill's euphoria over his accomplishments at the Arcadia Conference was short-lived. Back in London he was confronted with a new set of crises. The war in North Africa had swung against Britain, disappointing the British public because Churchill's bold promises of destroying the *Afrika Korps* and marching to the Tunis border had evaporated. In Southeast Asia the rapid and unexpected success of the Japanese onslaught magnified years of British neglect. The British people still lionized the prime minister for his determined leadership against German aggression in 1940, but by early 1942 critics questioned the government's many strategic missteps and errors. The press, as well as members of Parliament, lobbied to have Churchill relinquish his concurrent dual roles as prime minister and minister of defence. Separating government and strategic responsibilities, they insisted, would result in a more efficient conduct of the war. Churchill, however, believed that only as prime minister could he convince the British military to adopt a war-winning strategy, and only concurrently as defense minister could he manage the chiefs of staff, and conduct the day-to-day operations of the war to implement that strategy. As a consequence, Prime Minister Churchill dismissed the proposal and instead requested a vote of confidence from the House of Commons. This was a parliamentary procedure to gauge the support of the government for his leadership.[3]

A majority "no" vote, which would have brought down Churchill and his cabinet, was most unlikely. Instead, Churchill sought a ringing affirmation of his wartime leadership. He addressed the House of Commons over 27–29 January 1942 to emphasize his recent accomplishments at Arcadia and to manage public expectations by warning the people of hard times ahead. Churchill assured his Commons audience that his relationship with President Roosevelt was "not only of comradeship, but I think I may say, of friendship" that allowed them to speak openly and honestly about any problem, evidenced by the president's parting words to him ("We will fight through to the bitter end, whatever the cost may be").[4]

The arrival of four thousand American soldiers in Belfast, Northern Ireland, four days earlier bolstered Churchill's claims about the new British-American alliance. It reassured the British public, as did Churchill's promise that these troops were just the vanguard of hundreds of thousands of American reinforcements coming to Great Britain. Numerous bomber and fighter groups would aid in the defense of the British Isles and be key to future offensive operations against Germany. The prime minister stressed how much the industrial might of the United States would benefit Britain. Indeed, according to Churchill, the "colossal programmes" for American production of war matériel in 1942 and 1943 were so staggering that they shocked the Germans to the point of incredulity. But he insisted that the projected numbers were realistic.[5]

Churchill then shifted to his wartime leadership against Germany and Italy. He conceded that he was overly optimistic about the recapture of Cyrenaica and the destruction of the German Army in Libya. Indeed, the two months of fighting had "turned out very differently from what was foreseen." He still emphasized British success in capturing 36,500 German and Italian soldiers and claimed that the British had killed or wounded another 11,000 German and 13,000 Italian soldiers. Nevertheless, hard-hitting German counterattacks had reversed almost all the British territorial gains, and German reinforcements left the future in the western desert in doubt. "Another battle is even now in progress, and I make it a rule to never try and prophesy beforehand how battles will turn out." It was fortuitous that he avoided predictions because the Germans recaptured Benghazi on the final day of the Vote of Confidence.[6]

Even following the German desert victories, the Southeast Asia situation seemed more dire. The Japanese advance threatened British colonies everywhere. "We have had a great deal of bad news lately from the Far East, and I think it is highly probable . . . that we shall have a great deal more. Wrapped up in this bad news will be many tales of blunders and shortcomings, both in foresight and action." Churchill, however, refused to accept responsibility for the failures in Southeast Asia. Fighting Germany and Italy, Britain lacked the resources to simultaneously engage the Japanese in Burma and the Malay Peninsula. He asserted that Japan had seventy mobile divisions, a powerful navy and air force, and, because of the destruction of the American Pacific Fleet, the initiative in the Pacific. Scattering British forces to meet multiple overwhelming Japanese attacks would only result in defeat.[7]

Churchill likewise assumed no responsibility for the Malay disasters. He defended his decision to dispatch the battleships *Prince of Wales* and *Repulse* to Singapore even though both were quickly sunk by Japanese aircraft. Truth be told, he had anticipated the Japanese threat and had quickly moved reinforcements to Singapore although he admitted that it may have been too little, too late. His only forecast was that considerably reinforced British, Australian, and Indian troops would fight "to the last inch." Although 1942 would be a difficult year, he anticipated that by the end of the year the British-American forces would regain naval command of the seas.[8]

After a short deliberation, the House of Commons overwhelmingly voted 464 to 1 in support of Churchill's leadership.[9]

The prime minister had his striking endorsement. Lord Beaverbrook cabled Harry Hopkins in Washington that the prime minister was now "established in authority and power exceeding all that had gone before." Roosevelt quickly responded with warm congratulations and told the prime minister that it was "fun to be in the same decade as you." Churchill quickly responded, thanking Roosevelt and assuring him that the two leaders would have "no disagreements."[10]

Singapore was a disaster that was twenty years in the making. The First World War had drained the British treasury, leaving London almost bankrupt and unable to afford the defense of its far-flung empire. With the abrogation of the Anglo-Japanese Naval Treaty and Japanese expansion in the Pacific and East Asia, the Commonwealth nations, especially Australia and Canada, expected that Britain would protect them against Japanese aggression, particularly after their sacrifices in the recent war. Post–World War I Britain could not afford to build and maintain two fleets, however, one in the Atlantic and the other in the Pacific. In 1919, as the secretary for war and air, Churchill agreed with the "ten-year-rule" consensus that because a major war was unlikely during the next decade, military spending could be reduced accordingly. In 1928, as chancellor of the exchequer, Churchill made the consensus self-perpetuating. New Zealand prime minister W. F. Massey summed up the Commonwealth nations' fear of Japan when he warned the British government at the 1923 Imperial Conference that rearmament, especially in capital ships, was a lengthy process.[11]

To appease the Commonwealth nations, Britain agreed in 1921 to build a large naval base in Singapore and to deploy the fleet from the Atlantic to this base within seventy days should a threat arise. Singapore's strategic location made it the natural site for the naval base, to be completed by 1925. Financial constraints and political bickering delayed completion until 1937, and during that period Labour Party majorities in Parliament continually reduced funding for the naval base and its fortifications. During the 1920s, even a Conservative like Churchill was denouncing the Admiralty for conjuring up an "imaginary" threat from Japan. He asserted that "he did not believe there was any danger to be apprehended from Japan."[12]

In 1937 Britain promised Australia and New Zealand that even in case of war with Germany, nothing would interfere with the dispatch of a fleet to the Far East. Two years later, the British reiterated their "full intention" of deploying a major fleet to endanger any serious Japanese expedition. The same year, 1939, Churchill returned to power as First Lord of the Admiralty and still downplayed any threat from Japan. He told Prime Minister Neville Chamberlain in March 1939 that Japan would not risk their limited forces on such a "wild adventure" as an attack on Singapore. Churchill was simply echoing Chamberlain's thinking and the government's official policy.[13]

Deployment of a major fleet to Singapore was problematic in 1937 and impossible by 1940. The interwar "main fleet to Singapore" strategy was an illusion because the British lacked the resources to back up imperial commitments. Yet the British could not admit to the Dominions an inability to fulfill its defense obligations. The British government continued to assure Australia and New Zealand that the defense of Singapore ranked second in importance only to the defense of the British Isles. As late as November 1939, First Lord of the Admiralty Churchill unequivocally, if disingenuously, reiterated Britain's willingness to sacrifice the Mediterranean Sea lanes that moved its oil from the Middle East to defend Singapore.[14]

By 1940 Churchill was prime minister at war with Germany and Italy and now depended on the United States Navy to secure British interests and commitments in East Asia. A powerful US Pacific Fleet checked Japanese ambitions in the region and maintained the illusion that Britain was still capable of defending the Dominions. In 1941 the British even proposed the United States move a portion of their fleet from Pearl Harbor, Hawaii, to Singapore because the latter was the key to the defense of the Far East. The chagrined Americans saw no reason to shift resources to Singapore. After the disaster at Pearl Harbor and the accompanying destruction of the powerful American Pacific Fleet, the Japanese, not the British or the Americans, held supremacy in Asian waters.[15]

Churchill did not fully grasp conditions in Singapore. Original plans from the 1920s called for a defense against an attack from the sea and assumed that large ground units would find the heavily jungled Malay Peninsula impassable. Economic development on the peninsula during the 1930s changed this equation. British and colonial engineers built an extensive road and rail network and improved port facilities to better exploit Malaya's rich natural resources. The

British military grasped the need to defend the entire peninsula, but with London decreeing ground troops too costly and unavailable, they opted to rely on the Royal Air Force (RAF) for overall defense. Beginning in the mid-1930s, the RAF built numerous airfields, but London was not forthcoming with the promised numbers of aircraft. By 1940 aerial reinforcement was moot, as the demands of the Battle of Britain in 1940 and Mediterranean campaigns in 1941 left few aircraft to spare for Singapore. In short, the defense of the entire peninsula and a naval base without ships rested on an army that lacked the troops to defend it.[16]

During the Arcadia Conference, Churchill projected confidence that Singapore could hold out for six months. It stunned him when the Japanese swept aside all resistance and captured the entire Malay Peninsula in a mere seven weeks. Just when he had successfully fought off attempts to strip him of his powers as minister of defence, he confronted the spectacle of British forces withdrawing to Singapore Island. News that Singapore's naval base was vulnerable to an attack from the north "staggered" him.[17]

It was clear that something was seriously wrong in Britain's Malaya colony. Lord Moran, Churchill's personal physician, remarked that "the Prime Minister's Parliamentary triumph was only a momentary gleam in a dark winter."[18]

Churchill tried to control the public access to the bad news as Japanese forces closed in on Singapore. He directed Gen. Archibald Wavell, the commander in the Far East, to institute censorship to block the "stream of information now pouring out from Singapore." But the fast-moving Japanese advance made it impossible to conceal military defeats from the British people.[19]

Churchill also fired off a series of cables to his commanders that were better suited for the Victorian Age. His indifference to the welfare of his soldiers makes for painful reading even eighty years later. He notified Gen. Hastings Ismay, secretary to the Chiefs of Staff Committee, to defend Singapore "to the death." Surrender was unthinkable and senior officers should die fighting at their posts. He commanded Gen. Archibald Wavell, commander in the Far East, to fight a protracted battle in the ruins of Singapore, defending "every inch of ground" and leaving the enemy nothing but scorched earth.[20]

TWO COLONIES 41

Japanese invasion of Malaya, 1941–42 (US Army/Public Domain)

Churchill realized a naval base without warships was useless but sought to save face among the Allies by protracting its defense as long as possible to tie down Japanese forces. The doomed garrison would somehow reassure the Dominion nations of Britain's commitment to them and convince the Americans of the British Army's fighting spirit. As the beleaguered American and Filipino forces fought desperately on Bataan in the Philippines, Churchill feared that an ignominious defeat in Singapore would diminish British prestige and undermine his position within the new British-American Alliance. On 10 February, he reiterated to General Wavell the necessity to fight to the bitter end for the honor of the army and empire. A gallant last stand would rival the Russians' struggle against Hitler's legions and the stubborn American resistance on Luzon. In Churchill's mind, if the British Army could not save the island, it could at least save British prestige.[21]

Five days later the British commander in Singapore, Gen. Arthur Percival, surrendered to the Japanese. The seventy-day campaign had lasted thirty days fewer than Japanese planners had anticipated and was the most humiliating British defeat of the war. Almost 140,000 British empire troops surrendered to a Japanese force one-third their numbers. It was, Churchill lamented, "the greatest disaster to British arms in our history." The strategic, economic, and psychological ramifications for Britain and its empire rippled across the globe.[22]

Strategically, the fall of Singapore meant the loss of British naval mastery in Southeast Asia and opened maritime routes to the Indian Ocean and the Netherlands East Indies to the Japanese. It secured the Japanese southern flank, enabling their air and ground forces to capture Rangoon, Burma, and close its port (heretofore used by the Americans to supply China). Economically, Malaya's and Burma's natural resources of rubber, tin, oil, and rice, so desperately needed by the Allies, fell into Japanese hands. Japan now had the raw materials to extend the war and to continue their expansion. Psychologically, the populations of the Dominions resented British incompetence. The white population of the Dominions feared a Japanese invasion, and indigenous Asians, witnessing the overthrow of British power firsthand, took a wait-and-see attitude toward their new Asian

Surrender table at the Ford Motor Factory. Lt. Gen. A. E. Percival, general officer commanding, Malaya (front right), unconditionally surrenders all British forces on Singapore Island. Lt. Gen. T. Yamashita, commander in chief, is on the left (Imperial War Museum Photo)

masters. Churchill never fully appreciated how much the collapse of Singapore damaged the once unquestionable image of an invincible Britain that had propped up the empire. The unimaginable defeat by a non-European army frayed the bonds of the British Empire in East Asia and beyond.[23]

The fall of the "impregnable" fortress was a terrible blow to the people of Australia and New Zealand. For decades, the British led the Dominions to believe that Britain would protect them from any threat in the East Asia. Singapore was the proof of that determination and the cornerstone of that regional defense. A generation of colonial British subjects believed in Singapore as a symbol of British military and racial superiority. The Japanese ability to rapidly push the British forces five hundred miles down the Malay Peninsula and to capture the fortress in Singapore in less than ten weeks shattered the myth of Anglo-Saxon military prowess and left stereotypes of racial superiority in tatters.[24]

In the short term, Singapore's fall exerted a profound psychological effect on Churchill and senior British military leaders present during strategic discussions with the Americans throughout the remainder of 1942. Rather than an objective assessment of the strategic missteps of the past twenty years, Churchill blamed defeat on the army and questioned its courage and quality. In brief, he felt the current generation of British soldiers were not as good as their fathers. "In 1915, our men fought on even when they only had one shell left and were under a fierce barrage. Now they cannot resist dive-bombers. We have so many men in Singapore, so many men—they should have done better." Churchill thought that the army displayed a similar lack of fortitude in Libya. He persisted in the belief that the army suffered serious morale problems and felt that it had let him down personally.[25]

Writing after the war, Churchill still shouldered no responsibility for the Singapore disaster. Yes, there were financial limitations; yes, there was a lack of skilled labor to construct defenses; and yes, the troops had only limited training; but still "the Army's role was to protect the naval base," and it had failed.[26]

In the immediate aftermath of Singapore's loss, the prime minister took out his frustration on the army chief, General Brooke, by chiding him at cabinet meetings for not having "a single general in the army who can win battles." In Churchill's estimation, generals lacking ideas meant continual lost battles.[27]

Other government bureaucrats echoed this sentiment. Alexander Cadogan, permanent undersecretary at the Foreign Office, complained of useless generals and non-fighting troops. "Indian Brigades" or "Colonials" were always in the front line, making our army "the mockery of the world." Other government officials shared his attitude when seeking a scapegoat for the fall of Singapore.[28]

Army leaders also questioned the British soldiers' fighting spirit after Singapore. A few days before Singapore's surrender, Gen. Alan Brooke, the chief of the Imperial General Staff, expressed his decade-long feeling that the decaying British Empire was in decline, but it fell to pieces quicker than he anticipated. A week later he wondered, "If the Army cannot fight better than it is at present we shall deserve to lose our Empire!"[29]

General Brooke rationalized the failure as a result of losing the best leaders of the British Army during the First World War. Those losses left the army without a pool of quality senior officers to lead large formations in the Second World War. Even if he fired half his corps and division commanders as "totally unfit" there were no suitable replacements. Brooke's reasoning failed to explain why the German army, which suffered even worse attrition in the ranks of its junior commanders during the First World War, did not have similar problems.[30]

Brooke's deputy, Maj. Gen. John Kennedy, the assistant chief of the Imperial General Staff, agreed that Singapore's fall created unease about the British Army's fighting qualities. British soldiers not only failed to compare well with the German or Russian soldiers and were being outclassed by the Japanese; commanders at two army training centers reported that new recruits "lack enthusiasm and interest in the war." Kennedy concluded, "This nation has become very soft.... The people do not want to fight for the Empire. Mostly, I suppose, they do not care if they have an empire or not so long as they have an easy and quiet life. They do not realize that German domination will be very unpleasant."[31]

The feeling of unease and lack of confidence in the army extended far outside London. General Wavell cabled Churchill on 18 February to blame the fall of Malaya and Singapore on a "lack of fighting spirit" among the troops in Malaya and also in Burma. "Neither British, Australians or Indians have shown any real toughness of mind or body," although the Australians did fight well in Johore.[32]

Such comments reinforced Churchill's prejudices, particularly regarding the performance of the Indian troops on Malaya and Singapore, blaming them more than the other Dominion troops for the catastrophe. The Indian Army was "too big, too lacking in fighting quality—and of dubious reliability." India, for example, had more than nine hundred thousand men under arms by February 1941, but one-third of these troops were deployed overseas to Iraq, Malaya, and the Middle East. The remainder were stationed in India, with a quarter of them serving on the northwest frontier or on internal security missions. Approximately three hundred thousand troops were new recruits undergoing training. Each month brought fifty thousand new recruits into the rapidly expanding army. These newly raised units were woefully short on weapons and equipment, however, and lacked sufficient numbers of experienced officers and noncommissioned officers to lead them in combat. Regardless, they went into combat.[33]

The British Army did learn from their experience in Singapore. Gen. Henry Pownall, a keen observer, made positive recommendations on how to improve the army. As Wavell's chief of staff, he was in a unique position to see the flaws in the army. He realized that the small prewar army had been scattered throughout the empire and had no opportunity for large scale maneuvers during peacetime. Budget restrictions limited the creation of armor units, and recruiting for the army was difficult. In terms of the defense budget, the army was fourth, behind the Royal Air Force, antiaircraft units defending the homeland, and the Royal Navy. Recent wartime expansion had been haphazard and confused, especially for the Indian Army units, which were constantly "milked" of experienced officer and noncommissioned officer talent to create cadres for new formations. Pownall told General Kennedy that Britain needed a "tougher Army" that only harder training, not "exercises timed to suit mealtimes," could supply. "We must," Pownell concluded, "cultivate mobility of mind as well as body, i.e., imagination," along with a common fighting doctrine. A long-overdue revitalization of the army started shortly thereafter. Throughout 1942, British doubts about their army resulted in a reluctance to undertake offensive operations on the continent. This lack of confidence in their own forces led to a projection of similar doubts about the training, leadership, and fighting quality of the US Army.[34]

In the midst of Singapore's death throes, on 11–12 February another challenge closer to home confronted Churchill. Three German cruisers, *Scharnhorst*, *Gneisenau*, and *Prinz Eugen* departed anchorage at Brest and sailed through the English Channel to dock in the German port at Wilhelmshaven. Their transit caused a larger outcry in Britain than the disaster enveloping Singapore. The British public was outraged and panicked that these warships could slip past British guns and the Royal Navy to sail unmolested through the English Channel.

Would they steam up the Thames River and bombard London next? Frightened, people questioned the professionalism and competence of both the Royal Navy and Royal Air Force to protect them. (The ships in fact were damaged when they ran into British minefields, but Churchill could not tell the public because this information was revealed through enigma decrypts.)[35]

The loss of Singapore and the so-called Channel Dash by the German warships revived questions about Churchill's concurrent role as minister of defence. Churchill sought to reassure and rally the British populace. His 15 February broadcast again expressed gratitude for the British-American alliance, but his tone quickly shifted when he attributed much of the recent British misfortune in Southeast Asia to the Pearl Harbor disaster. Without the US Pacific Fleet to check Japan's aggression, the Japanese were free to rampage across the region, seizing British colonies at will.[36]

This buck-passing irritated Americans who listened to his broadcast. Numerous senior US policy officials complained that Britain was self-serving in shifting responsibility for their own defeats to the Americans. President Roosevelt appreciated Churchill's position and remained a resolute friend and supporter. When American complaints about the broadcast reached him, he simply remarked, "Winston had to say something."[37]

John Winant, the American ambassador to Great Britain, wired the president that Churchill looked very tired and was under a great deal of political pressure from opponents angered by the loss of Singapore and other military setbacks. Winant suggested the president try to lift Churchill's spirits, as "a cheery word from you and Harry [Hopkins] always lightens his load." Roosevelt immediately cabled Churchill of his utmost confidence in the prime minister's leadership, while acknowledging the adverse effect the fall of Singapore exerted on him and the British people. Now was not the time for looking back, however. The British-American alliance "must constantly look forward to the next moves that need to be made to hit the enemy."[38]

The United States' focus in the Far East was the Philippines, not Singapore. The Americans were better situated in the Philippines than the British were in Singapore. The Treaty of Paris ceded the archipelago to America in 1898 at the conclusion of the Spanish-American War. As early as 1905, the United States recognized Japan as the only potential threat in the region. Subsequently, a massive construction project to seal off the entrance to Manila Bay was undertaken. By 1914, a series of state-of-the-art defenses were built on the island of Corregidor and adjoining islands. These fortresses were so strong that Manila was nicknamed the "Gibraltar of the East." They were dug deep and reinforced to withstand an attack from the heaviest surface vessels then in existence. These strongholds were designed and built before military aviation became a serious threat. The rapid technological advances in air power during the 1920s undermined their effectiveness. This flaw could not be corrected because the Washington Naval Treaty of 1922 prohibited the United States from modernizing the fortifications on Corregidor and adjacent islands. The only work allowed was the addition of antiaircraft batteries and deep tunnels to store supplies. Nevertheless, the American defenses were in far better shape than those of the British on Singapore.[39]

Army and navy planners deduced by 1924 that the United States did not possess enough forces to defend all of the Philippines against a Japanese invasion. Politically, however, the American public would not accept an abandonment of American posts and civilians in the Far East. The planners adopted War Plan Orange, which specified that the US Army would hold Manila Bay as a base for the navy until the fleet arrived. Although never formally abandoned, the war plan was modified in 1935 from holding all of Manila Bay to just holding the entrances to the harbor. Unfortunately, the army and navy planners failed to synchronize the war plan. The plan's strategic flaw was the assumption that the US Navy would relieve the Philippine garrison within six months. Otherwise, the beleaguered garrison would fall. Navy planners, however, estimated that it would take two years, not six months, for the Pacific Fleet to relieve the Philippines. This was never resolved prior to the Japanese invasion.[40]

That same year, General MacArthur was appointed as the military advisor to the commonwealth governor of the Philippines. His plan for the newly established American-Filipino army was to withdraw to the mountainous jungle on the Bataan Peninsula, which is situated on the northern arm of Manila Bay, if he could not prevent the enemy from landing on the main island of Luzon. From there he could coordinate a defense with the fortresses on Corregidor and other islands to deny the Japanese access to Manila Harbor until the US Navy arrived. Prior to the Japanese invasion, the American-Filipino forces conducted extensive site surveys and reconnaissance of the difficult terrain on Bataan. This familiarity with the geography and terrain later proved a distinct advantage in December–April 1942.[41]

The Japanese expected an easier fight in the Philippines than in Singapore. Japanese planners anticipated that it would take fifty days to occupy the Philippines, half the time it would take to capture Singapore. Anticipating a quick victory, they scheduled the withdrawal of several veteran units for operations elsewhere. Although they realized this might hinder the Japanese advance, it was a risk they were willing to take. The Japanese grossly underestimated the American-Filipino force and assumed the capture of Manila would precipitate the collapse of the Filipino will to continue resisting. They did not expect the Allied withdrawal to Bataan and were totally unprepared for the difficult terrain and spirited defense.[42]

In May 1934, President Roosevelt and Congress passed the Tydings-McDuffie Law. A strong anti-colonialist, Roosevelt was a major advocate for granting Philippine independence in 1946. This legislation set the stage for a ten-year transition for the Philippine Commonwealth to establish protocols for defense, economic development, and national integration. Guaranteed independence proved a positive psychological and political factor as the Filipino people resisted the Japanese invasion.[43]

During January and February 1942, the Americans repulsed Japanese advances in the Philippines. With Singapore occupied, Japan wanted to finish the Philippines campaign to secure their Pacific lines of communication. The Americans faced a dilemma in the Philippines. It made military sense to write off the isolated islands and dedicate their limited resources to the defense of those locations that were defensible. This was the US Navy's position because without the main forces of the Pacific Fleet they were unwilling to

CHAPTER 2

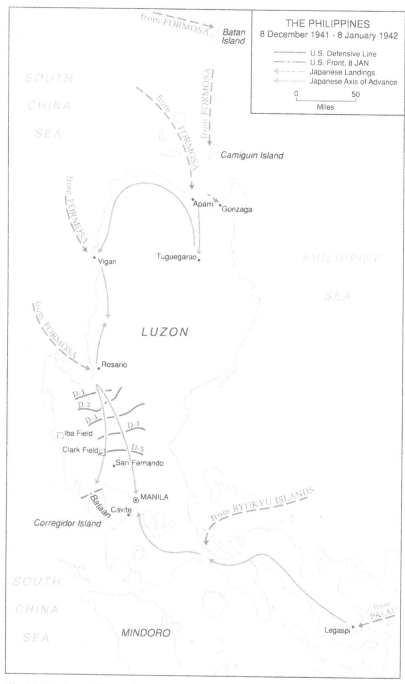

The Philippines, 8 December 1941–8 January 1942 (courtesy of US Army Center of Military History)

risk scarce resources on a forlorn hope. The US Army and President Roosevelt were unwilling to do this. Roosevelt recognized that America would be judged on the performance of its soldiers and rejected any defeatist attitude, insisting that every effort would be made to keep open the lines of communication between the US mainland and American and Filipino forces fighting on Bataan.[44]

This became impossible when the United States could not break through the Japanese blockade of the Philippines. By 8 February, a frustrated Manuel Quezon, the president of the Philippines, told Roosevelt: "The situation in my country has become so desperate that I feel positive action is demanded. Militarily it is evident that no help will reach us from the United States in time either to rescue the beleaguered garrison now fighting so gallantly or to prevent the complete overrunning of the entire Philippine Archipelago.... All our soldiers in the field were animated by the belief that help would be forthcoming. This help has not and evidently will not be realized."[45]

Gen. Douglas MacArthur and Manuel Quezon, president of the Philippines (courtesy of the George C. Marshall Foundation, Lexington, Virginia, USA)

Quezon proposed that the United States grant the Philippines immediate independence. He would then declare the Philippines a neutral country, expecting both US and Japanese forces to accept his declaration and withdraw accordingly. For his part, Quezon would immediately disband the Filipino army. Quezon thought that Roosevelt, embarrassed by his inability to provide aid and succor to the islands' defenders, would endorse the plan. Quezon's frustration was understandable, but his plan was unworkable. The Japanese had invested too much effort into capturing the archipelago to simply accept a declaration of neutrality and leave.[46]

Roosevelt responded bluntly, rejecting the proposal and reminding Quezon that the United States had previously promised the Philippines complete independence in 1946. American soldiers would fulfill the United States' obligation to the Philippines to the "bitter end" and eventually the Americans would drive the Japanese invaders from the islands.[47] The president also notified Gen. Douglas MacArthur, commander of American-Filipino forces, of his rejection of Quezon's proposal. There was no bombastic rhetoric to "fight to the death" similar to that which Churchill sent to his commanders in Singapore. Rather, Roosevelt trusted MacArthur, allowing him to surrender the Filipino element of his command if he deemed it appropriate, while insisting that "American forces will keep our flag flying in the Philippines so long as their remains any possibility of resistance." The president informed MacArthur that he was fully aware of the dire military situation, but the United States had an obligation to resist "Japanese aggression to the last," not only to fulfill its duty to the Philippines but also to demonstrate American determination and will to all peoples.[48]

On 12 February Quezon accepted the US president's decision. MacArthur likewise reassured the president that he had no intention of surrendering Filipino units and that his wife and son would remain with him to share the "fate of the garrison."[49]

Secretary of war Henry Stimson thought that the decision, "consigning as it did a brave garrison to fight to the finish," was highly emotional for all concerned. He sent personal notes to Quezon

The guiding genius of Bataan was Gen. Douglas MacArthur (right), shown here with Maj. Gen. Jonathan Wainwright, who assumed command when MacArthur was ordered to Australia (Library of Congress)

and MacArthur, assuring them that the president recognized their "superb courage and fidelity." General Marshall was also impressed by Roosevelt's resolute handling of such a difficult and sensitive issue and believed the president showed great courage in ordering MacArthur to fight to the last man. He later said that was the moment he realized that Roosevelt was a great man.[50]

The tenacity and courage of the Filipino soldiers had impressed Roosevelt. Regardless of MacArthur's early errors, once the American and Filipino forces reached Bataan they fought extremely well and the Filipino forces maintained a high level of morale and esprit de corps, despite a lack of training, food, medicine, and equipment. Although unable to repulse the Japanese landings, they inflicted heavy losses on the invaders and delayed the capture of Corregidor Island in Manila Bay. Prewar plans expected to deny the Japanese use of Manila Harbor for six months. Corregidor surrendered one day short of five months.[51]

CHAPTER 2

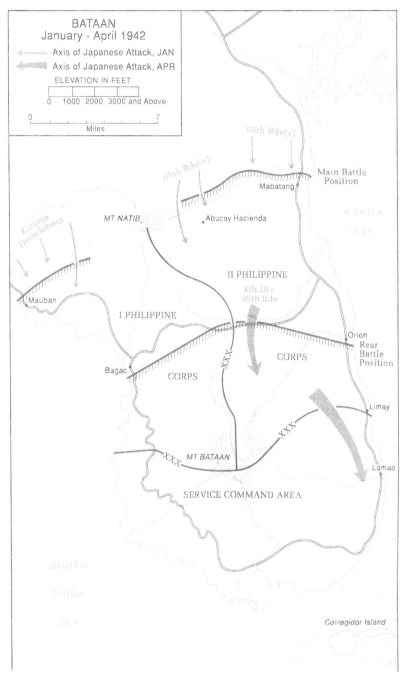

Bataan, January–April 1942 (courtesy of US Army Center of Military History)

After the Singapore debacle it was perhaps inevitable that unfavorable comparisons were made between the American and Filipino troops in the Philippines and the British Dominion forces in Malaya and Singapore. The resolute Filipino forces fighting loyally with the Americans seemed to some to be an example of the trust free governments placed in the United States. Critics of imperialism were quick to point out that Filipino soldiers resisted to the end and did not join forces with the Japanese, as was the case of many Indian troops after the fall of Malaya and Singapore. Roosevelt was convinced that Britain's imperialistic policies toward India were the root cause of the differing performance between the Filipino and Indian troops.[52]

Recent developments in Malaya and east India influenced Roosevelt so profoundly that on 25 February he sent Churchill a highly confidential note recommending that Britain take steps toward granting India independence. According to the president, Churchill's imperial attitude played into Japan's hands and made their "Asia for Asiatics" proposals more appealing. Roosevelt detected Indian resentment with the British government that might reduce India's willingness to fight Japan. This was the first of Roosevelt's repeated suggestions to Churchill to consider greater autonomy for India and was not well received by the British prime minister.[53]

During the Arcadia Conference, General Marshall, with strong backing from the president, had proposed a single theater commander who, it was hoped, could rise above service and national demands and decide conflicting directives to formulate an effective and cohesive operational strategy. Churchill and the British agreed, and Gen. Archibald Wavell was appointed as the theater commander of the American-British-Dutch-Australian (ABDA) Command. Through January and February 1942, the recently formed Combined Chiefs of Staff struggled to support ABDA.

The command consisted of the four nations, all of which recognized the importance of controlling the Malay Barrier to prevent Japanese expansion southward into the Netherlands East Indies (NEI). Beyond that, each had its own diverse objectives in East Asia. Wavell, as commander, was beset with arguments on protocol and priorities from constituent governments; helplessly searching for scarce resources to inflict damage on the Japanese; and barraged with cables from home governments demanding too much from a situation they did not fully understand.[54]

Singapore's loss was a crushing blow to the ABDA because its defense was central to the security of the NEI, Australia, New Zealand, and India. The swift-moving Japanese campaign made an invasion of Java imminent. Wavell doubted that the Allies could hold Java and instead proposed saving Burma. He recommended that the two Australian divisions currently en route by ship from the Middle East to reinforce Java be diverted, preferably to Burma. The Australians and the Dutch vigorously dissented; the former wanted their troops at home to protect Australia, and the latter wanted to hold Java. Both dismissed the entire ABDA command as a sham to divert resources to protect the British Empire in the Far East.[55]

Australia had supported the British war effort by deploying three of its best divisions to the Middle East, plus a fourth lost at Singapore. Australian prime minister John Curtin was in no mood to acquiesce to further British demands on Australian troops. Churchill initially appealed to Curtin's sense of duty: "I suppose you realize your leading division ... is the only force that can reach Rangoon in time to prevent its loss and the severance of communication with China.... There is nothing else in the world that can fill the gap.... We are all in favor of Australian troops returning home to defend their native soil.... But a vital war emergency cannot be ignored."[56]

Curtin was unmoved and demanded the immediate return of Australia's divisions. Churchill convinced himself that Curtin would soon change his mind and arbitrarily diverted the Australian troop convoy to Rangoon without Curtin's permission. The incensed Australian prime minister demanded the return of his troops. Darwin had been bombed, and a Japanese submarine had recently attacked ships in Sydney Harbor. Australians feared an imminent Japanese invasion and believed Britain ignored the threat they faced. Churchill then asked Roosevelt to send US divisions to Australia to replace the units that he would send to Rangoon. Curtin rejected that offer and notified Churchill of his priority to save Australia, whose northern defenses were "gone or going." Unable to overcome Curtin's determined opposition, Churchill had no choice but to redirect the ships to Australia.[57]

Discord between Churchill and Curtin suggests a wider problem within the alliance. In the early months of 1942, Australia grew more and more disgusted by Britain's lack of support and looked more and more to the Americans for support and resources. Curtin told the press that Australia looked "to America, free of any pangs as to (her) traditional links or kinship with the United Kingdom." Help was on the way. Roosevelt promised a US division regardless of Curtin's decision on the troop diversion and Adm. Ernest King continued to push for more resources to protect the lines of communication between Hawaii and Australia and the southwest Pacific.[58]

The Combined Chiefs of Staff discussed resources for the ABDA on 17 February. They concurred with Wavell's assessment that Java was indefensible, and that Burma and Australia were more important. They deferred judgment on the diversion of Australian troops to Rangoon because it was a political decision between London and Canberra. They acknowledged that Burma was effectively cut off from the rest of the ABDA and would be best controlled from India, a position the British had desired from the outset.[59]

On 21 February, General Wavell closed the ABDA Command after six miserable weeks. No one blamed Wavell for the failure of this first attempt at unified command in the Pacific. Two days later the Combined Chiefs of Staff officially dissolved the ABDA Command, with far-reaching implications. Britain and the United States agreed to establish areas of responsibility in the Far East. Burma would pass to British control in India, and the British would be responsible for the defense of India and the Indian Ocean. The Philippines, which had only nominally been under the supervision of the ABDA, reverted to American control. Australia took responsibility for the defense of its northern states. The Dutch opposed ABDA's dissolution because it would spell the end of Allied assistance to the Netherlands East Indies. Not wanting to appear to have abandoned the Dutch, the Combined Chiefs promised that supplies and matériel would continue being sent to Java and the NEI[60]

This ended the Allies' initial attempt at creating a unified command in a single theater. Although the Combined Chiefs could find reinforcements for the ABDA, lack of shipping resulted in only a trickle of replacements arriving in theater. At sea, the warships that might have challenged the Japanese fleet were scattered, protecting the vast lines of communication. The command did not accomplish all that Marshall hoped when he proposed the concept of a single theater command. But many lessons were learned, and the concept's validity was proven. In the future, when it was time to create other unified commands, the Combined Chiefs benefited from the harsh discussions and disagreements that arose trying to support the ABDA. It would prove the blueprint that the commands in North Africa, Southeast Asia, and western Europe followed.[61]

General Brooke, a member of the Combined Chiefs of Staff by virtue of being the chief of the Imperial General Staff, was ecstatic over ABDA's dissolution. Brooke had opposed the unified command concept from its creation at Arcadia, a conference he had not attended, and was vociferously opposed to several of Arcadia's agreements. "So far there is very little that was settled at Washington which is surviving the test of time." He hoped that the Combined Chiefs of Staff would be dissolved next. After the war, he explained, "I had little faith in this organization at the time . . . I think mainly due to the fact it had been set up in Washington with the USA as the predominant partner whilst they had . . . not much knowledge in running the war and certainly little experience."[62] After Singapore, Brooke still did not view the war from a combined perspective. His parochialism limited his vision to the paramount British needs in the alliance.

Dissolving the ABDA did not end the demands and frantic appeals for help from the Far East. Churchill and the British wanted the United States to send troops to Australia and New Zealand, as well as additional naval units for the southwest Pacific. The prime minister also proposed that the United States supply shipping to transport British troops to the Indian Ocean and commence air offensives in China, northeast India, and the Aleutians.[63]

Marshall, on the other hand, was dealing with the war in the Far East more holistically. Marshall was responsible for allocating the bulk of the resources to the theater, and, despite the disagreements in the Combined Chiefs meetings, the ABDA concept was a huge help in deciding how to fairly divide resources amongst the allies. He was loath to see the ABDA command organization, which had been so laboriously established, be completely abolished.[64]

Aside from Churchill's incessant demands, the Americans' bigger problem was the lack of interservice coordination between the army and navy. Throughout January and February, the navy increased their demands for more resources in the Pacific in order to build air bases along the lines of communication between Hawaii and Australia that would protect the sea lanes. This frustrated Brigadier General Eisenhower, the lead army planner for the Far East, who noted in his diary during mid-February, "The navy wants to take all the islands in the Pacific, have them held by army troops, to become bases for army pursuit and bombers. Then the navy will have a safe place to sail its vessels. But they will go no further than our air (army) can assure superiority. The amount of air required for this slow, laborious, and indecisive type of warfare is going to be something that will keep us from going to Russia's aid in time." The culprit, as Eisenhower saw it, was Admiral King, commander in chief of the US fleet, who was the "arbitrary, stubborn type, with not too much brains and a tendency towards bullying his subordinates."[65]

Adm. Ernest King (Navy History and Heritage Command Photograph, UA 02.06.01)

Support to the Far East had to be balanced with the Arcadia agreement on grand strategy, which stated that "only the minimum of force necessary for the safeguarding of vital interests in other theaters should be diverted from operations against Germany." No one, however, defined what this meant. It was obvious though before the conference ended that limited shipping resources originally intended for the Atlantic would have to be diverted to check the Japanese thrust in the southwest Pacific.[66]

The rapid Japanese advances in January and February 1942 forced the Allies to make emergency transfers of American soldiers and sailors with their equipment to the Pacific. There was no established plan for the concentration of limited resources, and, given the wide disparity in military leaders' opinions on requirements for the Pacific, the result was a series of disjointed, ad hoc distributions of supplies. The Combined Chiefs of Staff found themselves overwhelmed by constant demands for resources. In the first week of February alone, they received four British requests to send aircraft to Australia, New Zealand, and Fiji; Dutch demands for fighter aircraft for the NEI; and American planners' pleas for bombers needed in New Guinea and Australia.[67]

By 21 February 1942, the shipping shortage had become so acute that Maj. Gen. Brehon Somervell, the American assistant chief of staff, G-4, told the British that unless they made Gymnast the top priority, planning for the operation was "nebulous." On 25 February British planners admitted that the Gymnast plan for an invasion of North Africa was no longer possible during 1942. By the end of the month even Churchill considered postponing his long-cherished Gymnast plan.[68]

In late February, Secretary of War Stimson and General Marshall were concerned that despite the Germany First strategy most resources seemed destined for the Far East, where demand was growing, not slowing. The two believed that the British-Americans were dispersing forces to plug gaps in response to each new Pacific crisis. They feared that the Allies were losing sight of the main objective, the defeat of Germany, and sought to concentrate resources and effort on Germany, or, as Stimson put it, "strike an offensive blow at the heart of the enemy."[69]

On 24 February, Stimson told General Arnold that it was time to limit men and supplies being sent to the southwestern Pacific because the region was slowly becoming the major theater of the war. Stimson directed the army to send seven thousand troops to Ireland instead of using the shipping for the Pacific operations. This was Stimson's attempt to refocus the alliance on Germany and the deferred Arcadia commitments. Marshall's efforts to check the piecemeal dispersion of Allied forces globally involved directing General Eisenhower and the newly formed Army Operations Division to prepare plans for a cross-channel attack in northwestern Europe. This was the priority target, allowing Marshall to assign resources and prevent future dispersions of forces.[70]

3

Dispersion Unchecked

March 1942

At the Arcadia Conference, the British-American allies agreed that Nazi Germany was their primary enemy, but by March 1942 halting the spread of Imperial Japan's aggression in East Asia became the Allies' immediate concern. British and American strategies in Asia diverged according to their respective national interests. For the British, the defense of their Far East empire meant protecting India. For the Americans, the Army and Navy's unwillingness to cooperate undercut any attempt to offer a united front in strategic discussions. The US Navy wanted more resources to support a Pacific offensive, while the US Army wanted to focus the American and British navies on the main enemy, Nazi Germany.

Japanese forces had destroyed Allied naval power in the Netherlands East Indies (NEI), and after a series of brief land campaigns they occupied the entire oil-rich Dutch colony. Japanese attention shifted to Burma, where the Japanese army wanted to cut off the "Burma Road," the sole logistical lifeline open to China for desperately needed military equipment and munitions from the United States. Closing the Burma Road would isolate China, which, the Japanese believed, would then collapse, thereby freeing the large numbers of Japanese ground and air forces fighting in China for redeployment against the US forces in the Pacific.[1]

The forlorn Burma campaign illustrated how the strategic problems of divided command in a secondary theater disrupted meaningful operational planning. Great Britain and the United States held

Burma, 1942 (courtesy of US Army Center of Military History)

widely divergent strategic views about Burma's role in the defeat of Japan. Roosevelt thought Burma was vital to the Allied effort because supplies flowing through Burma kept China, which was tying down the bulk of the Japanese army, active in the war. The president considered China a great power and, as a member of the Big Four—China, Great Britain, the Soviet Union, and the United States—an essential postwar partner. American strategy thus emphasized reopening the Burma Road by operations in northern Burma near the Chinese-Burmese border.[2]

The British regarded Burma as, at best, a defensive barrier and buffer between India and the Japanese forces in China. They dismissed China as more of a liability than a great power and were loath to allocate scarce resources to the Chinese, who would only squander them. Above all, the British premised their Far East strategy on the defense of India and would fight along the Indo-Burmese border to preserve their empire. American leaders, and especially President Roosevelt, considered the European colonial empires anachronisms and championed their independence after the war.[3]

General Wavell, recently reappointed as commander in chief in India, was unaware of just how dire the situation was in Burma. It was plain that the poorly trained and equipped Anglo-Indian troops could not hold Rangoon, and Wavell ordered the port city evacuated and troops withdrawn to upper Burma before the Japanese cut off and destroyed his forces. Intact forces positioned in central Burma could at least help to defend India.[4]

Rangoon's loss was a serious blow to the Allied cause in Asia. China was cut off from the allies and its vital supply route through Burma. American strategists worried that, without the means to continue to resist, China might capitulate to Japanese aggression. The British estimated the impact of defeat in terms of lost natural resources; the Burmese rice bowl, which fed India's huge population, was gone, as was the main British source of refined aviation fuel. Gone, too, were British airbases near Rangoon and the Allies' air defenses with them. The Japanese enjoyed unimpeded maritime passage to reinforce Burma from Malaya, a much faster and more efficient method than the difficult overland route.[5]

The conflicting strategic goals of Britain, China, and the United States bore much of the blame for the disaster in Burma. Britain lacked the forces to defend her Burmese colony but refused to allow two Chinese field armies into Burma to stiffen its defenses. Chinese Generalissimo Chiang Kai-shek took the British rejection personally and, after Rangoon fell in early March, was convinced the British really had no intention to fight the Japanese invaders and refused to cooperate further with the British.[6]

Chiang turned instead to Gen. Joseph Stilwell, his new American chief of staff. Stilwell arrived in China and met with Chiang for the first time on 6 March. Stilwell was Marshall and Stimson's personal choice for this challenging role. He had years of experience in China and spoke the language fluently. Roosevelt wanted Stilwell to increase the effectiveness of US aid to China and improve the combat efficiency of the Chinese army. To accomplish this the president authorized Stilwell to accept any command position offered by the generalissimo. At his initial meeting, Chiang informed his new chief

General Stilwell marches out of Burma, May 1942 (National Archives Photograph)

of staff that he was "fed up with the British retreat and lethargy ... and was suspicious of their motives and intentions." On 9 March, the generalissimo, concerned that the British were only concerned with India and not China, informed Roosevelt of his dissatisfaction with the British and recommended that Stilwell assume command of the Allied (Chinese and British) effort in Burma.[7]

Wavell opposed Stilwell's independent command of Chinese forces (approximately six divisions) and proposed that Churchill protest any new command arrangements directly to Roosevelt. Churchill agreed and recommended to the US president that Stilwell serve under British command (General Alexander) because Burma was British territory, and they were responsible for supply matters.[8]

Churchill's plea failed to account for both Roosevelt's strong anti-colonial feelings and the president's concern with long-term Sino-American relations. When discussing the contretemps on 19 March, Roosevelt and Stimson agreed that Wavell lacked tact in dealing with the Chinese and that Stilwell would be more supportive to a British senior officer than would a Chinese commander. Roosevelt's reply to Churchill endorsed Stilwell over any Chinese commander because Stilwell was "an immensely capable and resourceful individual" with an intimate knowledge of the Chinese. He concluded that the command status be left unchanged and underlined his faith that Stilwell would cooperate with the British.[9]

British Field Marshal Dill in Washington, DC, actually drafted Roosevelt's reply. When the president received Churchill's cable, he sent it to Marshall for comment. Marshall discussed the contents with Dill, remarking that "the important thing at the moment is that Stilwell provides in himself a possible means of cooperation, whereas a Chinese commander probably would make the situation impossible." Dill grasped both Churchill's desire to control all the forces defending Burma and India as well as the American desire to aid Chiang. He contacted Stilwell directly and reviewed the command relationship in Burma before advising the continuation of the current arrangement. Marshall forwarded Dill's recommendation to the president who in turn submitted it verbatim in his cable to Churchill.[10]

The discussion between the Americans and British on command relations in Burma was irrelevant. Dill was correct in his assessment

DISPERSION UNCHECKED

Japanese conquest of Burma, April–May 1942 (courtesy of US Army Center of Military History)

that Alexander and Stilwell could work with each other. After the two met face-to-face on 21 March, Alexander agreed that he would get more support from the Chinese through Stilwell than working directly through the Chinese commanders. Despite the discussions on command and control, by the end of the month the Allies were in complete retreat in Burma.[11]

As the defeats in the Pacific and Southeast Asia mounted, so, too, did the strains on the new British-American alliance. American public opinion openly criticized the Germany First strategy and demanded greater effort to fight Japan. A depressed prime minister shared his concerns with the US president in early March. "When I reflect how I have longed and prayed for the entry of the United States into the war, I find it difficult to realize how gravely our British affairs have deteriorated by what has happened since December seven." Singapore's surrender, he told the president, was the "greatest disaster in our history," and indeed Churchill could not foresee any limits on Japanese expansion in the near term. He worried that the Japanese would be unstoppable in 1942 because the Allies lacked the troops and equipment to hold them at bay in the broad Pacific.[12]

Churchill nonetheless still sought to influence the next Allied steps in the Indian and Pacific Oceans. His early March counsel to the president only reflected Churchill's firm conviction that the United States had unlimited resources available to underwrite his war-winning strategy in Asia. Churchill questioned what the American Navy was doing in the Far East. "I have not been able to form a full picture of the United States plans by sea, air and land against Japan. I am hoping that by May your naval superiority in the Pacific will be restored and that this will be a continuing preoccupation to the enemy." He insisted that the US Navy initiate immediate and strong action to tie down the Japanese fleet in the Pacific in order to prevent a Japanese invasion of India via the Indian Ocean. The prime minister's lengthy specifications left the impression that his strategy consisted of a series of piecemeal attacks against the periphery of the Japanese empire. American readers could not help but notice the similarities between his strategic concepts for defeating Japan and Germany.[13]

Churchill, for instance, wanted American bombers deployed to northern India, from which they could strike enemy bases in Siam (Thailand) and Indochina. The United States, in his opinion, should simultaneously establish operational air bases in the Aleutian Islands, several thousand miles removed from northern India. Furthermore, the United States had to ship a US division to both New Zealand and Australia, respectively, to bolster their defenses and deploy "main naval forces" to protect the ANZAC area. He justified this recommendation by noting that the Allied counterstroke against Japan would originate from bases in the ANZAC area. Finally, he proposed that US commandos raid outlying Japanese islands to siphon off resources. Churchill's rambling cable ruffled the US Joint Chiefs of Staff because it required dispersing scarce or even nonexistent resources throughout the Far East at the expense of those needed to defeat Germany.[14]

That same day, 5 March, Roosevelt consulted with Hopkins, Stimson, and the Joint Chiefs to coordinate a reply to Churchill. The president well understood the British feelings after the fall of Singapore and the imminent evacuation of Rangoon. He simply commented that "Churchill needed a pat on the back." Stimson was less charitable, describing the cable as "an appeal for further dispersion on the already over-extended world front and it suggested that we would now be unable to get our victory in '43 but would have to wait till '44." Churchill's latest note frustrated the secretary of war because it was a continuation of the ad hoc dispersion and "plugging of leaks" approach that had dominated strategy in the Far East for two months. Stimson knew that the United States did not have unlimited resources to disperse all over the globe, and he felt that the Allies were losing the Germany First focus decided at the Arcadia conference. He believed that it was time for a new and bolder strategy and proposed one to the president that would send "an overwhelming force to the British Isles" to "threaten an attack on the Germans in France." The very arrival of American troops would greatly boost the sagging British morale. Stimson noted that Marshall and Arnold were enthusiastic about his suggestion, but Admiral King and the US Navy were not. Roosevelt appeared very impressed by Stimson's recommendation.[15]

Later that day the president consulted with the British chiefs to learn their opinion of Churchill's cable. They had not seen this latest message but had received separate instructions from London to request greater American help in various locations, especially diverting additional resources to the Indian Ocean. Per Roosevelt's instructions, General Arnold updated the British chiefs on the earlier discussion on the advantages of offensive operations conducted from Britain against the Germans in occupied France. Taken off guard by the US proposal for an offensive into France, the British chiefs were reticent to give an opinion on so major a proposition and preferred any agreements be made in London. After a short discussion, Roosevelt ended the meeting by urging the British chiefs to consider the idea of a "second front" in France.[16]

The following day Stimson met with Marshall and Eisenhower to design a strategy to offset the dispersion of resources around the world. The secretary asked Eisenhower, the lead war planner, for his views on strategy. Eisenhower emphasized that the United States must clarify the limits on its resources for the Far East. Furthermore, the current ad hoc US policy of providing men and matériel was unsustainable. All three agreed that Japan was a secondary theater and that even Japan's defeat would not end the war against Germany. The primary goal for the Allies, Eisenhower believed, was keeping Soviet Russia in the war. If Germany defeated the Soviets, the best the British-American alliance could hope for was a stalemate. To accomplish this strategy, Eisenhower would build up US forces in Britain to prepare for a powerful attack into France. Stimson endorsed his concept, but Eisenhower warned that the navy would oppose it because Admiral King envisioned a "slow step by step creeping movement through the islands of New Caledonia, New Britain, etc." in the Pacific. Such an approach would only drain Allied resources and time but "would not get anywhere in solving the big situation as it is being fought out in Europe."[17]

Yet the deteriorating situation in the Pacific did require the diversion of scarce shipping to transport US troops to the Far East. To Eisenhower's thinking, the lack of shipping ruled out sending US troops to the Middle East in 1942 for operations that American planners had previously declared impractical. Still, they spent disproportionate energy responding to the prime minister, who insisted that a combined British-American operation in north and northwest Africa to drive the Axis forces from the Middle East was vital. Marshall and Eisenhower wanted Roosevelt to intervene and end this tedious planning cycle.[18]

On 7 March, the Joint Chiefs of Staff met formally for the fourth time to discuss strategy and review the president's preliminary draft response to Churchill. General Marshall firmly reiterated his opposition to the continued dispersion of resources, insisting that "we must never lose sight of the eventual necessity of fighting the Germans in Germany." Marshall would concentrate the major effort against the Axis on land operations on the European continent, staged from bases in Britain and conducted as soon as possible. Marshall made the same recommendation that morning to the president, raising an issue that the British-American allies had avoided for two months as they scrambled to halt the Japanese rampage in the Far East.[19]

The British mission in Washington had an opportunity to review the president's proposed reply before it was sent to the prime minister. They made few changes, and after two days of meetings and discussions Roosevelt finally answered Churchill. The president acknowledged "the magnitude of the problems confronting you [Churchill] in the Indian Ocean," but he pointed out that the United States was "equally concerned over those which confront us in the Pacific." Roosevelt observed that the United States had already assumed responsibility for the defense of Australia and New Zealand as well as guarding the sea lanes around them. He agreed to furnish two additional American divisions to Australia and New Zealand but told Churchill that reallocation of shipping for the deployment forced the cancellation of the French North Africa operation, cautioning Churchill that finite resources required such tradeoffs. Assets sent to protect the dominions in Asia had to come from the troops and supplies available for deployment to the Indian Ocean, the Middle East, or Britain. That meant that "Gymnast cannot be undertaken." This uncharacteristically firm reply urged

Churchill to look at the war holistically and not focus simply on the welfare of the British Empire.[20]

This cable ended months of equivocation on the Middle East. Three days later the American and British chiefs formally agreed that it was no longer necessary "for the Combined Chiefs of Staff to present any paper to the President or Prime Minister on the subject of Super Gymnast." On the advice of his key military advisors, however, Roosevelt somewhat surprisingly broached as a replacement for Gymnast the option of building up Allied forces in Britain in preparation for an offensive against Germany in 1942.[21]

The cables exchanged between Churchill and Roosevelt on global priorities led to a strategic division of responsibility. At an 8 March meeting with Stimson, Hopkins, and Marshall, the president sought a method to coordinate global grand strategy. The president recommended dividing the world into three main areas of operation: (1) the Pacific would be an American area of responsibility; (2) the Indian Ocean and Middle East would be a British responsibility; and (3) the Atlantic, including Europe, would be a joint responsibility. Stimson liked the concept because it simplified the present command situations and "took the initiative [in the Pacific] out of the hands of Churchill." Roosevelt dispatched the proposal to Churchill the next day.[22]

Churchill and the British chiefs agreed to Roosevelt's proposal to divide the world into three theaters of operations, but with certain reservations. Churchill concurred in principle with the simplification resulting from the American control of the Pacific sphere and the British control of the Indian Sphere. Nowhere, however, was mentioned the joint control of the European-Atlantic Sphere nor of the future front on the European continent. Churchill feared that the United States might opt for naval superiority in the Pacific at the expense of naval security in the Indian Ocean. To avoid this eventuality Churchill proposed to establish two Pacific war councils to provide input on strategy, one in Washington and the other in London. The London council soon disbanded because the United States contributed the lion's share of the resources destined for the Pacific theater. Some senior British officials, like General Brooke, took a more sinister

Gen. Alan Brooke (Australian War Museum Photo)

view of the proposal, describing it as an attempt by the Americans "to bust up the Empire" by coopting Australia and New Zealand.[23]

The virtual abandonment of the Gymnast operation also created a dilemma for the president. Without Gymnast the United States no longer had a significant ground operation against Germany planned for 1942. But at the Democratic National Committee dinner on 23 February, the president had promised the American people that British-American forces would soon take the offensive in the Atlantic. The Soviets were also clamoring for an Allied "second front" to divert German resources from the Russian front. Roosevelt told Marshall on 8 March that he and the prime minister were under a great deal of Russian pressure to act. The president cautioned Marshall that he did not want Russia to pressure the Allies into making an attack that was precipitous or militarily unsound. But something had to be done. Could an air campaign alone reduce German momentum on the eastern front? Roosevelt was also beginning to consider the possibilities of a land offensive on the continent, but it had to be successful.[24]

In a 9 March message to Churchill, Roosevelt again broached the need for "definite plans for the establishment of a new front on the

European Continent" and proposed a third operational theater, the Atlantic-European area, as a joint responsibility of the United States and Great Britain. An invasion of western Europe was also more attractive than any Mediterranean undertaking because the shorter distance made "shipping and supplies . . . infinitely easier for us to participate." Roosevelt thought the new front might open in the summer of 1942, but he did not press Churchill for an immediate answer, asking only "I wish you would think this over."[25]

The prime minister never responded during March to the president's proposal of an attack on the continent. Churchill's concerns and priorities were elsewhere, specifically in the Indian Ocean and the defense of India. In mid-March, he instructed Field Marshal Dill in Washington on how to guide the strategy discussions in the Combined Chiefs of Staff meetings. There were three points. First, the US Navy should seize the initiative against Japan by attacking Japanese-held islands in the Pacific or disrupting their lines of communication. Second, a continuation of the heavy bombing campaign against Germany was the best way to help Russia. Third, and most important, it was essential that the British should defend the Middle East and Indian Ocean to protect India from invasion and preserve British communications in the Middle East from attack. He told Dill that the British chiefs' opinion was that accomplishing the last objective could only be done if the US Pacific Fleet launched an immediate offensive to "hold a large part of the Japanese fleet in those waters."[26]

Churchill's recommendation demonstrates the gulf between British and American thinking. Dill appreciated how nationalistic and biased it would sound to Americans ears. He had a keen sense of the US Navy's growing frustration over Churchill's continued demands for action against the Japanese fleet in the Pacific. The US Navy was already stretched thin trying to protect the lines of communication in the Pacific after Pearl Harbor, and the new responsibility for defending the British dominions of Australia and New Zealand only stretched their resources further. Brig. Vivian Dykes, the British secretary for the Combined Chiefs of Staff, recalled that Dill spent the next day drafting a response to the prime minister "on a rather stupid telegram about what our strategic policy should be." For his part Dykes realized that the constant harping by the prime minister for the Americans to act in the Pacific was grating, and "it merely infuriates [Admiral] King and makes him stubborn."[27]

Churchill was undeterred. A separate cable advised the president of the critical importance of regaining the initiative against Japan, emphasizing that the Combined Chiefs of Staff must coordinate any "large-scale method" for accomplishing this to avoid the United States taking unilateral action in the Pacific. In another cable he asked Roosevelt to send "two battleships, an aircraft carrier, some cruisers and destroyers" to the Mediterranean to temporarily replace the British fleet at Gibraltar. This would enable the British fleet to deploy to the Indian Ocean to prevent the Japanese from establishing a base at the deep-water port of Diego-Suarez on French Madagascar. The British hoped that the Vichy regime would not retaliate against the American fleet in the Mediterranean if the British seized Madagascar. Roosevelt agreed to help but followed Admiral King's recommendation and sent US naval reinforcements to the Home Fleet rather than Gibraltar, ostensibly because the distance the reinforcing fleet had to travel was shorter.[28]

The British planners, under Churchill's dynamic leadership, always presented a united front when coordinating with their US counterparts. The same could not be said for the Americans because their army and navy possessed widely different strategic visions of the war, which also contributed to the dispersion of forces. The US Navy, despite Russia's tenuous position against Germany, wanted to strengthen the Pacific theater, insisting that reinforcements were necessary to check the Japanese offensive and meet the minimum-security requirements for the strategic defense of the Pacific. Besides keeping open the line of communication to Australia, Admiral King, with Australian and New Zealand support, recommended the capture of South Pacific island bases to use as strong points in an advance through the New Hebrides, Solomons, and Bismarck Archipelago. The mid-March Japanese landings at Lae and Salamaua on the northeast coast of New Guinea alarmed the Australian government, who believed they would be invaded next. Under heavy political pressure at home, Prime Minister Curtin demanded the return of the veteran 9th Australian Imperial Force Division from the Middle East. The Australians were adamant, regardless of Churchill's pleas to keep the veteran division in Libya. Support for additional resources for the Pacific was further bolstered symbolically on 17 March with the arrival in Australia of US Gen. Douglas MacArthur from the beleaguered Philippines. President Roosevelt had expressly ordered MacArthur to escape from the Philippines and take command of the newly organized southwest Pacific area in Australia. Stimson astutely noted in his diary that the general might also be a potential problem: "MacArthur will make great demands upon us and will not always be easy to manage in respect to other theaters of action which may become more important than his. But he is a great asset and skillful fighter." Others were less certain. Brigadier General Eisenhower of War Plans in Washington, DC, had served under MacArthur in the prewar Philippines. He wondered about MacArthur's suitability for such a command. "He is doing a good job where he is, but I'm doubtful that he'd do so well in more complicated situations. Bataan is made to order for him. It's in the public eye; it has made him a public hero; it has all the essentials of drama; and he is acknowledged king on the spot. If brought out, public opinion will force him into a position where his love of the limelight may ruin him."[29]

Marshall and the army planners realized that increasing the strength of the reinforcements sent to the Pacific could only be accomplished at the expense of operations in the Atlantic. The army was willing to accept risk in the Far East, in order to build up forces in the United Kingdom for an offensive against Germany. Eisenhower, the lead planner, summed up the army's fear in his diary: "If we use our shipping for the SW Pacific, we will lose the war."[30]

Shipping was the most critical logistic shortfall for the Allies in 1942. Although Churchill later wrote, "Shipping was at once the stranglehold and sole foundation of our Strategy," in fact, the prime minister had no idea of the scarcity of limited US shipping assets. Roosevelt notified him that as of March 1942 the United States only possessed the shipping to move a total of 130,000 troops. That number would increase by an additional 35,000 as American shipyards completed ship conversions in 1942. In 1943, the United States would

DISPERSION UNCHECKED 77

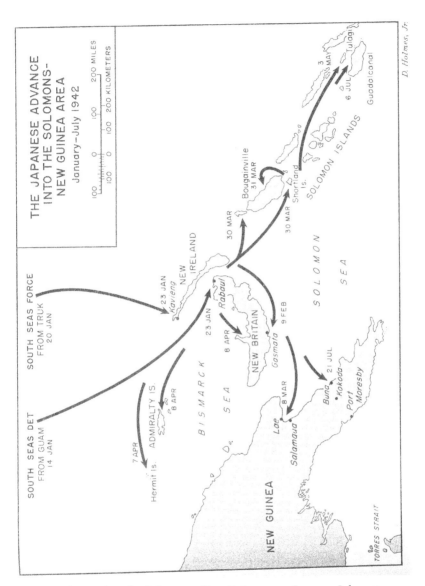

Japanese advance into the Solomons–New Guinea area, January–July 1942 (courtesy of US Army Center of Military History)

produce sufficient shipping to move 140,000 more troops and by June 1944 another 100,000. According to US staff officers, barring any losses of troop transports, "the total troop-carrying capacity of U.S. vessels by June 1944 will be 400,000 men." The discrepancy between operational requirements and available shipping was so serious that the fifth meeting of the Combined Chiefs of Staff pondered the possibility of choosing between defending the Far East or the Middle East.[31]

Besides production issues, a separate problem confronting the Allies was the recent spike in shipping losses to German submarines. Two factors drove the latest German successes. First, the Germans introduced a new cipher system for their U-boats. The undersea navy

The Combined Chiefs of Staff meet in the Public Health Building in Washington, DC, circa 1942. Clockwise from left: Cmdr. Richard D. Coleridge, Royal Navy; Adm. Wilfrid R. Patterson, Royal Navy; Field Marshal Sir John Dill, British Army; Brig. Vivian Dykes, British Army; Lt. Gen. Gordon MacReady, British Army; Air Marshal Douglas Evill, Royal Air Force; Col. T. H. Hammond, US Army; Gen. J. T. McNarney, US Army; Gen. George C. Marshall, US Army; Brig. Gen. John R. Deane, US Army; Adm. William D. Leahy, US Navy; Adm. Ernest J. King, US Navy; and Adm. Frederick J. Horne, US Navy (courtesy of the George C. Marshall Foundation, Lexington, Virginia, USA)

had originally used the same Enigma machines and encipherment systems as other German naval vessels. That ended in late January 1942 when the U-boat fleet introduced a new Enigma machine designed exclusively for their use. The British had decrypted the original German communications method during the summer of 1941, which enabled the Admiralty to accurately track Nazi U-boats. The new, much more secure system, however, was unreadable. This development coincided with a marked increase in the size of the U-boat fleet and its deployment to the US East Coast. As a consequence, the first six months of 1942 witnessed a considerable increase in the loss of Allied merchant shipping, especially oil tankers. At a cost of fewer than fourteen U-boats sunk in the Atlantic, the Germans sunk five hundred Allied merchant ships that amounted to three million tons of shipping. Put differently, during early 1942 the Germans were building U-boats faster than the Allies could sink them, and conversely, the Allies were losing merchant ships faster than they could replace them. Despite a dramatic increase in shipbuilding, American shipyards could not balance losses with new construction until late May 1942, and the Allies as a whole did not achieve this goal until late August.[32]

By mid-March, the American Joint Planners recommended to the American chiefs of staff that they had to establish priorities. Lacking an agreement on the principal effort, it was almost impossible to predict where, in what strength, and in what priority future deployments should occur. Arcadia had not addressed two central issues in the grand strategy bargain: First, what were the Pacific theater's minimum force requirements and their priority in relationship to conducting the war against Germany? Second, what and where was the main effort in 1942 against Germany? The frustrated Joint Planners asked the US chiefs to "at once decide on a clear course of action and execute this decision with the utmost vigor."[33]

The staff planners offered the American chiefs three options. First, to guarantee the absolute security of the Allied position in the Pacific, the Allies could deploy more forces than previously considered, although this would render any offensive against Germany impossible. Second, the Allies could take a risk in the Pacific by deploying some additional forces while simultaneously building up forces in the United Kingdom for an offensive against Germany as soon as it would be practical. Planners recognized that shipping constraints dictated that the British would have to provide the majority of the forces required for any 1942 operation. Third, they could mass the bulk of American forces in Britain for an offensive against Germany in western Europe to keep the Russians in the war. Until Germany's defeat, the western Allies risked "the possibility that the Southwest Pacific might be lost."[34]

At a contentious meeting of the Joint Chiefs of Staff on 16 March, the Joint US Strategic Committee (JUSSC) presented "A Plan for the invasion of Europe" for consideration for a cross-channel invasion of western Europe. The JUSSC proposal was aggressive but embarrassingly amateurish, characterized by a lack of detailed research and analysis. It called for twenty-eight divisions, upwards of six hundred thousand troops, to land in France between July and August 1942. These forces would be almost entirely British and far exceeded the number of British divisions then available. No logistical or naval support plans accompanied the recommendation. According to the JUSSC, the Allies had to invade the western European continent that summer "to assure Russia is not defeated" by Germany. The committee argued that "if the British are not willing to implement this concept adopted at Arcadia by launching an offensive in the European Theater this year, the agreed strategic concept should be re-evaluated, and the possibility of concentrating U.S. offensive effort in the Pacific Area considered." The American planners had unilaterally drafted more of an ultimatum than a measured proposal and ignored Arcadia's disinclination to discuss, much less agree on, a time or location for a cross-channel return to Europe. The Joint Chiefs of Staff made no decision on the JUSSC's recommendation for an invasion of western Europe in 1942 and simply reiterated the established concept of giving priority to an offensive in Europe.[35]

Hopkins and Roosevelt also shared the planners' frustration with the continual haphazard deployments of forces around the world without a discernable strategic objective. Both worried that continued German gains on the eastern front might cause the Soviets to negotiate a separate peace with Germany. The US military attaché in

Cairo had recently reported that a senior Russian general, Alexander Repin, remarked, "If the Allies of Russia do not initiate an offensive on a large scale in the west, the Russian people would be justified in making a separate peace." Because the Russian front was not only tying down the bulk of the German army and air forces but also inflicting massive casualties on the Germans, both American leaders realized it was critical to the Allied war effort that Russia continue to do so.[36]

Hopkins believed that three strategic objectives guided the president's decisions in March 1942: the Russians had to be kept in the war by opening a second front in 1942; cooperation with the British was essential to maintain the British-American alliance; and the United States had to actively fight the Germans somewhere in 1942. Hopkins agreed. "I doubt any single thing is as important as getting some sort of front this summer against Germany. This will have to be worked out carefully between you and Marshall, in the first instance, and you and Churchill, in the second. I don't think there is any time to be lost because if we are going to do it plans need to be made at once." Hopkins and the president did not share their concerns with the chiefs of staff or with Stimson, although these worries reinforced Roosevelt's determination to open an American second-front "somewhere" in 1942. Coming to grips on a second front with the Germans narrowed "somewhere" to either western Europe or North Africa. This put Gymnast back on the table, unbeknownst to Marshall.[37]

At their 16 March meeting, the Joint Chiefs of Staff agreed to send JUSSC's "Plan for the Invasion of Europe" to the British, with caveats. They also informed the British representatives in Washington that the United States would provide only the current commitments in the Pacific and recommended a build-up "in the United Kingdom [of] forces intended for offense at the earliest practicable time." This sudden and unilateral plan surprised the British. They were focused on the Japanese advance in the Indian Ocean and the threat to India. Still, they responded quickly by providing the Americans with their own version of a plan for a cross-channel invasion, which they had prepared before Arcadia but never shown to the Americans.[38]

The British plan, "Operation Round-Up," dated from late December 1941 and demonstrated anew how far apart the two sides were on the possibility of a cross-channel attack. The British argued that an invasion could not be undertaken until "Germany had suffered a severe deterioration of military power" and possessed "no remaining prospect for victory." An Allied invasion would disrupt the orderly German withdrawal from the occupied territories and was consistent with their preferred peripheral strategy that relegated an offensive in Europe to a last resort. They did not presume American participation in the assault, which would occur during 1943 at the earliest. The British only offered the concept as a thought piece to generate discussion and identify risks, but the Americans took it as a clear insight into the British position on a second front in Europe.[39]

On the evening of 16 March, Brooke and the British Chiefs of Staff Committee discussed the feasibility of an offensive in France. They had obtained a copy of the JUSSC's plan to invade Europe and thought the entire concept was suicidal. They were appalled by the American planners' oversimplifications, their inability to think strategically, and the absence of basic analytical research. As far as the British chiefs were concerned the issue could not have come up at a worse time. At home the British press was beating the drums for a second front in France, and the aroused public was lending its increasingly vocal support. Several key government officials were also pushing for an invasion, leaving the General Staff feeling isolated in its opposition. Brooke was upset with the Americans and the uncoordinated JUSSC plan and told his deputy general, John Kennedy, that "the advocates of the Second Front always miss the point that sooner or later a force landed in France must fight a battle with the German Army. We must not be confused by ideas of the French rising, etc. the battle is the thing. We must wait until we have a chance at winning the battle, that cannot be until the Germans are cracking up." Kennedy spoke to Gen. Bernard Paget, the commander in chief of the Home Forces, who agreed "that offensive operations on the Continent were quite beyond our powers at the time." The best that Britain could accomplish was an aerial offensive that might draw some German aircraft or air defense units from the eastern front.[40]

The day following his discussions with Paget and Kennedy, Brooke had a very "difficult" Chiefs of Staff Committee meeting because there was little that could be done to draw off German ground or air forces from Russia. The chief of the Imperial General Staff echoed Paget when he told the committee that the most Britain could accomplish was an air offensive that siphoned German airpower from the eastern front. Brooke's frustration with the subject increased the next day, 18 March, when Roosevelt's cable to Churchill alerted the prime minister that he would send him "a more definite plan of a joint attack in Europe itself."[41]

On 23 March the CCS directed the Combined Staff Planners to reconcile the widely divergent American and British strategies with three options: first, landing sufficient ground forces on the European continent in 1942 to maintain a foothold; second, an Allied invasion of the continent in 1943, contingent upon the planners' exact determination of troops and matériel required; and third, assuming a cross-channel invasion was infeasible during 1942, determining what resources the Allies could instead deploy to the Middle East. Dill notified the CCS that British officers from each service were coming to the United States to share their wartime experiences conducting combined operations (air, sea, and land). Ever tactful, he explained that these officers were only to advise on tactical and technical issues and would not interfere with planning. Dill's hope was that the British officers' perspective might inject some realism into the American planners about the inherent difficulties of an invasion of the continent.[42]

That evening Stimson took advantage of a farewell dinner for the Australian ambassador to the United States held at the British Embassy to discuss the possibility of an invasion of the continent with another guest, Field Marshal Dill. Dill was surprised and in an awkward position as the head of the British mission in Washington. He did not want to offend Stimson, a staunch supporter of Britain, but he knew that an invasion was not even remotely feasible at this time. Dill's experience as a corps commander in France in 1940 made him acutely aware of German military capabilities as well as the operational and logistical requirements of such an operation. Polite and diplomatic, Dill voiced moderate concerns about the JUSSC plan, but Stimson misinterpreted his restraint as obstinance. He "had it out" with Dill, who "was very conservative about it [the invasion], altogether too much so I thought."[43]

Stimson was of course an unwavering supporter of a cross-channel invasion. He thought that a firm Allied commitment against the main enemy, Germany, would end the global dispersion of assets to support secondary theaters. He also believed that a second front in Europe was the fastest and surest way to ensure that Soviet Russia stayed in the war. Stimson's lawyerly appeals to evidence and argument failed to sway the field marshal, who realized that the British high command would never support an independent British invasion of the continent in 1942.[44]

On 20 March, Stimson met Roosevelt at the White House to again discuss dispersion. The secretary later described the frank interchange as "one of the best talks I ever had with him." Stimson told the president that the best way to end the ad hoc deployments was for the army and navy to develop a coordinated policy for an offensive against Germany during the summer of 1942, which was consistent with the president's desire to have American forces engage Germany that year. The president agreed to meet on 25 March, when Marshall would brief him on a proposed plan, although no date for an offensive had yet been determined. Marshall realized the JUSSC proposal was unrealistic and instructed General Eisenhower to prepare a separate plan for an invasion of Europe. Eisenhower's planning group, however, had a very broad concept, focusing on obtaining presidential approval to give priority to a buildup of US forces in Britain for a future offensive in western Europe. Specifics such as the timing, landing sites, objectives, and forces required were yet to be determined. Marshall's aim was to have the president formally recognize that the operation in Europe took precedence over operations in the Middle East and the Pacific. Pending presidential agreement, the planners would work out the details for the invasion of the European continent.[45]

Five days later General Eisenhower handed Marshall the army's plan, "Critical Points in the Development of Coordinated Viewpoint as Major Tasks of the War." This was a unilateral American plan that argued for the selection of a single theater for the first major offensive by the Allies. This would be beneficial to army planners because it would "constitute a basis on which subsidiary decisions, involving necessary dispersion of forces, will be made." The plan laid out four "mandatory" tasks for the Allies: (1) protection of the continental United States; (2) security of Great Britain; (3) retention of Russia as an ally in the war; and (4) defense of the Middle East. Planners recommended Germany as the principal target for the first offensive, to be conducted through western Europe.[46]

Eisenhower next outlined the advantages to this proposal. Since the air and sea lines of communication to England were already protected by air and naval units, it required no additional planes or warships. The line of communication was the shortest distance by sea and allowed the Americans to maintain large forces with the minimum strain on shipping. A buildup of ground and air forces in Britain would threaten Germany and prevent it from concentrating their full military strength against Russia. The airfields and logistical support at the forward air bases in Britain enabled the Allies to achieve air superiority over the east coast of France. The continent's proximity to Britain would also allow the British to use major forces for the invasion without stripping its home defenses. Finally, the Allies could directly attack Germany while German armies were engaged on several widely separated fronts.[47]

The plan's success depended on the Combined Chiefs of Staff endorsement and agreement with a strategy to attack Germany through western Europe. Eisenhower felt so strongly that the Combined Chiefs of Staff should select Germany as the principal target that he added the caveat that "unless this plan is adopted as the eventual aim of all our efforts, we must turn our backs upon the Eastern Atlantic and go, full out, as quickly as possible against Japan!" Nowhere does the document mention a cross-channel attack in 1942.[48]

That same day, Marshall briefed the president along with Hopkins, Stimson, Knox, Arnold, and King on the army's plan to invade western Europe. The president opened the meeting by discussing the Middle East, suggesting that in Roosevelt's mind, at least, operations there were still possible. Marshall, however, persuaded the president of the greater potential of a western Europe offensive than one in the Middle East. Roosevelt was ready to send the plan to the Combined

Chiefs of Staff for review and was surprised when both his military and civilian advisors opposed staffing the plan with the British delegation in Washington. Hopkins recommended that it not be sent to the Combined Chiefs of Staff because it would just be "pulled to pieces and emasculated." He suggested that instead that Marshall personally brief the plan to Churchill, Brooke, Pound, and Portal. Roosevelt concurred and gave the attendees one week to review and expand the proposal before another meeting with him.[49]

During the last week in March, the western Europe proposal underwent numerous rewrites and additions. By 27 March the army planners had complemented their preliminary thoughts on an invasion with potential landing sites, timing, and required forces. Marshall personally reworked several versions of this revised plan, ultimately known as the Marshall Memorandum. The British mission in Washington was not involved. On 27 March Stimson recommended to Roosevelt that "you should not submit it to the secondary British Chiefs of Staff here for amendment. They know about it, and, if they have comment, they can send their comments independently to Great Britain." This was unfortunate because British rigorous analysis and constructive criticism would have benefited the plan. But the British-American allies had yet to develop that degree of trust and confidence in each other.[50]

Even among senior American military leaders there were qualms about Marshall's 25 March presentation to the president. Admiral King, for instance, paid lip service to the "Europe First" strategy but was loyal to his service. US Navy officers doubted the long-term suitability of assuming the tactical defensive in the Pacific. Rather, navy planners thought that the fleet should seize opportunities for limited tactical offensives against Japan while the United States built up forces not only to defend Allied territory in the Pacific but also to advance into enemy occupied areas on the long road to Japan. This meant ensuring the air and sea lines of communication linking Hawaii to Australia. King needed resources for a Pacific offensive, and if Marshall was not going to use the army divisions immediately, King would. King wanted to hit the Japanese, gain the initiative, and keep on hitting them. He likened actions in the Pacific to a boxing match.

King's 29 March request for forces for such an offensive fell on Eisenhower and Marshall. Eisenhower found himself writing yet another memo opposing the dispersion of resources, an especially galling task because just days earlier the president gave general approval to the offensive in western Europe. This issue of war aims and the effort allocated to the Pacific continued for months and ultimately forced the president to decide it.[51]

In late March, India overshadowed British interest in the American plans for an offensive in Europe. An Imperial Japanese Navy strike force of five aircraft carriers sortied into the Indian Ocean. Its objective was to destroy the British fleet or, failing that, to knock out airfields, dockyards, and shipping anchored in the harbors. That accomplished, the Japanese could proceed to the Bay of Bengal to secure the lines of communication for Japanese convoys to Rangoon. They also expected that the naval victories would foment political unrest in India.[52]

Meanwhile there was growing tension between Churchill and Roosevelt over India. The fall of Singapore and the retreat in Burma seriously damaged British prestige in Asia. A surge of refugees from Burma into India added to discontent. Mahatma Gandhi and the Indian National Congress party, the leading Indian nationalist group, demanded concessions from the British, and Roosevelt pressured Churchill to negotiate a compromise to assure India's continued support of the war effort. The president felt that the promise of independence might offset India's receptiveness to Japan's anti-white, Pan-Asiatic propaganda and was the key to India's support of the war. "I feel that there is a real danger in India now in that there is too much suspicion and dissatisfaction in too many places, and that resistance to Japan would therefore not be nearly as sincere and wholehearted as it should be. I wonder if there is sufficient spirit to fight among the Indian people." Independence was out of the question for Churchill, and the most he would consider was dominion status after the war, and only if the elected constituent assembly formally requested it. The Indian National Congress quickly rejected the prime minister's offer. Throughout March, Roosevelt sent several cables to Churchill recommending compromises, and the prime minister grew more agitated in his responses to what he viewed as meddling in internal British affairs. Roosevelt, however, persisted and sent a special representative to India to assist with negotiations between Britain and the Indian colony, which only irritated Churchill more. The relationship between the two leaders was fraying over this issue by the end of the month.[53]

March ended with the British-American alliance still lacking a unified focus, the US Army and Navy still at odds on strategy, a powerful Japanese fleet still advancing into the Indian Ocean, and the Churchill-Roosevelt personal relationship still unsettled. It was not the most opportune moment to introduce a major shift in British-American strategic thinking.

4

A Tentative Agreement on an Offensive against Germany

April 1942

Ten weeks after the Arcadia Conference, the British-American Alliance had yet to reconcile the American desire to strike decisively at the heart of German military power on the northwestern European continent with the British peripheral approach along the littoral edges. The result was a dispersion of scarce resources in the absence of an agreed-upon strategic focus.

During the last week of March, the newly promoted Major General Eisenhower and his team of US Army planners prepared a plan for an offensive against Germany in accordance with the president's desire to open a second front. On 1 April, Eisenhower briefed Marshall on a general concept of operations, including troops required, timing, and landing sites. Eisenhower also included a brief strategic justification for a second front in Europe. Marshall approved the broad outline and, with minor edits, carried it to the White House that day. His goal was to secure presidential approval of the strategic concept in order to coordinate and focus troop levies, training, and deployment on a single objective.[1]

Before meeting with the president, Harry Hopkins lunched with Marshall and Arnold to review the concept and identify any potential problems. Hopkins expected that US Navy and senior British leaders would oppose the plan and believed that Americans should present their concept in person to Churchill and the British Chiefs of Staff in London. Churchill would go along, he said, since "due to the political situation in England he wouldn't dare do anything but to go with us, as the temper of the people at this time is for an 'all-out' offensive with the least possible delay." Admiral King's support for the plan became pivotal, and for that reason the three agreed that the admiral should attend the meeting with the president. King required resources for the Pacific, and his needs competed with Marshall's proposal for a second front in Europe. Hopkins and Stimson hoped to force King into either accepting the plan or voicing his objections directly to the president.[2]

The attendees—Hopkins, Stimson, Knox, Stark, King, Arnold, and Marshall—all entered the president's office through the back door and left the same way to ensure the complete secrecy that the president had insisted was necessary to prevent leaks to the American press or public until after the British were informed. Marshall's presentation took two and one-half hours as Roosevelt combed through the proposal paragraph by paragraph and asked numerous detailed questions. The strategic premises of the plan, later known as the Marshall Memorandum, were that the United States and Great Britain had to open an offensive against Germany before the Nazi war machine defeated the Soviet Union and current neutrals such as Portugal and Turkey were "drawn into the ranks of the enemy." Moscow's continued participation in the war was essential to the defeat of Nazi Germany, and therefore the Soviets had to receive maximum support from the western Allies. The best way to support the USSR was to invade western Europe from British bases. Marshall pronounced western Europe the decisive theater because an attack through France offered the most direct route to the heart of Germany while British bases provided the best staging areas for the invasion.[3]

Marshall's plan had four basic assumptions: (1) the Alaska-Hawaii-Samoa-Australia line would hold, and US troop strength in the Pacific would increase from 175,000 to a maximum of 300,000 men; (2) the United States would meet its agreed commitments in Australia, New Zealand, and China; (3) the USSR would continue to fight and tie down the bulk of the German Army; and (4) the Axis forces would remain as powerful as their April 1942 strength.[4]

There were three main phases. The preparatory phase, which became known by the codename "Bolero," would witness Allied air operations and raids along the coast of France. The United States would gradually build up a force of one million men—approximately thirty divisions—and 3250 combat aircraft for an invasion scheduled for 1 April 1943. The British would add eighteen more divisions and 2,550 more combat aircraft to the American force. Phase two, code-named "Roundup," was a landing in France on a six-division front somewhere between Le Havre and Boulogne. The combined strength of forty-eight divisions and 5800 aircraft was sufficient to establish air superiority and sustain the beachhead. Marshall estimated that the Allies could reinforce the landing beachhead at a rate of one hundred thousand men per week, which was faster than the Germans could reinforce their defenses in France. In phase three, the Allies would consolidate and expand the beachhead, break through the German defenses, and advance to the Belgian port of Antwerp.[5]

The plan had several advantages. Shipping resources were at a premium, and the north Atlantic route placed the least additional burden on the American Navy, which was already responsible for maintaining the sea lines of communication between the United States and Britain. Unlike a North African operation, no additional sea lanes needed to be secured. Air bases in Britain were ideally located to provide air cover for the invasion. The buildup of American forces in Britain guaranteed additional security against a German invasion of the British Isles. Most importantly to Marshall, a direct approach to Germany would prevent American involvement in secondary operations that drained resources, were indecisive, and did little to aid the Soviet Union.[6]

Marshall candidly explained to the president the proposal's serious logistical flaw. The United States lacked the merchant shipping and landing craft essential for the operation. The required shipping was unavailable to transport the necessary troops, ammunition, and military equipment to Britain by April 1943. The president asked the secretary of the navy, Henry Knox, about solutions to the shipping and landing craft deficiencies. Knox thought "that by stepping on the gas and stepping up production" that the United States could dramatically increase the number of landing craft programmed for construction. With the president's endorsement, Hopkins, Stimson, and Knox agreed that a reordering of the US production program was needed to meet the invasion's goals. Arnold further appealed to the president for greater access to US manufactured war equipment. The plan's success hinged upon Allied air superiority over France, and that in turn demanded more US aircraft to beat down the Germans. Roosevelt agreed and directed Stimson to give the Americans' aircraft priority.[7]

Marshall's briefing to the president focused on an invasion of France in 1943 and differed significantly from the earlier JUSSC draft, which assumed an attack in 1942. Marshall, however, also introduced a "Modified Plan" for an "emergency" landing in France in September or October 1942, codenamed "Sledgehammer." (A major reason Marshall included this proposal was to fend off diversions from Bolero in 1942.) This contingency operation would occur only if the Soviet Union was on the verge of collapse. In such circumstances, American leaders believed that only a British-American attack in the west would save the USSR from utter defeat. British troops (between five to nine divisions) would make the "sacrifice" (Marshall's word) because limitations of shipping and landing craft precluded a large-scale American effort during 1942. Marshall well understood that this was a suicidal undertaking but viewed it as a "sacrifice for the common good" of Allied forces to save Russia. Marshall and the American planners had not yet learned to "walk to the other side of the table" and examine the proposal from their ally's perspective. They did not fully realize, after Dunkirk and Singapore, how insensitive, unrealistic, and outlandish this proposal would appear to the British.[8]

Marshall's arguments and presentation impressed Roosevelt. The president agreed with his military advisors that the focus on Germany would reduce the helter-skelter dispersions of recent months, counter Soviet propaganda urging a second front, and focus American public opinion on the Soviet-German struggle, thereby undercutting the public clamor demanding priority be given to the war with Japan.

Hopkins demanded the participants' unanimous agreement to the strategy. He knew that the navy wanted more resources for its Pacific operations because two days earlier Admiral King had asked for additional aircraft "to implement surely and effectively the strategic concept on which the detailed [navy] plans are based." Hopkins questioned King, "Do you see any reason why this cannot be carried out?" King replied, "No, I do not." Hopkins then pressed King, "Assuming that commitments in the Far East stand as they are without any further reinforcements, will this program interfere with your operations, and will you have sufficient airplanes?" King carefully responded that although the navy would not have as much as he wanted, they would make do. That did not satisfy Hopkins, who then asked King pointblank in front of the president if he could simultaneously support this plan and conduct his Pacific operations. King, mouse-trapped, had to say, "Yes."[9]

The meeting ended with the president directing Marshall and Hopkins to depart for London in the next couple of days to "sell" the concept to the British. The Americans thought the Royal Air Force and Royal Navy would support the plan but anticipated General Brooke and the army would violently oppose the strategy.[10]

Roosevelt immediately informed Churchill that a thorough examination of the immediate and long-range strategic issues confronting the British-American alliance led him "to certain conclusions which are so vital that I want you to know the whole picture and to ask your approval." Hopkins and Marshall would brief Churchill in person on the "salient points." Churchill responded enthusiastically and Roosevelt in turn replied that his "heart and mind" were firmly convinced that a second front was needed to relieve German pressure on the Russians whose fighting presence was essential for the Allied war effort.[11]

The following day, Stimson and Marshall met with the former Canadian ambassador to the United States and a friend of the Roosevelt administration, William Duncan Herridge. Herridge had just returned from Britain and sought to share his observations of the mood in London. He believed that the British public was anxious for a second front in western Europe, and that without a British-American offensive in 1942 the "British Army will go stale and lose its morale." Herridge explained that waning morale after a long string of defeats was corroding the British Army. The junior officers and other ranks wanted to take the fight to Germany, but older, conservative senior leaders in the army held them back. Marshall and Stimson heard only what they wanted to hear and drew incorrect conclusions about the strategic thinking in London. They believed the British Army favored a second front, but failed to grasp the political and military implications that the "sacrifice" of seven divisions would have on their ally if the Sledgehammer contingency was executed.[12]

Hopkins and Marshall departed for London by plane on 4 April. They had kept their plan a secret because they did not want the British to have time to review the proposal and prepare counterarguments before the Americans could even present their rationale for an invasion of western Europe. Despite the desire for secrecy, the British surreptitiously received an advance copy of the Marshall Memorandum that day from the British mission in Washington.[13]

Although the British-Americans were supposedly equal partners, American and British planners remained reticent to share information with each other. They operated in an environment of suspicion dominated by national prerogatives. As one American planner, Paul Carraway, described, "Certain of our top-secret Intelligence information they were not allowed to see, because a lot of it came from undisclosed channels or whatever, much of it through the British without their knowledge." He went on to describe the reluctance to share papers with the British before a meeting because they "would be able to check our positions."[14]

The two secretaries of the Combined Chiefs Staff, Brig. Vivian Dykes (British) and Brig. Gen. Walter Bedell Smith (American) were unusual in this regard. The two officers enjoyed the utmost confidence of their superiors, had developed a close rapport with each other, and were willing to cooperate with one another. When Marshall wanted some idea of the British perspective on operations against Germany, Smith asked Dykes for help. Dykes shared a highly classified paper, "Grand Strategy," which incorporated the latest British strategic thinking. In exchange, Smith showed Dykes a copy of the Marshall Memorandum. Dykes sent a précis of the memo to Dill, who forwarded it to London on 4 April for review by the British chiefs. When Hopkins and Marshall's plane was delayed three days in Bermuda due to engine trouble, the British chiefs enjoyed four full days to review the proposal and prepare their rebuttal of the strategy.[15]

The British chiefs devoted their effort over the next four days to a careful study of the Sledgehammer operation (the emergency landing in France in 1942 if Russia was on the verge of collapse). They were appalled. They had no objection to Bolero, the buildup of American forces in Britain; in fact, they welcomed it. On Roundup, which was scheduled to take place in 1943, they felt they had enough time to review and analyze the operation. On 7 April, the day before Marshall and Hopkins arrived in London, the War Cabinet Chiefs of Staff Committee presented an analysis identifying fatal dangers inherent in Marshall's Sledgehammer proposal and highlighting five key risks. (1) If the operation failed and seven divisions were destroyed, the reduced UK forces remaining in Britain would imperil the nation's security. (2) Success depended on securing the bridgehead within five days, but weather conditions might make this impossible. (3) A two-division German reinforcement of the area or strengthened coastal defenses would mean mission failure. (4) The bridgehead could not be made impregnable. German counterattacks would destroy all the Allies' equipment and most of their troops. (5) The assault force would be unsustainable because the beaches selected were deficient for landing resupplies.[16]

The British insisted that strategic surprise was unattainable because preparations for the invasion could not be concealed. The landing zone was only six miles wide, its open beaches covered by German guns, and air cover over the beaches was problematic. Unpredictable autumn weather and high tides hampered any landing. Besides, the Allies lacked landing craft and could only transport twenty thousand troops on the first day. So small a force without proper logistic support was vulnerable to annihilation. They estimated that the twenty-nine German divisions in France could easily deal with the six-division invasion force, meaning that the Axis would not need to withdraw troops from Russia. In a worst-case scenario, Berlin could redeploy German troops from Italy.[17]

The British chiefs concluded that a Sledgehammer-like operation should only be executed if Germany was overextended, German morale was breaking, and a Russian victory was probable. As an alternative, the British agreed that planning for Roundup (the 1943 cross-channel attack) should begin at once. During the interim, the Allies could conduct large raids on the continent during the training and assembly period for Roundup.[18]

The British did understand the gravity of the Russian situation and cabled Dill and the British Joint Staff Mission, "We consider (that) importance of helping Russia in 1942 is so great that consideration of an (an) offensive in 1943 should not prevent us from doing anything we can, however, small, this summer." However, after the Dunkirk disaster of 1940 and the recent setbacks in North Africa, Singapore, and Burma during 1941–42, the British military was in no mood to undertake a "sacrifice for the common good." They accepted that, while the British public was pushing for an offensive in Europe, the popular psyche could not withstand another catastrophic defeat like Singapore. The loss of seven more divisions on top of all the other setbacks might prove fatal to the army. General Brooke met with his deputy, Maj. Gen. John Kennedy, who described the initial British reaction as general agreement "that there could be no question of landing an army in France and holding a front for long." Brooke thought that the Germans could easily turn on the landing force and "wipe them out." Brooke succinctly appraised Sledgehammer (the 1942 emergency landing): "Plan they had put up was a thoroughly bad one."[19]

Furthermore, events in the Indian Ocean diverted Churchill's attention and that of his military advisors from a cross-channel attack. At the end of March, a Japanese fleet composed of a small aircraft carrier, six cruisers, and eight destroyers sailed into the Bay of Bengal to support the invasion of the Andaman Islands and to attack British merchant shipping. This fleet sank twenty-three merchantmen (over 112,000 tons), mostly off the coast of India, and brought the war to Indian soil for the first time by bombing the port cities of Cocanada and Vizagapatam. On 5 April, a second Japanese fleet, with five aircraft carriers, four battleships, and five cruisers, destroyed the British naval base infrastructure at Colombo, Ceylon, in the Indian Ocean. Four days later, the Japanese fleet demolished the port facilities and workshops at the British naval base at Trincomalee, Ceylon, and thereafter roamed the Indian Ocean with impunity, sinking a British aircraft carrier, two heavy cruisers, and two destroyers, as well as several merchant ships (over 56,000 tons total). The outnumbered and outgunned British Eastern Fleet withdrew from the Indian Ocean to Kilindi, East Africa.[20]

The Japanese Indian Ocean raid was another humiliation for British arms. The damage inflicted on the naval facilities at Ceylon and the losses at sea crippled the Eastern Fleet and left the Royal Navy unable to protect British interests in the Indian Ocean. For a hundred and fifty years the Royal Navy had dominated the region; in one week the Japanese had shattered any remaining illusion of British naval superiority.[21]

The Japanese foray into the Indian Ocean created a near panic in London. On 6 April, Brooke was surprised to learn that the Japanese fleet was maneuvering in the Indian Ocean and the British Eastern Fleet retiring westward. He feared an imminent full-scale invasion of Ceylon and wanted Admiral Pound to convince the US Navy to attack the Japanese somewhere in order to divert them from the Indian Ocean foray. Brooke confided to his diary, "I suppose this empire has never been in such a precarious position throughout its history! I do not like the look of things. And yet a miracle saved us at Dunkirk, and we may pull through this time. But I wish I could see daylight as to how we are to keep going through 1942."[22]

Churchill was shocked. On 7 April, he asked Roosevelt for help, because the weakened British Eastern Fleet could not cope with the powerful Japanese fleets creating a "situation . . . of grave anxiety." Like Brooke, he wanted the US Pacific Fleet to attack somewhere to draw the Japanese away from the Indian Ocean. Churchill somehow believed that US naval forces were "decidedly superior" to Japan's in the Pacific, presenting the Americans with the chance somehow "to compel" the Japanese fleets in the Indian Ocean to return to the Pacific, and removing the danger of invasion to Britain's colonies. On 8 April, Roosevelt instructed Hopkins to inform the prime minister that "movements were already in hand which should tend to give some relief from current pressure in critical area of enemy naval concentration." This intentionally vague response alluded to the top-secret mission of a carrier task force operation that was moving to conduct a surprise air attack on Japan. Churchill received no specifics until the raid was over.[23]

Since the Americans apparently were not going to help, Churchill recommended that the British chiefs immediately move six fighter squadrons from the Middle East to India. The chiefs advised against this recommendation, arguing that such a move was precipitous because they had no idea of Japanese intentions for the Indian Ocean. Furthermore, stripping the British forces in Libya of six fighter squadrons would seriously cripple operations in the Middle East and, because all the theaters were interconnected, only contribute to the piecemeal diversion of resources. They reminded Churchill that "the strategy which we have agreed to with the Americans is that we should attempt to deal first with Germany, who must be regarded as the main enemy." Any decisions should wait until they heard Marshall because "the proposals he is bringing are certain to affect them profoundly."[24]

When Hopkins and Marshall finally arrived in London, they immediately met with Churchill at 10 Downing Street. The prime minister was charming and gracious, and, genuinely glad to see the Americans, he did his best to put them at ease and make them feel welcome. No one realized that this was the eve of the most stressful period of the alliance. There was nothing "special" about the British-American relationship, and their latest meeting was the start of five long months of frustrating transatlantic negotiations in a fleeting quest to agree on a common grand strategy. Marshall immediately presented a broad outline of the proposal to the prime minister. Churchill surprised the Americans by remarking that he had personally reviewed the proposal and that his staff had given it careful consideration. He mentioned that the British chiefs had analyzed the proposal for several weeks, suggesting a comparative study of both the 14 March JUSSC plan and Marshall's intended proposal. Nevertheless, just as Hopkins had predicted, Churchill told his chiefs that he was willing to support the American proposals despite the difficulties.[25]

Churchill noted some objections that his chiefs had made on the risks of a 1942 cross-channel attack, but much to Marshall's relief he was generally supportive of the proposals. The prime minister's immediate major concern was the military situation in the Indian Ocean, and he quickly shifted the discussion to that topic. His general strategic overview of the Middle East expressed disappointment in Gen. Claude Auchinleck, the commander in Libya. Churchill also shared with Hopkins and Marshall his concerns about the British Army's lack of fighting spirit. He complained at length about the loss of Singapore, where the British Army had just folded up and let him down badly. This attitude would heavily influence the risks the British military would accept in 1942, but neither Hopkins nor Marshall fully understood the ramifications of the admission.[26]

Afterwards Hopkins and Marshall dined with Churchill and General Brooke. Churchill dominated the discussion, displaying his vast knowledge of American military history. Little else was accomplished on the grand strategy proposals for Europe. Brooke noted that "neither Hopkins nor Marshall disclosed their proposed plans for which they have come over." After the dinner, Hopkins cabled Roosevelt that Churchill seemed sympathetic to the American strategic proposals.[27]

The following day, Marshall met with the War Cabinet Chiefs of Staff Committee. The British were cordial, and the meeting minutes convey a more collegial atmosphere than future historians would describe. Despite their misgivings, the British listened to Marshall, a valued ally, present his case for an agreement in principle on where and when the main British-American effort should occur. He favored a cross-channel attack in 1943. This was necessary in order to focus the production and allocation of matériel, as well as train and move troops for the main strategic objective. He candidly explained to the British that American commitments to the Far East, Ireland, and Iceland plus shipping shortages precluded a large American force in Great Britain until 1943. His fear was that an imminent Russian collapse might force the British-American allies to execute an emergency operation on the continent to keep the USSR in the war. If this emergency occurred, British troops would comprise the bulk of the forces used in the operation. Marshall concluded with a plea for the two allies to agree on a common strategy in order to coordinate planning.[28]

Brooke responded first for the British chiefs, addressed only Sledgehammer, and said in their opinion that it could be executed only if Germany was on the verge of collapse. He doubted that a ground offensive by so small a force in France would help Russia. The best that the British-Americans could accomplished in 1942 was an air campaign against Germany combined with raids along the European coast. Brooke was frank that the British could not endure another defeat on the continent as recent deployments to the Middle East and Far East had already stretched thin homeland defenses. Adm. Louis Mountbatten, the chief of Combined Operations, then stated that although the shortage of landing craft was an issue in 1942 it should be resolved by 1943. Air Marshal Portal estimated that the Allies lacked the fighter strength to defend the beachhead and instead recommended a bombing campaign against Germany to help Russia. British criticism centered on Sledgehammer, which Marshall apparently gave little thought, considering it an emergency contingency. Marshall bluntly responded that he understood American assistance was not available in case the emergency operation had to be executed in September 1942. "Losses might be sustained and these they were ready to accept."[29]

In other words, the Americans were not going to share the risks and potential losses with their British ally in case of a disaster. Marshall never seemed to realize how cavalier with his ally's lives his comments appeared or to comprehend the depth of British resentment. Britain needed a victory, and Brooke did not see any way that Sledgehammer could achieve one.[30]

Brooke displayed a respectful demeanor at this meeting and during the remainder of Marshall's London visit despite his private biting comments about the American general. "He is, I think, a good general at raising armies and providing the necessary links between the military and political worlds. But his strategic ability does not impress me at all!!!" Brooke had to react to immediate near-term Axis threats in India, the Indian Ocean, Australia, and the Middle East. Western Europe remained beyond his ken. "They [Marshall and Hopkins] have not begun to realize all the implications of this plan and all the difficulties that lie ahead of us! The fear I have is that they should concentrate on this offensive at the expense of all else! We have therefore been pressing on them the importance of providing American assistance in the Indian Ocean and Middle East." Years later, Brooke's estimation remained unchanged. "I found that his [Marshall's] stunted strategic outlook made it very difficult to discuss strategic plans with him, for the good reason that he did not understand them personally but backed the briefs prepared by his staff." Nowhere is such an attitude evident in the meeting minutes. The "special relationship" would have benefited by a more honest exchange of ideas.[31]

While Marshall met with the British chiefs, Hopkins met privately with Churchill, whose attention was on the situation in India and the Indian Ocean, not the Marshall Memorandum. The prime minister resented American interference in the British negotiations in India, in particular the role of Roosevelt's representative in India, Louis Johnson, an advocate of having an Indian in charge of the Defense Ministry. Nor did the prime minister appreciate American interference in the British negotiations with the Indian National Congress. Hopkins unsuccessfully tried to mollify Churchill by blaming Johnson for overstepping his instructions. Churchill also shared his fears that Ceylon could not withstand a Japanese invasion. He complained that the US Navy was secretive and did not share their plans and responded to requests on Pacific strategy with the simple comment "we have the matter in hand."[32]

While Churchill wanted to discuss the empire and the war with Japan, Hopkins turned the discussion back to Marshall's recommendations, which he informed the prime minister enjoyed the president's full support. Hopkins reminded Churchill that the American people sought revenge against Japan (Bataan had just surrendered that day) and if the British could not support Marshall's strategy, then the US forces described in the plan would be sent to the Pacific instead of England. Churchill understood and promised to pass on Hopkins's remarks to his advisors.[33]

Next Roosevelt interjected himself into the British negotiations with the Indian National Congress. Churchill notified the president on 11 April that the British offered postwar independence to India but only if an elected Constituent Assembly formally requested it. The Indian National Congress rejected this recommendation and demanded immediate independence. Churchill was opposed, believing that it would be detrimental to the defense of India. He informed the president that he was ending negotiations and bringing his representative at the talks home. Roosevelt's immediate response reminded Churchill that American public opinion was on the side of India. "The feeling is almost universally held that the deadlock has been caused by the unwillingness of the British Government to concede to the Indians the right of self-government, notwithstanding the willingness of the Indians to entrust technical, military and naval defense control to the competent British authorities." If the negotiations collapsed and the Japanese then invaded India, "the prejudicial reaction on American public opinion can hardly be over-estimated."[34]

This cable arrived well after midnight on Sunday morning at the prime minister's country residence, Chequers. Regardless of the late hour, Churchill and Hopkins were still talking about war strategy. As he read the note, Churchill grew visibly angry and his temper exploded because Roosevelt was interfering directly in British domestic politics. Hopkins was amazed "how the string of cuss words lasted for two hours in the middle of the night." Churchill threatened to resign because immediate independence would throw the entire Indian subcontinent into total confusion with the Japanese already prowling along the Indian-Burma frontier. Churchill dashed off a particularly ill-tempered reply and showed Hopkins the draft. Hopkins had remained imperturbable throughout Churchill's profanity-laced temper tantrum. But an abusive written communiqué to the American president was entirely different matter. After reading the draft, Hopkins stonily told Churchill that "he had better write a more decent one than that." Chastened, Churchill did so.[35]

The successful Japanese naval sorties in the Indian Ocean and the contretemps over Indian independence left Churchill in an awkward position with the Americans over their proposal for the second front in western Europe. The British desperately needed American resources to defend their empire in India and to execute their operations in the Middle East. The disagreement on India strained the personal bond between the two leaders that was essential to the British-American alliance. Churchill knew that Roosevelt strongly endorsed the Marshall Memorandum and realized that opposing the memo risked the Americans shifting all their resources to the Pacific, against Japan. The prime minister was averse to a 1942 cross-channel attack but realized that Britain needed American resources to flow to the Atlantic. He conceded and cabled Roosevelt on 12 April, "I have read with earnest attention your masterly document about the future of the war and the great operations proposed. I am in entire agreement in principle with all you propose, so are the Chiefs of Staff." Churchill's only caveat was that "we must of course meet day to day emergencies in the east and far east while preparing for the main stroke." As for Sledgehammer, he informed Roosevelt, "I may say that I thought the proposals made for an interim operation in certain contingencies this year met the difficulties and uncertainties in an absolutely sound manner." He furthermore assured the president that he expected the Defence Committee would give their complete agreement at the 14 April meeting with Marshall and Hopkins. This was disingenuous. The previous meetings of the British Chiefs of Staff Committee on 8 and 9 April demonstrate that they had numerous reservations and objections to Sledgehammer. Churchill's postwar revisionism stated that he really meant that the British were only willing to study Sledgehammer. Nonetheless, the Americans could (and did) interpret his cable as a firm commitment to Marshall's proposals.[36]

On 13 April, the British chiefs of staff met to finalize their response to Marshall and Hopkins. They frankly expressed their opinions, concerns, and objections. They agreed with the Roundup proposal for a combined British-American invasion of the continent in 1943 and believed operational planning should begin as soon as possible. Sledgehammer, however, was especially contentious. They still believed that a 1942 landing should occur only if Germany was on the verge of collapse, but they acknowledged that some sort of mission might be necessary if the Soviet Union seemed likely to capitulate. The latest crisis in the Indian Ocean, though, continually disrupted their deliberations. The British chiefs would have preferred to discuss

American naval operations in the Pacific to relieve the pressure on the British rather than a second front in western Europe. Brooke also had to reconcile the Royal Air Force's reluctance to provide close air support for ground operations, because the RAF's limited resources were needed for the strategic bombing campaign against Germany. This diversion wasted time but brought no solution.[37]

The next day, the British chiefs met Marshall and summarized their endorsement of his proposals. They accepted the Roundup recommendations, but Sledgehammer remained the sticking point. They recognized the paramount importance of "keeping Russia in the field" and agreed that "we may be compelled to take some action on the Continent in 1942." Their primary concern remained the Japanese threat to their empire, and they insisted that the Japanese advance be halted before other operations were undertaken.[38]

Marshall anticipated these British had reservations because of the current Japanese threat to their empire. Before the meeting, he had cabled his deputy, Lt. Gen. Joseph McNarney, "It appears that our proposal will be accepted in principle," but with British demands for men and matériel for India, Australia, and the Middle East. He told McNarney that he was hesitant to predict an outcome to the negotiations because "virtually everyone agrees with us in principle but many if not most hold reservations regarding this or that." Stimson's appraisal was much harsher. Although Marshall's negotiations were progressing satisfactorily, "he evidently has no illusions as to the chiseling and other efforts that will be made to slow us down and nullify our work."[39]

At 10:00 p.m. Marshall and Hopkins attended a Defence Committee meeting chaired by the prime minister and attended by most of his cabinet ministers. Churchill endorsed "concentration against the main enemy" with the broad reservation that "it was essential to carry on the defense of India and the Middle East." The prime minister emphasized imperial prerogatives as the priority over the Marshall's proposals.[40]

Marshall expressed "great relief" over "a basic agreement on general principles," and "complete agreement on what was to be done in 1943." He then addressed Sledgehammer, admitting that shipping shortages rendered any American contribution modest during 1942, due to shipping constraints, but that Britain could use whatever was available.[41]

Brooke voiced no concerns. Rather, he reiterated Churchill's arguments regarding the Japanese advance toward India. In brief, he concentrated his remarks on the dire situation in the Indian Ocean, not Marshall's proposals.[42]

Churchill again pleaded for the US Pacific Fleet to act against the Japanese because the British lacked the localized naval strength to "cope unaided" with a threat in the Indian Ocean. Marshall agreed to advise the president and Admiral King of Churchill's request. Hopkins then added that if public opinion in America had its way, smashing Japan first would be the priority of the war effort. He said the president, in contrast, wanted Americans to fight in western Europe, where they could decisively engage the enemy on air, sea, and land. Roosevelt was not sending American troops to Britain to sit idle; he wanted to quickly engage the enemy and win the war.[43]

From left to right: Gen. George Marshall; John G. Winant, US ambassador to Great Britain; and Harry Hopkins, 20 April 1942 (courtesy of the George C. Marshall Foundation, Lexington, Virginia, USA)

Churchill wrapped up the meeting praising the "complete unanimity on the framework," which would enable the British-Americans to march forward. Again, he offered no modifications to either Roundup or Sledgehammer. All Churchill wanted was resources for the Indian Ocean "without which the whole plan would be fatally compromised."[44]

Marshall believed that he had a firm commitment and cabled Stimson that the British "formally accepted" the American proposal. Hopkins likewise cabled Roosevelt that day of Churchill's enthusiastic support of the American proposals. Three days later, Churchill cabled Roosevelt his passionate and unequivocal acceptance of Marshall's proposals. "We wholeheartedly agree with your conception of concentration against the main enemy, and we cordially accept your plan with one broad qualification . . . it is essential that we should prevent a junction of the Japanese and the Germans." Churchill expressed no reservations and was so enthusiastic that even the normally somber Hopkins thought the British had accepted the concept and that it was "not only an agreement in principle but a real meeting of minds."[45]

This was seemingly a watershed agreement by the Allies. The Americans had presented a plan for directly attacking the main enemy on the continent, and for the first time the British, who had heretofore endorsed a peripheral approach, agreed. The British commitment, however, was not as comprehensive as the Americans thought. Even the British chiefs were puzzled by Churchill's complete acceptance without revisions or changes to Marshall's proposals. Lord Moran, the prime minister's personal physician, asked Churchill why he had not pushed back against an obviously flawed American plan. According to Churchill, with American public opinion pressuring the president to send more resources to the Pacific, this was not the time to argue with the Americans.[46]

After Hopkins and Marshall had returned to Washington, the prime minister exposed his inner feelings to Averell Harriman, the president's envoy to Churchill and Stalin. The prime minister told Harriman that "Sledgehammer was impossible, disastrous." Churchill worried that a combination of limited British resources and the minimal American assistance would doom the operation to failure. He still lacked confidence in the fighting ability and poor equipment of the British Army and seemed so distraught that Harriman offered to fly to Washington to share Churchill's concerns with Roosevelt in person. Churchill did not think that necessary and in any case did not want to appear to renege on the agreement that he had just approved. He would wait and discuss the issue personally with Roosevelt at an opportune time.[47]

Gen. Hastings Ismay, a close advisor to the prime minister, granted that the final meeting with Marshall had created a false impression to the Americans that in the future would create mistrust and misunderstandings between the allies. Instead, the British kept their anxieties to themselves. Brooke's diary entry for 14 April reads: "A momentous meeting at which we accepted their proposals for offensive action in Europe in 1942 perhaps and in 1943 for certain." Two days later, his private diary acknowledged that his greatest fear was that Germany would get the best of Russia and the western Allies might have to actually invade France in 1942. He thought "this is the most dangerous set of circumstances for us." Perhaps if Brooke had been as blunt during the London meetings as he was in his diary, the "special relationship" would have benefited and these later misunderstandings been avoided.[48]

Ismay believed that the British leaders should have been forthright and worked out their objections with American planning in an open forum. According to Ismay, a better approach would be to tell the Americans, "We agree in principle with Roundup, but would not as yet like to commit ourselves to so early a date as September 1943. On the other hand, we regard Sledgehammer as an extremely doubtful proposition, and wonder whether you have given sufficient weight to its immense difficulties and embarrassing implications." If Sledgehammer failed, Ismay feared the catastrophic results would in the long run delay Roundup. But the British said nothing.[49]

Churchill's memoirs acknowledge that he misled the Americans. India was his primary concern in 1942, and he considered the defense of India was just as important as keeping Russia in the war with a cross-channel attack. Although he welcomed the buildup of

American forces in Britain, he completely opposed Sledgehammer. He realized troops could not sit idle during 1942 but thought that other limited operations were possible in Norway or North Africa. Churchill refrained from mentioning these fears because he wanted harmonious relations with the United States, "without whose aid nothing but ruin faced the world." His failure to openly express his concerns would sow seeds of mistrust later.[50]

As Marshall and Hopkins completed their London visit, in Washington, DC, Roosevelt was meeting with Canadian prime minister Mackenzie King at the opening of the Pacific Council, on 15 April. The Canadian prime minister's arrival coincided with word that Churchill had agreed to the American strategic proposals. Roosevelt valued King's opinion and made clear that he sought the destruction of the German Army. He explained that vengeance did not drive his goal, but like General U. S. Grant, who rose to command Union armies during the US Civil War, Roosevelt was willing to sacrifice troops to win battles that would end the war.[51]

Roosevelt was probably more committed to Sledgehammer in 1942 than Marshall. Marshall viewed it as a contingency plan for a strategic emergency. Roosevelt wanted American ground troops in action in 1942 and thought Sledgehammer should be executed that year. Roosevelt asked the Canadian prime minister, whose view he respected, for his thoughts on the American plans for a cross-channel attack. King opposed Sledgehammer and pointed out numerous problems such as proper timing, shipping shortages, the unavailability of reinforcements, and the lack of intelligence on German dispositions in France. King realized that Canadian troops would be part of Sledgehammer, and, like the British leaders, he was reluctant to sacrifice his citizen soldiers in an anticipated massacre. Surprised, King asked if the president knew how many divisions Britain had. The president reckoned about one hundred, and King informed him the number was more like sixteen. If half the divisions defending Britain were destroyed in France, Britain would be ripe for German invasion. King was shocked by how little British and American planners knew about each other. King's cautions left the president unsure about where the Americans should engage the Germans in 1942.[52]

Later, Prime Minister King met in private with Admiral Pound and asked him about a cross-channel invasion in 1942. King voiced concern about a premature offensive. He felt that the Americans did not understand how few British troops were available and how difficult it would be to land troops in Europe. Pound was sympathetic to what Marshall was trying to accomplish. He told King that Marshall was deploying troops to Australia and New Zealand, as well as East Asia, and had to promise an offensive in Europe, if only to reinforce the Allies in that theater. Pound concurred that Sledgehammer needed refinements, but he did not anticipate an offensive in Europe that year. King "felt considerably relieved" after speaking to the head of the Royal Navy.[53]

On 16 April, Roosevelt again met Mackenzie King and mentioned that several disturbing cables from Churchill had given him a rough night. The telegrams clearly show that the prime minister's attention was not on a return to western Europe but on the British Empire in the Pacific. Roosevelt shared that the messages were "the most depressing of anything I have read. They [the British] seem to be terribly alarmed about the situation in the Indian Ocean." Roosevelt reviewed the cables, which restated Churchill's apprehensions about the possible loss of India and the necessity of an immediate US Navy offensive to compel the Japanese fleet to pull back from the Indian Ocean and concentrate in the Pacific. If that was impossible, Churchill wanted an American aircraft carrier and battleship sent to the Indian Ocean to reinforce that area. After reading these British cables, Roosevelt remarked to the Canadian prime minister that Churchill "had the worst case of jitters in Britain than he thought they ever had."[54]

This latest exchange between Churchill and Roosevelt continued to highlight different national priorities between allies. The British feared that an early cross-channel attack would preclude a buildup of Allied naval might in the Indian Ocean. Admiral King, a well-known Anglophobe, suspected the British were exaggerating the threat and advised Roosevelt that the Japanese incursion into the Indian Ocean was a raid, not an invasion. The president sided with his admiral and informed Churchill that he would not deploy US warships to build up a fleet in the Indian Ocean, and he made another vague allusion to imminent actions in the Pacific that would alleviate the current situation.[55]

The president's veiled reference was to the planned aerial bombardment of Tokyo. Without informing the British, on 1 April sixteen B-25 bombers were loaded on the aircraft carrier *Hornet* with orders to proceed to within two hundred miles of the Japanese coast from where, in an unprecedented and daring operation, the medium bombers would strike the Japanese mainland. Despite complications, the raid, led by Lt. Col. James Doolittle, was successful and a great propaganda coup for the Americans.[56]

Tactically, the damage from the bombing was minimal, but strategically the raid exceeded all expectations. The Japanese army and navy were humiliated because they failed to protect the nation's capital from an attack. The Japanese navy immediately withdrew the fleet in the Indian Ocean to protect the homeland from further

Doolittle raid on Japan, April 1942 (Official US Navy Photograph 80-G-41196, now in the collections of the US National Archives)

attacks. The commander in chief of the Japanese fleet, Adm. Isoroku Yamamoto, overrode all objections to his proposed offensive to draw the US Pacific Fleet into a decisive battle at Midway. There he hoped to destroy the American carriers and end any further aerial threat to the Japanese homeland.[57]

The withdrawal of the Japanese fleet from the Indian Ocean did not end British concerns for their empire in the Far East. India and Australia were still threatened, and the British needed more resources for the Middle East. Meanwhile, the US Army and Navy still pursued competing strategies and vied for scarce resources. Nevertheless, April 1942 witnessed an important step in the evolving relationship between the British-American allies. Marshall had general approval for a plan that allowed him to counter the ad hoc dispersion of resources, as for the first time both sides agreed on a general strategic approach to defeat Germany. Although the destruction of the German army received priority, national prerogatives were still the determining influence on Allied operations. For his part, Churchill had successfully prevented the Americans from turning their focus and resources to the war against Japan and had received a US commitment for a massive buildup of men and matériel in Britain. To achieve this end, he had to agree to Sledgehammer, which Roosevelt, as evidenced by his discussion with McKenzie King, viewed as more than a mere emergency operation. Both sides still operated in an atmosphere of secrecy and suspicion about the other's motives. They had, however, seemingly established a tentative strategic goal for planning purposes.

5

Second Thoughts on a Second Front
May 1942

Upon leaving London at the end of April, Marshall believed that the British War Cabinet and the American Joint Chiefs of Staff agreed on Bolero (the buildup of US forces in Britain) and Roundup (the cross-channel invasion in 1943). The Combined Chiefs of Staff concurred with his decision to establish two committees, one in London and the other in Washington, DC, to facilitate Bolero. London assumed responsibility for port logistics and the accommodation of the US troops deployed in Britain. Washington oversaw all production and maintenance issues related to the sustainment of the American troops in the United Kingdom. Marshall assigned additional American logisticians and operational planners to work with the London committee to ensure the committees' close cooperation as they coordinated logistics and troop movements between the United States and Great Britain. He recommended appointing a corps commander and staff to Britain to coordinate detailed tactical planning.[1]

Marshall presumed that he had Roosevelt's full support for his Bolero strategy and expected to build a massive US force in Britain in preparation for the 1943 invasion. Thus, the president's 1 May directive to divert men and planes to the Pacific left him nonplussed. The US Army would increase the number of American troops in Australia to one hundred thousand and the total number of aircraft to one thousand, an increase of twenty-five thousand troops and one hundred planes.[2]

Marshall was away on an inspection trip when the presidential directive appeared, and upon returning to Washington on 3 May, he apprised Roosevelt of the implications of this order. An increase of twenty-five thousand US troops in Australia was the equivalent of a division and a half, but due to the shipping shortage and the great distance between Australia and the US West Coast, the time involved would reduce the buildup in Britain by three divisions. This in turn would eliminate any American ground participation in Sledgehammer (the possible emergency 1942 landing on the continent) and would seriously hinder the potential buildup for the April 1943 invasion. Marshall urged the president to reconsider the decision to increase the forces in Australia at the expense of reducing the buildup in Britain.[3]

This exchange came at a critical juncture in the Pacific. The day after Marshall asked for reconsideration of the transfer of forces to the Pacific, Lt. Gen. Jonathan Wainwright cabled Washington that the end was near in the Philippines. The American and Filipino forces had held against heavy odds for five months. After the fall of Bataan,

Gen. Jonathan Wainwright broadcasts his surrender message, following the capture of Corregidor by the Japanese, May 1942 (Naval History and Heritage Command, NH 73582)

Filipino-American forces regrouped on Corregidor Island, which the Japanese subjected to six consecutive weeks of relentless aerial and artillery bombardment. Food and ammunition were low, and the defenders could not repulse a Japanese assault on Corregidor. Two days later, on 6 May, Wainwright surrendered to the Japanese invaders.[4]

As the president deliberated the deployment of additional reinforcements to the Pacific, Admiral King weighed in with a memo, "Defense of Island Bases in the Pacific," sent to the Joint Chiefs of Staff and the president. King argued that supporting Bolero (the buildup of American forces in Britain) should not interfere with the vital interests in the Pacific. He contended that Bolero and the Pacific were equally important and the situation in the latter was currently more urgent. He wanted more than two hundred airplanes (bombers and fighters) sent to the Pacific area, because the Allies were spread too thin. Indeed, the Allies had lost Burma and much of East Asia because of a lack of resources. Coming as it did on the eve of Corregidor's impending surrender, King's memo resonated with the president.[5]

King's push for mores resources and the president's instruction to send more forces to Australia threatened to cancel the Bolero agreements with Britain. Marshall's plan to mass forces in Britain in preparation for a large-scale assault on the continent in 1943 was unraveling. On 6 May Marshall's note to the president summarized the resource issues involved in the conflict between the Pacific theater and Bolero. He appealed to the president's determination to keep the Soviet Union in the war. Because the fighting in Russia in the next few months would be critical to the Allied war effort, Marshall insisted that the western Allies make every effort to draw German forces from the eastern front. A British-American assault on western Europe was the best method to accomplish that goal, hence the urgency for the rapid buildup of US forces in Britain. Marshall warned Roosevelt that if Bolero was not America's main priority, then Washington should formally notify the British of the change and abrogate the recently concluded April agreements. Lacking a JCS consensus, Marshall had no choice but to ask for Roosevelt's decision, as commander in chief, and request for formal guidance on what to do next.[6]

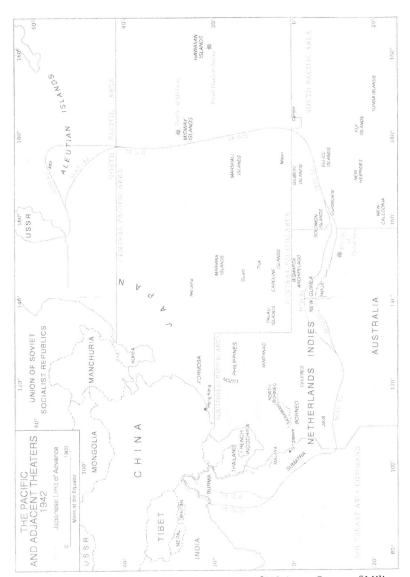

Pacific and adjacent theaters, May 1942 (courtesy of US Army Center of Military History)

Roosevelt's same-day reply sided with Marshall. It was all a misunderstanding. The president had not meant to order the deployment of troops and planes to Australia but had merely asked if it was possible. He understood that it was inadvisable at the present time. The president also rejected King's request for more aircraft, remarking that only a sufficient number of bombers and fighters should be sent to the Pacific to maintain the current objectives. With the declaration, "I do not want Bolero slowed down," he made it clear that the buildup in Britain had priority over the Pacific Theater.[7]

Roosevelt's close-hold memo, also sent on 6 May, for Stimson, Knox, Marshall, King, Arnold, and Hopkins, clearly laid out this strategic thinking and was the formal strategic guidance that Marshall had requested. Marshall's appeal to aid the USSR struck the correct note with a president who said the principal strategic objective of the United States was to help Russia. As Roosevelt put it, "Russian armies are killing more Germans and destroying more Axis material than all twenty-five united nations combined." The United States could help Russia in two ways: First, by supplying much-needed military equipment via the northern sea route; and second, by opening a second front that would compel Germany to withdraw air and ground forces from the eastern front. He recognized that assembling powerful air forces in Britain would allow the Allies to control the skies over western Europe. Combined air and ground raids would aid Russia by destroying as many German units and as much war matériel as possible. As for the Pacific theater, the president simply advocated the "maintenance of existing positions and existing strength" over the next few months.[8]

In his memorandum, the president caveated his support of Marshall's buildup of US forces in Britain preparatory for a large-scale invasion of the continent in 1943. Roosevelt was concerned with the growing public and congressional clamor for a second front against Germany and wrote that wartime "necessities" called for the United States to act in 1942 and not wait until 1943. The president's caveat deemed it "essential that active operations be conducted in 1942" and warned the navy that he found their constant objections and negativity about undertaking operations in Europe disturbing. Neither

Marshall nor the army and navy planners realized that this statement would exert such a profound impact on Allied strategic discussions during the coming months.[9]

Marshall anticipated an invasion of western Europe in 1943. There was no plan for 1942, except for a contingency operation (Sledgehammer), which envisioned an emergency seven-division invasion of the continent if the Soviet Union appeared on the verge of collapse. With only two American divisions in Britain, the United States had to depend almost entirely on British forces for the operation. The British vigorously opposed Sledgehammer in April. But Roosevelt's decision that US forces must fight Germans in 1942 doomed Sledgehammer because of its overreliance on British troops. Although Churchill and his advisors were not yet fully aware of it, they now controlled the destiny of the near-term strategic discussions.[10]

Roosevelt's decision on 6 May to support Bolero over the Pacific theater came at a dangerous time in the South Pacific. The Imperial Japanese Navy had enjoyed an unparalleled string of victories over the Allies and had yet to be checked anywhere in the Pacific or Indian Oceans. During the first week of May, as the American JCS argued amongst themselves, a Japanese fleet moved into the Coral Sea. They planned to seize Port Moresby on the southeastern tip of Papua New Guinea, only eighty nautical miles from Australia's north coast. From airfields near Port Moresby and in the Solomon Islands, they could strike convoys in the Coral Sea and attack Australia to cut the supply line between the United States and Australia.[11]

The Japanese scheduled the Port Moresby landing for 10 May. However, on 7 and 8 May the American fleet surprised the Japanese task force in the Coral Sea and sank one enemy aircraft carrier and damaged another. The Japanese, unwilling to risk the destruction of their troopships, cancelled the Moresby invasion and retreated north. This naval battle was the first major setback for the Japanese navy, halted the Japanese southward thrust, and secured Australia from invasion. It also relieved some of the pressure on the president to send more resources to the Pacific and buttressed his desire to build-up American forces in Britain in preparation for a cross-channel attack.[12]

On 7 May, as the Battle of the Coral Sea raged, Churchill met with the War Cabinet and the Chiefs of Staff Committee (COS) to discuss Sledgehammer. The British were having second thoughts on the April agreements that included Sledgehammer. They fully supported the buildup of troops and equipment in Britain but opposed any emergency landing in France in 1942 due to the overwhelming consensus that "this is not a sound military operation." There were two major problems. First, the British had troops deployed all around the globe and only a few units still available in the British Isles. If the invasion of western Europe in 1942 failed, the British Army would not have sufficient troops left to defend the home islands. Second, they believed that a landing in 1942 would jeopardize the success of the main assault (Roundup) in 1943. Local populations might rise against the Germans in 1942, but without adequate support the uprising would fail and would not likely be repeated the following year when the main assault occurred. Churchill's advisors insisted that Sledgehammer be undertaken only if German morale cracked and Germany was on the verge of collapse. This was, in short, the total opposite of the American concept of Sledgehammer.[13]

During May the president closely watched the Soviet military situation, which grew increasingly grim in the following few weeks. He told his military advisors that the United States' principal objective was to aid Russia. Roosevelt was not alone in keeping a close eye on the situation on the eastern front. As May wore on, Churchill's apprehension deepened because Britain might have to launch Sledgehammer to rescue the Soviet Union. Regardless of his personal feelings, he had after all promised Roosevelt that the British would execute Sledgehammer should the situation on the eastern front worsen. The Russians' failure on 12 May to recapture Kharkov, the administrative and railway center of eastern Ukraine, exposed the overextended Russian units to German counterattacks, and within five days converging German pincer movements surrounded the huge Russian forces. Soviet losses were staggering; 250,000 troops and twelve hundred tanks lost during just two weeks of brutal fighting. The Germans were now poised to resume their offensive against Moscow and Stalingrad. After this latest catastrophe, the Soviets appeared on the verge of collapse, which made a second front in

Pres. Franklin Roosevelt, Field Marshal John Dill, Gen. George Marshall, Capt. John MaCrea, and Adm. Ernest King reviewing parade, 1 May 1942 (courtesy of the George C. Marshall Foundation, Lexington, Virginia, USA)

western Europe to draw German forces from the east the only likely way to keep Russia in the war. Sledgehammer seemed inevitable, and Churchill recognized that he had to tell Roosevelt his reservations about its impracticality.[14]

The Kharkov debacle also led Stalin to increase pressure on the British and Americans for a second front. Three days after the German counterattack, the Soviet foreign minister, Vyacheslav Molotov, arrived in London to discuss two issues, a British-Soviet Treaty and a second front. The Soviets wanted a treaty with Great Britain that recognized the Soviet western border as of June 1941 when Germany invaded. This territory included Soviet-occupied eastern Poland. This was unacceptable to the British because the German invasion of Poland was Britain's original reason for declaring war against Germany. Molotov also proposed a secret agreement recognizing Soviet occupation of sections of Rumania after the war. Churchill realized that the Americans would never stand for such an arrangement and adamantly refused to consider it. Faced with British intractability, Molotov suggested deferring the topic and moving to the main reason for his visit—a second front in 1942.[15]

On 22 May, Molotov informed Churchill about the dire situation on the eastern front and Stalin's concerns. The Kharkov debacle was very much on his mind. While the Soviets appreciated the military equipment sent from the United States and Britain, they needed more substantial help against the vast German forces arrayed against them. Stalin's proposal carried by Molotov was simple. The Soviet premier wanted the British and Americans to launch an attack in western Europe during 1942 that would tie down forty German divisions. According to Molotov, this would seal Hitler's doom.[16]

Churchill did not want to launch an invasion of western Europe in 1942 but neither did he want to alienate the ally who was currently fighting the bulk of the German army. He explained the inherent problems in undertaking a cross-channel attack in 1942—lack of air superiority, especially inland from the coast, and lack of landing craft, which would be unavailable until 1943 to put the troops ashore. He told Molotov about the British-American discussions in April and the planning for a large-scale invasion of one and a half million men in western Europe in 1943.[17]

Molotov was unmoved. Stalin wanted help in 1942, not 1943. Molotov pointedly asked exactly how many British troops were currently engaged in fighting Germans. Churchill replied that Britain was tying down twenty-five German divisions in France, eleven in Libya, and eight in Norway, or forty-four total. It was unlikely that any British-American move in 1942 would draw a large number of German forces from the eastern front. Besides, according to British intelligence, the Germans were not as powerful as they were in 1941, so their anticipated spring offensive would not be as dangerous as the previous year's.[18]

Molotov remained unimpressed and asked what Britain would do if the Soviet army failed to hold against a German maximum effort expected in the next weeks. Churchill assured him that Britain would fight on regardless, maintain their blockade of Germany, and await the American buildup of large air and ground forces. A combined

British-American strategic bombing campaign would then devastate German industry before a landing on the continent. Molotov simply replied that he would report the British position to Stalin.[19]

After his disappointing meeting in London, Molotov flew on to Washington, DC, to ask Roosevelt about a second front in 1942. On the eve of Molotov's 27 May departure, Churchill cabled Roosevelt an update on his discussions with the Soviet foreign minister, emphasizing his successful negotiation of a British-Soviet Treaty that did not include any territorial concessions. Churchill made no mention of his talks on the second front, because he had not yet told Roosevelt of his concerns about a 1942 attack on western Europe. He recognized that he had been more forthcoming about his objections to a 1942 invasion with Molotov than with the Americans.[20]

Roosevelt's attention was on the second front, not the British-Soviet treaty. He immediately requested Churchill provide a summary of

V. M. Molotov in Washington, DC, 29 May–1 June 1942. From left to right: Adm. Ernest King, Vyacheslav Molotov, Maxim Litvinov, Cordell Hull, and Gen. George Marshall (courtesy of the George C. Marshall Foundation, Lexington, Virginia, USA)

his second front discussions with Molotov. In this request, Roosevelt mistakenly used the codename Bolero (the buildup of forces in Britain for the 1943 cross-channel attack) instead of Sledgehammer (the possible 1942 invasion of France), something that he would do frequently over the next two months that confused both Churchill and Roosevelt's own advisors. In this case, however, Churchill understood that the president's concern was with promises that the prime minister had made to Molotov regarding a second front for 1942. This left Churchill in a quandary. He had to reveal his misgivings about Sledgehammer to Roosevelt (since Molotov certainly would) and risk Roosevelt's wrath for negotiating in bad faith with Marshall and Hopkins in April.[21]

Churchill's carefully worded reply summarized his discussions with Molotov and for the first time expressed his doubts about Sledgehammer. Despite diligent collaboration by his military advisors with their American counterparts, Sledgehammer suffered from serious difficulties. Without elaborating on what these might be, Churchill recommended that Vice Adm. Louis Mountbatten come to Washington and discuss them in person with the president. As an alternative, Churchill brought up a draft plan to occupy northern Norway to improve the flow of British-American convoys to Russia along the northern supply route. He had promised to hand it to Molotov when the Soviet diplomat returned to London the following week. Churchill ended with the nebulous comment that "we must never let Gymnast [the invasion of North Africa by American forces] pass from our minds." This comment surprised Roosevelt's military advisors, whose opposition to a North Africa operation since the Arcadia Conference was well-known to the British leaders.[22]

Molotov arrived in Washington and on 30 May met with the president, Hopkins, King, and Marshall to discuss a second front in 1942. While Soviet morale remained high, Molotov feared the Germans were capable of a crushing blow in 1942. He believed that a British-American second front in western Europe would draw off forty German divisions from the eastern front and give the Soviets a respite that would either enable them to defeat Hitler in 1942 or at least assure his eventual defeat. Molotov insisted that the German troops in France were mostly "second-rate" units and asked if the Americans were prepared to undertake a second front in 1942, acknowledging that he had posed the same question to the British but had received no commitment. If the British-Americans refused, then the Soviets would fight on alone as best they could. After Marshall assured Roosevelt that American plans for a second front were sufficiently developed, the president told Molotov that he could notify Stalin to expect a second front during 1942.[23]

The president's commitment to a second front in 1942 made Marshall uncomfortable. Marshal's plan (Roundup) set a cross-channel attack in 1943. He interjected that the Americans had the troops, munitions, planes, and tanks for a second front, but lacked the shipping to move all those troops and matériel overseas. Requirements to ship matériel to Murmansk and heavy airplanes to the British Isles before they could fly on to Russia exacerbated shipping problems. Like Churchill, Marshall also stressed the difficulties involved in establishing air superiority and moving troops and their equipment across the channel.[24]

On 1 June, Roosevelt and Molotov met again, and the president addressed the issue of shipping. Put simply, to open a second front in 1942, the Americans needed more transports. The JCS suggested that reducing lend-lease shipping to Russia from 4,100,000 tons to 1,800,000 tons in the last six months of 1942 would release enough American ships to transport munitions and military equipment to Britain for the second front. Molotov opposed this recommendation because Stalin wanted a second front as well as the shipment of war matériel to Murmansk by the northern convoy route. Molotov bluntly announced his fears that the Americans would cut lend-lease shipments to the Soviets, precluding a second front. Roosevelt remarked that the ships could not be in two places simultaneously and the Soviets "could not eat their cake and have it too." Molotov was suspicious of this solution. What should he tell Stalin about a second front? Roosevelt answered that the Allies "expected to establish a second front" in 1942.[25]

Roosevelt updated Churchill on his discussions with Molotov and also dismissed Churchill's critique of a cross-channel attack in 1942.

He emphasized his concern over the Russian situation on the eastern front. The Soviet situation was "precarious" and might worsen over the next few weeks as the German spring offensive gained momentum. Therefore, he was anxious to execute Bolero in 1942. Once again, the president interchanged the codenames and used Bolero instead of Sledgehammer, further confusing matters. Roosevelt also told Churchill of his plan to reduce lend-lease shipments to Murmansk to make shipping available to build up resources in Britain.[26]

Roosevelt's press release on Molotov's visit further surprised Churchill because it announced an understanding on a second front in 1942. Molotov had drafted the release, which was his way of ensuring a written Allied commitment to a second front. Marshall felt the statement about a second front was overly optimistic and wanted it removed. In Marshall's mind, a 1942 invasion was a desperate contingency and his plan called for a landing in 1943. This was the second time the army chief tried to dissuade the president from committing to a second front in 1942. Roosevelt, however, overrode Marshall's objections and had the communiqué published almost as Molotov had written it. The Soviet foreign minister was ecstatic.[27]

Churchill's worst fears seemed to be coming to fruition. He had promised Roosevelt a second front in 1942 if Russia was on the verge of collapse. That now appeared to be the case. In a cabinet meeting on 27 May, Air Marshal Portal had candidly informed the prime minister that the deterioration on the eastern front might necessitate a landing in western Europe, even "at heavy cost to ourselves." Roosevelt had turned Churchill's promise of a potential operation into a firm commitment to the Soviets.[28]

Molotov returned to London and pressed the British for more details on their second front in 1942. Churchill lamely told him that preparations were underway, but he could not guarantee a second front in 1942. Molotov noted that in Washington the Soviets agreed to a reduction in supplies in exchange for a second front. The prime minister emphasized that the British-American plan called for an invasion of western Europe in 1943, but if it were possible to move it up to 1942 then the British would do it. Churchill's aide-memoire to Molotov read, "We can therefore give no promise in the matter [of a second front in 1942], but provided that it appears sound and sensible we shall not hesitate to put our plans into effect." Molotov returned to Moscow satisfied that his skillful diplomacy had secured the much sought-after second front during 1942.[29]

Roosevelt's press release had alarmed Churchill, who told General Brooke that it was time the two of them went to Washington to discuss the realities of a second front in 1942 with the president. Churchill realized that he needed an alternative to a cross-channel attack in 1942 and one that Roosevelt would support. This became his top priority during June.[30]

6

Sledgehammer, Gymnast, and the Second Washington Conference

June 1942

June 1942 opened with the Allies on the defensive everywhere. The British remained apprehensive about the Middle East, where Rommel's latest offensive in Libya on 26–27 May enjoyed early success but was unable to achieve a decisive advantage. On the eastern front the Germans decisively smashed the Soviets' massive Kharkov offensive and prepared for a major offensive of their own to capture Sevastopol. In the southwest Pacific, Japanese raids on Australia's southeastern coast surprised the Allies and reignited Commonwealth nations' fears of an impending Japanese invasion. The US Navy concentrated its forces in the central Pacific in anticipation of a decisive fleet action that would check Japanese expansion once and for all. In brief, British-American military leaders continued to emphasize and resource national objectives rather than a common unified strategy.[1]

The Japanese Combined Fleet commander, Adm. Isoroku Yamamoto, was determined, however, to engage the US Pacific Fleet decisively near Midway Island. The Doolittle air raid on Japan had embarrassed him personally by highlighting the Japanese homeland's vulnerability to air attack. Yamamoto wanted to expand the Japanese defensive perimeter. Air bases on Midway and Kiska would enable reconnaissance aircraft to patrol far-distant waters to detect approaching enemy warships before they could strike Japan. By surprising the Americans at Midway, the Japanese could capture the tiny island, which in turn would draw the American main fleet into a battle where the Japanese could annihilate it.[2]

Pres. Franklin Roosevelt, Gen. George Marshall, and Adm. Ernest King review Memorial Day Parade, 30 May 1942 (courtesy of the George C. Marshall Foundation, Lexington, Virginia, USA)

This was a compromise between the rival Japanese Combined Fleet and the Naval General Staff. The Combined Fleet (Yamamoto) sought a decisive naval battle to destroy the remaining American aircraft carriers and knock the US Navy out of the war. The Naval General Staff argued that the Midway operation was too dangerous and recommended a continuation of a southward advance to seize New Caledonia. In the resulting compromise, the Naval General Staff added numerous supporting operations, such as an attack on the Aleutians and submarine raids off the coast of Australia. These strikes would confuse the Americans, divert American resources from the main effort, and conceal Japan's actual objectives. The Japanese conducted the Midway operation with scant intelligence, casually expecting carrier-launched reconnaissance aircraft to locate the American fleet. As one historian noted, "Underlying the planned Midway offensive was a casual and yet insidious assumption that Japan was fated to continue its run of victories." As a result, the Midway plan was complex and marred by flaws and contradictions.[3]

Limited resources dictated a clear and concise American plan; ambush and destroy the Japanese aircraft carriers. Excellent intelligence allowed the US naval commander, Adm. Chester Nimitz, to set the trap. US Navy cryptanalysts had broken the Japanese code. One month earlier, the Americans could decipher about 15 percent of the Japanese code. However, Japanese failure to change their code book between 1 April and 1 June 1942 gave the navy cryptanalysts additional time to analyze Japanese communication systems. By the beginning of June, the codebreakers could decipher 90 percent of all Japanese naval messages. This provided Nimitz with the exact date, place, and time of arrival of the Midway invasion fleet.[4]

The Midway campaign began with a carrier-based Japanese air strike on the US Army and Navy facilities at Dutch Harbor, in the Aleutians Islands of Alaska, on 3 June 1942. Yamamoto's plan depended on the rapid capture of Midway and subsequent ambush of the American fleet dispatched to retake the island. Instead his fleet moved into Nimitz's trap and lost four heavy carriers to one US Navy aircraft carrier. Japan's limited industrial capacity exacerbated their ship losses. Within a few months Americans shipyards could replace or repair US warship losses. The Japanese never could.[5]

Japanese aircraft carrier *Hiryu* burning, shortly after sunrise on 5 June 1942, a few hours before it sank (Navy History and Heritage Command Photograph, NH 73064)

Without carriers, the Japanese navy no longer dared to risk a fleet action outside the range of their land-based bombers. The Midway victory eliminated any Japanese threat to Hawaii and the west coast of the United States. The decisive battle also silenced Roosevelt's critics who had clamored for a greater share of forces for the Pacific. The president was now free to move on his primary concern, keeping Russia in the war and the defeat of Germany. Second front discussions with the British on Sledgehammer, Roundup, and operations during 1942 took on greater urgency.[6]

Roosevelt exuberantly notified Churchill of the navy's accomplishments at Midway. Churchill immediately grasped that the loss of four aircraft carriers restrained any future Japanese operations. He informed Admiral Pound that the Japanese would need to husband large naval units, which improved the British position in the Indian Ocean and Bay of Bengal. With the elimination of the threat of a seaborne invasion on Ceylon or southeast India, General Wavell in India was free to move forces to the northeast India frontier and prepare a ground offensive in Burma. Likewise, Admiral Somerville, the commander in chief, Eastern Fleet, was free to repair the damage to the ports on Ceylon and secure the sea lanes in the Indian Ocean. Following Churchill's directives, Pound ordered Wavell and Somerville to plan British offensives against Japan.[7]

Churchill still had concerns. The US Navy's continued reluctance to share strategic intelligence and codebreaking discoveries with their British counterparts frustrated him. One British intelligence official claimed that it was difficult to coordinate with the US Navy codebreakers in the Pacific because the Americans believed they were ahead of their British counterparts and were thus reluctant to share data. A senior British intelligence officer described the American attitude on intelligence sharing as "what is yours is mine, and what is mine is my own." The US Navy was notoriously unwilling to share its intelligence not only with the British but also with the US Army. When army officers broached the subject of intelligence sharing, a high-ranking naval officer remarked that a Joint Intelligence Committee (JIC) would only be established "over my dead body." General Marshall lamented that he "was sorry to see so young a man die," but there would be a JIC.[8]

The lack of trust nettled Churchill, but after the war he glossed over his displeasure, acknowledging that the solution of the Japanese naval code system was decisive in the American victory at Midway, while complaining that he would have liked greater insight into American plans for the operation. He admitted, however, that secrecy was important and that the Americans had every right to be concerned about the consequences of a leak about critical intelligence reaching the enemy.[9]

Churchill also realized that American operations in the Pacific theater would no longer constrain American determination to open a second front against Germany. After the Molotov visit to Washington and Roosevelt's promise to Molotov of a cross-channel attack in 1942, Churchill had to quickly meet with Roosevelt to extricate himself from the April agreement for a second front against Germany. The prime minister sent Adm. Louis Mountbatten on 1 June to the United States, ostensibly to brief the Combined Chiefs of Staff on plans for Roundup (the cross-channel attack in 1943) but privately to meet with the president and explain the inherent obstacles to an invasion of France in 1942. He ordered Mountbatten, as chief of Combined Operations, to ascertain Roosevelt's zeal for an offensive in 1942 and sow the seeds of British rejection for Sledgehammer.[10]

On 4 June, before meeting with the president, Mountbatten outlined the status of London's second-front planning for the assembled Combined Chiefs of Staff in Washington. He explained that the British were considering two types of operations for an invasion of northwest Europe in 1943. The first assumed that the Russians still tied down the bulk of German arms along the eastern front. In that case, the British planned a landing on a wide front in northern France, capturing the port at Antwerp, and then rapidly driving to Berlin. The second anticipated a German redeployment from the eastern front, meaning that the western Allies would be facing the bulk of the German forces. In this event the invasion would occur farther east, to secure the Brittany peninsula and the French Atlantic ports. It was unnecessary at this time to decide between the two plans."

Mountbatten met with Marshall and King about landing craft several times between 5–8 June. The lack of landing craft was a key logistical shortfall in planning and executing a cross-channel attack in 1942. Disagreements between the two American services hampered design and production of the small vessels. Mountbatten had previously projected a requirement for between twenty to thirty thousand officers and men to man the landing craft for the invasion of northern France. Admiral King balked at this number because he opposed training thousands of naval personnel to serve as crews on landing craft for a cross-channel invasion that was primarily an army operation. During a private session with Mountbatten, King and Marshall argued heatedly over the manning of landing craft. Marshall finally told King that the army would provide and train the crews; in effect, Marshall would be creating his own navy.[12]

Afterwards Mountbatten bluntly told King, as one sailor to another, not to let the army do the navy's job, because it was short-sighted and erroneous to deny support to the army. Mountbatten admitted that in the future the British Army would boast of its accomplishment in landing on France's shores, but the British navy could say their landing craft put the army ashore. King's attitude would cede full credit to the army, leaving the navy forgotten. He warned King that the invasion of Europe was inevitable and turning the complete landing mission over to the army was "selling the birthright of the Navy."[13]

King followed Mountbatten's recommendations, which included appointing a senior admiral to work with the British to develop plans for the construction of landing crafts and training of crews. Rear Adm. H. Kent Hewitt headed the American planning team on amphibious operations in London. Hewitt, with King's support, breathed new life into the stagnant landing craft program. When learning of this decision, Marshall thanked Mountbatten for his successful intervention.[14]

Mountbatten met alone with the president for five hours on 9 June to discuss the challenges inherent in a 1942 cross-channel attack. Churchill had pushed for such a meeting, and the president was interested in hearing the British perspective and concerns on the viability of an invasion. During their discussion, Mountbatten reviewed the inherent difficulties of any invasion of northern France in 1942. Roosevelt, however, was insistent that the Americans had to engage the German army as soon as possible. The president continued that

Churchill had committed to Sledgehammer, the sacrificial landing in France by six British divisions, to divert the Germans if the Russians appeared on the verge of collapse that summer.[15]

Mountbatten opposed Sledgehammer on strategic grounds. He believed that a landing would not draw any German troops or aircraft from the eastern front. While the Allies could get ashore, the shortage of landing craft precluded transporting sufficient troops and equipment to hold any beachhead. The twenty-five German divisions stationed in France were more than enough to destroy Sledgehammer's small landing force. An Allied defeat in turn would boost German morale and not help the Soviet cause at all. A failure in 1942 would also make any future cross-channel attack more difficult because the Germans would reinforce their coastal defenses. As for the chances of a successful landing in northern France in September, Mountbatten resurrected the shopworn promise that the British would land in France in the autumn of 1942 if German morale cracked or the Russians were victorious in the east.[16]

This was not what the American president wanted to hear. Roosevelt insisted that he was unwilling to deploy one million American soldiers to Britain only to find that a Soviet collapse rendered a 1943 cross-channel attack to France impossible. To preclude that eventuality, Roosevelt wanted to know the possibility of conducting an offensive in France in 1942, even as late as December. Finally understanding the importance that the president attached to an offensive in 1942, Mountbatten recommended that the Allies look at an alternative operation and brought up Gymnast. Roosevelt made no commitments, although the president admitted that Churchill's recent cable about Operation Gymnast (invasion of French North Africa) intrigued him.[17]

Roosevelt informed neither Marshall nor King of this discussion nor his acknowledgement to Mountbatten that he was reconsidering a North Africa landing to help the Russians. This was consistent with Roosevelt's leadership style as a savvy politician who kept his cards close to his vest and usually told people what they wanted to hear and no more than they needed to know. He supported Marshall's plan for a 1943 invasion but spoke of action in 1942. He just could not have

Americans sit idle for another year, leaving the Soviets to fight the Germans alone. In early June, the president kept his own counsel; his options remained open, and he had yet to select a course of action for 1942.[18]

Churchill was gratified that Roosevelt remained interested in Gymnast, but the president's insistence on a cross-channel invasion during 1942 (Sledgehammer) disconcerted him so much that he made immediate arrangements to visit Washington, DC, to meet with Roosevelt in person. Churchill told General Brooke that "he considered Roosevelt getting a bit off the rails and some good talks as regards to the western front were required."[19]

But what alternative to Sledgehammer could Churchill offer to Roosevelt? The prime minister had already arbitrarily announced to his Chiefs of Staff Committee that the British would not carry out Sledgehammer. His definitive 8 June guidance emphasized that there would be no substantial landings in France unless the western Allies intended to stay there and the Germans were demoralized by their failure against the Soviet Union. The prime minister was frank, noting that "if Russia were in dire straits, it would not help her for us to come to a nasty cropper on our own."[20]

Churchill also entertained serious doubts about Roundup, despite telling Roosevelt and Stalin that the projected 1943 operation had his full support. He spoke from the other side of his mouth at the 11 June War Cabinet meeting, where he told the Chiefs of Staff Committee that the date for Roundup in 1943 would have to slide because "it was unlikely that the American forces would be trained in time." The prime minister had no evidence to support his remarks about the current quality of American training, and these comments apparently reflected his lack of confidence in the British Army. He also told the committee that Sledgehammer would delay the Roundup operation, but only three days earlier the prime minister had told his military chieftains that the British were not going to execute Sledgehammer.[21]

At the same meeting, Churchill and the War Cabinet also reviewed four second-front alternatives to Sledgehammer that might aid Russia. Since Marshall had envisioned Sledgehammer as a mainly British operation, three of the four alternatives excluded American forces.

Nonetheless, the prime minister preferred an operation that not only helped Russia but also endorsed Roosevelt's preference for US participation in combat operations during 1942.

The first alternative, Operation Imperator, was a solely British operation. A single division landing near Amiens or Abbeville was designed to draw German air forces from the eastern front. British planners considered it a suicide mission and rejected it because it could easily be defeated without a significant withdrawal of German resources from the eastern front.[22]

Second, Churchill advocated for Operation Jupiter, a British-American invasion of northern Norway and Finland, which the chiefs had previously considered and rejected three times. As this was his only option that included American participation, Churchill insisted passionately that a firm foothold in northern Norway would increase the security of the Allied convoys to Murmansk and "enable us to start to unroll Hitler's map of Europe from the top." The British chiefs again strongly opposed the plan and expressed their objections in an aide memoir for the prime minister.[23]

According to the chiefs' review, capturing the northern airfields would not significantly reduce German air attacks on the Allied convoys. Other German airfields to the south and west were operational and striking the convoys. The Allies would have to liberate and occupy most of Norway to eliminate the air threat. The large forces required would siphon shipping and landing craft resources needed for Bolero and potentially delay a cross-channel attack against northern France until 1944. In the chiefs' estimation, the operation had "little chance of success," and, even if successful, a second front in Norway was of "limited military value, since there would be no immediate threat to an objective vital to the Germans." This was not what the prime minister wanted to hear. On 11 June, he asked the chiefs to again rework this proposal and give it their "most earnest consideration."[24]

Third, Churchill urged consideration of Operation Jackpot, which involved the British occupation of Spitsbergen Island off the north coast of German-occupied Norway. The Germans had already established a meteorological base on the island, and the fear was that they would construct naval and air bases on the island, which was astride the northern supply route to Russia, from which they could further attack the Murmansk convoys. The British chiefs agreed that occupying the island was not essential to the protection of the convoys. The Chiefs of Staff Committee adamantly opposed reinforcing a small Norwegian expedition already ashore and instead recommended simply evacuating the survivors.[25]

Fourth, Churchill recommended yet another expedition in Norway, codenamed "Operation Viceroy." British forces would attack the German naval and air bases in the area of Kirkines and Petsamo in the extreme north of occupied Norway and in Finland. British planners were "wholly opposed to this project" for a variety of reasons. The landing force would be exposed to heavy German air attacks because the Allies lacked adequate air support to cover the landing areas; the expedition would be vulnerable to attack by German warships; British troops were not trained in arctic conditions and cold fall weather was fast approaching; and inadequate port facilities to support a landing meant that the Germans could reinforce the zone faster overland than the British could by sea.[26]

Two days later, on 13 June, Churchill's memorandum "Operation Round-Up" offered the chiefs of staff and the planning committee an alternative strategy for an invasion of Europe that bore no resemblance to Marshall's proposal. Instead of a single major assault by British and American forces in 1943, Churchill proposed "at least six heavy disembarkations in the first wave. The enemy should be further mystified by at least a half dozen feints.'" He recommended geographically separate landings and feints from Denmark to St. Nazaire, France, and expected the landing forces to rouse the populations to fight, disrupt German communications, and force the enemy to disperse resources over vast areas. The prime minister anticipated heavy fighting would occur at only one or two landing sites but otherwise the landings would be a walkover. A second wave would then reinforce the gaps where the invaders had encountered no resistance. The third wave would go ashore once a port was secured. He foresaw four hundred thousand troops landing within a week and an additional three hundred thousand as soon as a port was captured.[27]

This plan made no sense. In terms of logistics alone, if the Allies could not assemble sufficient landing craft and provide air cover for a single invasion site, there certainly was not enough support for landings at a dozen widely separate locations. Despite Churchill's postwar claims that this plan supported a second front in 1943, his 1942 proposal clearly suggests that the prime minister disagreed with Marshall's vision of a cross-channel invasion of France in 1943. Churchill should have realized that the resources for such a grandiose plan, with dispersed landings along the northwest coast of western Europe, would delay a cross-channel attack until at least 1944. He looked to his military chiefs for support before his meeting with Roosevelt in Washington. The British chiefs, however, were aghast at the proposal and quickly rejected it as unrealistic. Despite his own advisors' misgivings, Churchill remained determined to show it to the Americans.[28]

Opposed to Sledgehammer and lukewarm about Roundup, Churchill realized he had to provide Roosevelt with an alternative operation that could assist Russia and guarantee the continued flow of US resources to the war against Germany. The prime minister peppered his planning staff for analysis of possible operations in 1942. The War Cabinet also met several times to review the alternatives in the second week of June.

On 13 June, Churchill cabled Roosevelt that he spoke at length with Mountbatten in London and believed the two heads of state needed to meet face to face to discuss strategy and "all the many difficult points outstanding." Churchill wanted to come as soon as possible and offered to bring General Brooke with him. Roosevelt quickly agreed and offered to meet without any advisors at his home in Hyde Park, New York, on 19–20 June. After their meeting, the two heads of state would go by train to Washington to confer with their respective military advisors to discuss strategy.[29]

Churchill was soon to depart on 17 June for Washington and still needed an alternative to Sledgehammer to offer Roosevelt. Following the British chiefs and their planning staff's vehement rejection of Churchill's proposed four alternatives, the prime minister only had Gymnast as a substitute for Sledgehammer if Roosevelt insisted on some offensive operation in 1942. Hoping to generate more than a single alternative, the prime minister again ordered the British Chiefs of Staff committee to reconsider Jupiter. Churchill directed his Planning Committee to "set themselves to making a positive plan and overcoming the many difficulties." They were not to worry about the operation's desirability; that was his job, not theirs. They had three days to relook Jupiter and develop a "positive plan." To Churchill's thinking, the Jupiter strategy would reassure the Soviet Union of the Allies' goodwill by neutralizing the airstrips in northern Norway that menaced the supply route to Murmansk. It would also fulfill Roosevelt's desire to have US forces engage Germany in 1942. Churchill told the planners that it was the best alternative to Sledgehammer if the German occupation forces in France were not on the verge of collapse. His pleas did not change the planners' opinion of Jupiter, as they continued to point out the plan's flaws. Churchill's memoirs acknowledge that he did not receive much positive support for Jupiter. This left him only North Africa as an alternative to a landing in France.[30]

The prime minister had to convince the president that North Africa offered the western Allies their best opportunity for success. After all, during his meeting with Mountbatten, Roosevelt appeared sympathetic toward this strategy, and Churchill hoped to nurture that interest to guide the president's decision.[31]

On 17 June, President Roosevelt assembled his military and naval advisors for final preparations for his meeting with Churchill. The president's resurrection of the North Africa strategy surprised the group. Could Gymnast bring enough pressure on the Germans to save the USSR? Marshall and Stimson were stunned, having no inkling that the president was wavering on Bolero and Roundup in favor of Gymnast. It seemed to Stimson that the president's willingness to change course on Bolero imperiled the entire Allied strategy. Both Stimson and Marshall had yet to appreciate the president's anxiety to fight the Germans in 1942. Indeed, Stimson believed that Roosevelt may have brought up North Africa "in his foxy way" to forestall trouble during Churchill's impending visit.[32]

Mountbatten's earlier 10 June backbrief to the Combined Chiefs of Staff, on his meeting with the president, expressed British misgivings on Sledgehammer, raised questions about the feasibility of Roundup in 1943, and disquieted Marshall. This was the first indication the Americans had that the British were having second thoughts about their commitment to engage the Germans in France during 1942. If launching Sledgehammer in 1942 to save the Soviet Union from collapse was impractical, Marshall realized that the same argument could be used to postpone a landing in 1943. As a consequence, Marshall told his staff to prepare another detailed analysis of Gymnast in case the subject arose at the upcoming conference. Marshall used their findings with Roosevelt to oppose the North Africa operation for the usual reasons. Gymnast was risky and based on optimistic assumptions of full French cooperation, complete Spanish neutrality, and availability of British shipping. Marshall's major objection, however, was that undertaking Gymnast disrupted the Bolero strategy and pushed Roundup back from 1943 to 1944. Both he and Stimson spoke out passionately against the proposal, but the president asked that the two relook at Gymnast and "see if it could be done." For Stimson it was "altogether a disappointing afternoon."[33]

Learning of Churchill's impending meeting with Roosevelt in Washington, Canadian prime minister Mackenzie King in Ottawa, Canada, asked the British high commissioner, Malcolm MacDonald, on 19 June, if he knew what topics the two leaders would consider. King already resented not being invited to the strategic negotiations because there were Canadian troops in Britain, and he worried that the major Allies might launch a cross-channel attack in 1942 using Canadian troops but not telling him. MacDonald reassured him that Churchill strongly opposed any attack on France before the spring of 1943, if it could possibly be avoided. He accused the Americans of underestimating Germany's power and the requirements to attack France.[34]

The Second Washington Conference, codenamed "Argonaut," convened between 19–25 June 1942. Churchill arrived in Washington early on the morning of 19 June and met privately with Marshall, where he wasted no time in opposing Sledgehammer and endorsing Gymnast. Until Churchill's outburst, Marshall had assumed that the prime minister supported his April proposals. He accepted that the British had reservations on Sledgehammer but was stunned that Churchill was so single-minded in his support of Gymnast. A distressed Marshall told Stimson of Churchill's position, and the secretary of war in turn reminded the president in writing of Bolero's benefits and Gymnast's problems.[35]

Stimson's memorandum stressed the strategic continuity that Britain already accepted. It explained that Bolero provided the shortest and most direct route to the heart of Germany, and the British Isles were essential for this strategy because they offered only location where: (1) the United States could safely land air and ground forces without the aid of carrier-based air cover; (2) the Allies could launch both fighter and bombers against occupied Europe; (3) they could safely develop a logistics base for an invasion force against the continent; (4) they could gain air superiority over northern France to protect a beachhead.[36]

Stimson termed Gymnast as the "worst contingency possible." It weakened Bolero and delayed Roundup from 1943 to 1944. If Germany were successful against Russia in 1943, he feared Britain might be vulnerable to a surprise invasion if they weakened their home defenses by deploying more forces to North Africa. Conversely, if Germany failed in the east, the western Allied forces would not be in position to take advantage of the Nazi defeat. Gymnast would strain already scarce shipping and, because of the unavailability of local air support, require American aircraft carriers for Gymnast. Taken together this would retard future offensives in the Pacific. Stimson could only hope that Churchill's eloquence would not sway the president.[37]

While Churchill went to Hyde Park to meet privately with Roosevelt and Hopkins, the British chiefs of staff remained in Washington to confer with their American counterparts. Brooke outlined the situation from the British perspective for the Combined Chiefs of Staff. The British opposed a cross-channel attack in 1942, but Churchill was sympathetic to Roosevelt's desire to have American forces actively engage the Germans that year. Churchill was looking to dispatch substantial American forces direct to the Middle East to conduct some form of a Gymnast operation in 1942 rather than reinforcing the Middle East with British forces from the United Kingdom.[38]

Brooke then called attention to four options the British had considered in lieu of Sledgehammer. Of the four, a six-division landing in the vicinity of Pas de Calais had already been discarded, the landing force being too small to divert any German resources from Russia. A fifteen-division landing near Cherbourg or Brest merited further study, but it would take three months to assemble such a large force. Large scale raids for one or two days along the coast of France could be undertaken to tie down German forces in France and not allow them to redeploy to the eastern front. Even Jupiter, the Norway operation, made the list, although Brooke emphasized that the British chiefs had rejected the operation as too risky. It was clear to the audience that there was little stomach for large-scale operations in France.[39]

Brooke next met privately with Marshall, Eisenhower, Dill, and Ismay for a candid discussion about Bolero and possible offensives in either western Europe or northwest Africa in 1942. Both sides were surprised at how closely their military strategic views aligned. There was complete unanimity about the buildup of American forces in Britain (Bolero) for an offensive in Europe in 1943 (Roundup). Brooke opposed Gymnast because it would curtail reinforcements to the British Eighth Army with disastrous results for current British operations in Libya. Marshall agreed, as both concurred that Gymnast would disperse resources and delay the concentration of forces for Bolero and most likely delay the invasion of France until 1944. They also accepted that Sledgehammer should "be undertaken only in case of necessity or if an exceptionally favorable opportunity presented itself." Brooke was pleased that the two allies were in accord on strategic matters.[40]

The next morning, 20 June, the Combined Chiefs of Staff formally reviewed the minutes of Brooke and Marshall's discussion. Brooke explained that he "had been much encouraged to find that there was a complete unanimity of opinion between US and British staffs on general strategic policy and the merits of the Bolero plan as a whole." Brooke proved a strong advocate for Bolero because the deployment of a powerful American force in England would guarantee the nation's safety and more than compensate for the British troops currently fighting in the Middle East. The situation in Russia, Brooke believed, would be decided by September 1942. By that time, there would be enough American reinforcements to protect the United Kingdom if things went badly on the eastern front.[41]

Admiral King told the Combined Chiefs that he opposed Gymnast in 1942. King explained that the US Navy was currently responsible for escort and transportation duties on eight separate fronts. Adding a ninth in northwest Africa might break the navy. He enumerated the risks in the Pacific and advocated maximum support for Bolero rather than piecemealing naval forces to launch Gymnast. Admiral Little, the British naval representative to the Combined Chiefs of Staff, agreed and revealed that the head of the Royal Navy, Admiral Pound, also opposed Gymnast because the Royal Navy found operations in the Atlantic difficult enough without adding a large new commitment.[42]

Marshall and Brooke agreed that large-scale operations on the continent were not possible in 1943 unless the Allies concentrated forces in Britain and that a key benefit of the Bolero buildup was the security of the United Kingdom. Marshall likewise believed that the situation in Russia would be decided that summer and was willing to wait and see what happened there before deciding on any contingency operations. Brooke was of the same mind but made clear his opposition to Sledgehammer's sacrifice of six British divisions. Eisenhower interjected that Americans only saw Sledgehammer as an emergency contingency and "realized that the circumstances in which such an operation might be feasible were unlikely to arise."[43]

The committee recommended that the Combined Chiefs of Staff put these strategic agreements in writing for Churchill and Roosevelt. Although the British and American military chiefs had finally agreed on a cohesive strategy for defeating Germany, they knew that theirs was not the final word. Brooke spoke for all his colleagues: "But we fully appreciated that we might be up against many difficulties when confronted with the plans that the PM and the President had been brewing up together at 'Hyde Park'! We fear the worst and are certain that North Africa or North Norway plans for 1942 will loom large in their proposals, whilst we are convinced that they are not possible!"[44]

That afternoon, Churchill and Roosevelt discussed strategy. Harry Hopkins was the only other attendee. Churchill opposed Sledgehammer because it would lead to certain disaster, would not help the Russians, and would delay the main operation in 1943. In brief, Sledgehammer had no chance of success unless the Germans became completely demoralized, which was unlikely. While the British were willing to share risks and sacrifices with the United States, they would not make the sacrifices alone. Churchill then fired off a barrage of questions: "Have the American Staffs a plan? If so, what is it? What forces would be employed? At what points would they strike? What landing-craft and shipping are available? Who is the officer prepared to command the enterprise? What British forces and assistance are required?" Even if an invasion of France was beyond the western Allies in September 1942, Churchill did not intend to sit idle in the Atlantic theater. He called for Bolero to continue, along with the execution of Gymnast, which might "directly or indirectly to take some of the weight off Russia."[45]

This proposal resonated with Roosevelt. The president did not personally forward Churchill's memorandum to Marshall and King. Instead, he directed his military aide, US Navy Capt. John McCrea, to cable several questions for the American chiefs to study and discuss with him the following day. Roosevelt's key question was where American ground forces could attack German forces or Axis-controlled areas before mid-September 1942, possibly in locations where British forces might aid in achieving the same objective. The request caught Marshall and King off guard because Sledgehammer was only a worst-case contingency. Otherwise, they expected to invade the continent in 1943 and had no alternative plan.[46]

Official British history refers to 21 June as the "Day of the Dupes," a historical reference to the day in November 1630 when Cardinal Richelieu's enemies mistakenly thought they had convinced King Louis XIII to dismiss the cardinal from power. Similarly, the American and British chiefs mistakenly believed on 20 June that they concluded a strategic consensus for operations in Europe for 1942 and 1943. The CCS erroneously thought they had turned a corner in American and British military negotiations. The following day, Churchill and Roosevelt subtly nullified all that Marshall and Brooke had worked so diligently to carefully create.[47]

On 21 June, Churchill and Roosevelt returned to Washington, where the Combined Chiefs of Staffs had been meeting the past two days. The chiefs were prepared to present a memorandum dated 20

June that summarized their agreements. Their main conclusions endorsed Bolero, and since Roundup was still firmly set for the spring of 1943, advised that no alternative operations should be considered except in an unavoidable emergency. The chiefs had agreed that that the Allies should not undertake Gymnast given the current situation.

The chiefs never got the opportunity to formally present this report to the two heads of state. When apprised of the conclusions, Churchill was "very upset" because they contradicted what the prime minister had told the president the previous evening when advocating for operations in either North Africa or Norway in 1942. He vented his anger on Brooke and chastised his general for opposing Gymnast and Jupiter. Brooke laconically remarked in his diary that Churchill was "a bit peevish."[48]

Shortly after, on the morning of 21 June, the two heads of state met with Marshall, Brooke, Hopkins, and Ismay at the White House. It was quickly evident that Roosevelt and Churchill disagreed with the conclusions reached by their military subordinates. The political leaders opposed the chiefs' proposal to stand idle in 1942 and pushed instead for an offensive somewhere in Europe in 1942 to help the Russians as well as for domestic political reasons. If a landing in France was not possible, then an alternative like French North Africa must be conducted instead. This is the one thing the chiefs agreed they did not want.

Churchill opened the meeting with an emotional attack on Sledgehammer. Hopkins thought that the prime minister was especially eloquent in trying to secure the president's support for Gymnast. Roosevelt remained enigmatic. Regardless of his perceived agreements reached in private with Churchill the previous day, during this open session he strongly defended Marshall's strategy for a cross-channel return to the continent at the earliest possible date. Roosevelt reminded Churchill that the British had previously agreed to the emergency operation in 1942 if necessary, and on that basis the western Allies made promises to Stalin. On the other hand, Roosevelt accepted that Churchill was absolutely opposed to Sledgehammer, but the American president wanted US forces to engage Germany somewhere in 1942. Churchill understood this and revived Gymnast to satisfy the president's appeal for a second front. After the meeting, Stimson informed Marshall that Churchill's appeal resonated because Gymnast was, in Stimson's telling, "the President's great secret baby" and would satisfy his requirement for US troops to fight the Germans in 1942. Even so, Churchill was dissatisfied because Roosevelt held firm on Bolero and Roundup and refused to budge from the previous agreements. It was agreed that the buildup for Bolero would continue until 1 September, at which time Churchill would review the situation and determine if an attack on the continent could be made this year without ending in disaster. The meeting reached an impasse as the participants adjourned for lunch.[49]

Shortly after they reconvened for the afternoon session, Marshall interrupted the heads of state with a totally unexpected message for the prime minister. The British garrison at Tobruk, Libya, had surrendered. Thirty-two thousand British, South African, and Indian troops surrendered after a single day's siege. Churchill was devastated and embarrassed by the stunning defeat, which could not have come at a worse time. He feared his credibility was destroyed and his attempts to steer strategic discussions by appeals to superior British military planning in tatters. He could not hide his shock and disappointment from the president. "Not only were its military effects grievous, but it affected the reputation of the British armies. At Singapore 85,000 men had surrendered to inferior numbers of Japanese. Now at Tobruk... seasoned soldiers had laid down their arms to perhaps one-half their number." In yet another dark hour for Churchill, Roosevelt simply asked, "What can we do to help?" Churchill asked for as many new tanks as the Americans could spare. Marshall promptly promised to ship three hundred new tanks and one hundred self-propelled artillery guns to the British troops in Africa.[50]

Later that afternoon, Roosevelt and Churchill reconvened to discuss strategy with a small group, including Brooke, Marshall, Hopkins, and Ismay. The British appreciated Marshall's fast and positive response in providing tanks and weapons. Brooke thought the American's action contributed greatly to the friendship and understanding established during the war "between the President and Marshall on one hand and Churchill and myself on the other." Churchill, however, did not let gratitude interfere with his unrelenting pressure to launch Operation Gymnast. He ordered Ismay to draft a memorandum, based on the morning meeting, to the Combined Chiefs of Staff for formal approval. Ismay's draft stated that while plans and preparations proceeded for an offensive on the continent in 1943, the Allies had to take the offensive during 1942. If success was not possible in western Europe, the Allies needed an alternative, and because Gymnast was the best alternative for 1942, it should claim resources from Bolero for the operation. In short, Ismay's memo gave priority to Gymnast over Sledgehammer.[51]

Ismay's memo caused a minor furor among the military chiefs during the Second Washington Conference. Since the beginning of the conference, Ismay had tried to please Churchill by making the Combined Chiefs' recommendations compatible with the prime minister's desire for a North Africa operation. He had protested the agreement reached on 20 June between the Americans and British chiefs, supporting Bolero and opposing all alternative operations, because it directly opposed the prime minister's desires. Brigadier Dykes and General Smith, the CCS secretaries and the authors of the proposed 20 June memorandum to the heads of state, confronted Ismay when he attempted to slant their draft. Although that document was never formally presented, the determined efforts by Ismay to support Churchill's strategic objectives left a bad impression. Many on the CCS did not consider him the most objective choice to prepare the memorandum for this important meeting. When tasked the following day to write the formal memorandum of the 21 June CCS meeting with the heads of state, Ismay wrote the document to reflect Churchill's desires. Upon review Marshall ordered the document amended, and the American redraft stressed the importance of Sledgehammer. After further discussions and ruffled feathers, Ismay rewrote the meeting's minutes into a document that committed to planning and preparing for Bolero "on as large a scale as possible" and "with all speed and energy." The approved memorandum stated that the Allies "would not hesitate" with a sound plan to return to France in 1942, but with the caveat that if not, then there had to be a ready alternative. They would review Gymnast "carefully and conscientiously" should a successful operation in France during 1942 prove unlikely.[52]

CHAPTER 6

Ismay's revised memorandum, dated 24 June, seemed to support Marshall's plan because it recognized the that an invasion of France offered greater "political and strategic gains than operations in any other theater." But at the same time, by deeming it essential it that the United States and Great Britain act offensively in 1942, it reopened the door to Gymnast. Troops and weapons for Gymnast would have to be diverted from Bolero, and that would delay Roundup from 1943 to 1944. There are no minutes of this session because Roosevelt did not like notes taken during his meetings. By way of conjecture, however, four factors seemed to influence the decision to execute Gymnast: Roosevelt's overly optimistic assurances to Stalin and Molotov that there would be an Allied offensive in 1942; Roosevelt's increasing push for American action in the Atlantic in 1942; the president's firm support of a cross-channel attack, including Sledgehammer; and British pessimism about Sledgehammer and preference for an alternative.[53]

Gen. Albert Wedemeyer and Gen. Hastings Ismay (courtesy of the George C. Marshall Foundation, Lexington, Virginia, USA)

The final, revised 24 June CCS memorandum had a major flaw: no timetable was mentioned. Neither Churchill's 1 September deadline for a decision between the alternative operations of Gymnast and Sledgehammer nor Roosevelt's 15 September target date for committing American ground forces against Germany were included. With no timelines established, the result was a mushy compromise that required the CCS to continue preparations for Sledgehammer and at the same time plan for Gymnast. It would prove a recipe for confusion in the future. It appeared to the Americans that Marshall had successfully fought off Churchill's Gymnast scheme.[54]

The Tobruk disaster changed the nature of the Second Washington Conference. Marshall later related that Churchill was terribly shaken by Tobruk, and the British-American leaders had only one consideration: how to help the British through the disaster. The United States' willingness to send tanks and equipment to help the British did not mark a strategic shift toward the Middle East, but it did dispose Roosevelt to listen more carefully to Churchill's arguments for Gymnast.[55]

Churchill and Roosevelt held a late-night session on the 21st with the American and British chiefs at the White House. It lasted until one in the morning, and they discussed the deteriorating situation in the Middle East, where after the fall of Tobruk, the Germans' eastward offensive was approaching the Egyptian border. Roosevelt asked Marshall if the United States could send a large army to the Middle East to reinforce the British by covering the front between Alexandria and Tehran. The general replied that it was too late that evening to discuss such a venture, and a totally new operation meant the end of a cross-channel attack in 1943.[56]

Marshall put his words into writing two days later, recommending against deploying a large US force to the Middle East because of inadequate logistics, confused command relations, and the operation's vagueness. He pointed out that the United States was already supporting forces across great distances: the southwest Pacific at eight thousand miles; the central Pacific, three thousand miles; Alaska at two thousand miles; the Caribbean at one thousand miles; and Greenland and Iceland at two thousand miles. Moving a large force to the Middle East would not only stretch US shipping resources to the breaking point but also would undercut Bolero. Adamant that western Europe was the decisive theater, Marshall argued that opening a separate front in the Middle East would make a decisive American contribution to western Europe out of the question."[57]

Roosevelt was as shocked as Churchill by the fall of Tobruk and the sudden British defeat in North Africa. Although privately upset, he concealed his feelings from the prime minister and was publicly supportive. But he confided to his cousin that the "Germans are better trained and better generaled" and blamed the latest defeat on "partly Churchill and partly bad generals." If Egypt fell to the Germans, he feared that the Germans would go after the oil of Afghanistan, Arabia, and Syria next.[58]

The following day, 22 June, Roosevelt and Churchill met with Hopkins, Stimson, and Knox to review how the United States could support the British Eighth Army. The prime minister's diminished demeanor, evident in his manner and speech, surprised a sympathetic Stimson. Tobruk's loss had staggered Churchill, who attributed defeat to "just plain bad leadership." Rommel had "out-fought" the British defenders.[59]

Stimson offered to send bombers and transport planes, plus pursuit aircraft ferried by carriers, across the Atlantic to support the Eighth Army. Discussion about deploying an American armored division foundered because shortages of modern firepower rendered current units unready. Roosevelt then asked Stimson about sending a larger force to fill in the denuded frontier between Alexandria and Tehran. Before Stimson could respond, Churchill interjected that a large force to bolster the Eighth Army was welcome, but he was not asking for that. He did remark that troops earmarked for Bolero might be better used elsewhere, but Stimson's firm opposition caused the prime minister to drop the subject. Immediate reinforcements for the Eighth Army were far more important at the moment than rearguing the merits of Sledgehammer, Bolero, or Gymnast.[60]

Later that afternoon, Churchill met with Generals Eisenhower and Mark Clark. Marshall had selected Eisenhower as the new American Commanding General of the European Theater of Operations based on his demonstrated planning abilities. Eisenhower was scheduled to depart for London in two days, and Clark would accompany him as the corps commander. Churchill met with both to develop a good working relationship and, perhaps expecting to influence them, gave each a copy of his 15 June alternate to Roundup. He badly misjudged his audience. Eisenhower, and later Marshall, judged Churchill's alternative absurd and interpreted it as evidence of Churchill's reluctance to undertake any invasion of France.[61]

By 23 June, Rommel's advance continued unabated toward the Egyptian border. Heretofore Marshall had opposed reinforcements because they would be diverted from Bolero forces and might postpone Roundup. Faced with the need to stop the Nazi offensive crisis, however, he diverted tanks, self-propelled guns, and planes destined for Bolero to Egypt. Marshall also reassured Churchill that all was not lost and was anxious to show the prime minister that the Americans could defeat Germans. For that reason, Marshall, who had previously heard rumors of poor morale in the British army, invited Churchill to join him at Camp Jackson, South Carolina, to see the US infantry training and judge its quality of troops for himself.[62]

Late on the evening of 23 June, Churchill departed by train for Camp Jackson, along with Brooke, Ismay, Dill, Marshall, and the prime minister's personal physician, Sir Charles Wilson. Arriving mid-morning, Churchill observed three divisions with full combat gear pass in review designed to show the prime minister the true quality of the US Army. The three divisions were a diverse slice of the army: a Regular Army unit; a National Guard unit; and a newly activated unit with only two months service. They conducted armor, infantry, and artillery simulated combat exercises followed by a heavy airborne drop, complete with artillery. Afterwards Churchill and his advisors observed soldiers undergoing individual and small unit training such as marksmanship, artillery and tank gunnery, and calisthenics.[63]

Stimson, who had hosted the event, thought the exercises had convinced Churchill of the United States' ability to mass produce high quality combat units. Privately the British had a different opinion. Ismay found the exercises competent and professional but recognized

Winston Churchill at Fort Jackson, SC, 24 June 1942 (courtesy of the George C. Marshall Foundation, Lexington, Virginia, USA)

that the troops were "obviously very green" and thought "that it would be murder to pit them against continental soldiery." Brooke thought American individual and elementary training appeared excellent but had serious reservations about higher echelon training and was unsure the Americans "realized the standard of training required." Churchill, however, was impressed and told Ismay, "You're wrong. They are wonderful material and will learn quickly."[64]

Churchill unabashedly praised the exercises, although throughout the day he repeatedly reminded Stimson and Marshall that it took two years to make a soldier capable of meeting the Germans on an equal footing. Bearing the weight of serial defeats, Churchill and Brooke had doubts about their own army and were unwilling to believe that the newly organized US Army could best the Germans. Portal also later acknowledged that the American leaders exhibited greater confidence in US troops than the British displayed in theirs.[65]

Churchill and his party returned to Washington that evening. The conference would end the following day, 25 June, because Churchill had to return to London to deal with the Tobruk crisis in Britain, where a member of parliament demanded his censure. The British press carped that "defective military leadership" and logistical shortages led to the defeat. The *Times* attributed the defeat to "deficiencies of British tanks." The *Manchester Guardian* criticized the weapons design and procurement system. The *Daily Mail* declared British generalship was "too slow, too cautious, and too easily led into traps." In the same paper, the military correspondent, Basil Liddell Hart, blamed both British Army doctrine and the inability of tired senior leaders to adapt to the fast pace of armor warfare in the desert. Churchill was responsible for all these deficiencies.[66]

At the Combined Chiefs of Staff meeting the morning of the 25th, no one mentioned a second front in Europe. The only topic discussed was getting US reinforcements for the Middle East. Marshall shifted American bombers from India to Cairo; King planned to ferry pursuit planes to Ghana, from where they could fly on to Cairo. The Combined Chiefs prepared various alternative shipping plans to possibly move the US 2nd Armor Division to North Africa.[67]

As the conference ended on those sour notes, Roosevelt met with the Pacific War Council at the White House. Before the meeting, Churchill had gathered Dominion representatives (from Canada, New Zealand, Australia, South Africa, and India) for an update on the conference. Churchill expected that Russia would hold on the eastern front and spoke with false confidence of the certainty that the British could hold Egypt. As everyone in the room knew, the Japanese defeat at Midway had reduced the threat to Ceylon and India. He passionately insisted that there would be a second front in Europe but not until victory there was assured.[68]

Shortly after, Roosevelt opened the short, formal session of the Pacific War Council. He "had no particular news" and mentioned the US Navy's victory at Midway. The president then turned the forum over to Churchill to discuss the Atlantic. Churchill covered the same ground that he had in his earlier meeting with the Dominions, except that he made no mention of a second front in Europe in front of the president. McKenzie King, frustrated by his exclusion from the conference, acidly thought the main purpose of the Pacific War Council meeting was to end it quickly without allowing too many questions.[69]

Churchill and his party departed Washington on 26 June. Brooke felt that he and Marshall had finally begun to appreciate the problems each other faced. Brooke had observed firsthand the lack of cooperation between the US Army and Navy. King's influence and ability to gain resources for the Pacific was unexpected. Brooke also gained respect for Marshall's ability to disagree with the president and curb his plans by explaining the military implications of the president's ideas. The importance the president attached to Marshall's counsel left Brooke envious of Marshall's ability to counter Roosevelt's "wildish plans." In brief, he began to see from Marshall's perspective the difficulties in pushing the European strategy in Washington.

Marshall similarly saw firsthand Brooke's problems in dealing with Churchill. Brooke's sense was that the prime minister believed he had inherited the military genius of his famous ancestor the Duke of Marlborough and therefore knew more than his generals. Churchill did not like to listen and that made it difficult to wean him off many of his wildest and most dangerous proposals. Marshall and Brooke both recognized that the impulse of the heads of state to confer and plan without them would complicate future strategy formulation.[70]

The Argonaut Conference had started well. The American and British military chiefs wanted the Americans to build up forces in Britain. The British chiefs were willing to go along with the American goal of an invasion of France in 1943 because it gave them leeway to adjust plans according to the strategic situation before any final decision. Both military sides opposed Gymnast: the Americans because it diverted resources from Bolero and the British because of the danger in Libya. The British chiefs opposed Sledgehammer while the Americans viewed it as an emergency operation awaiting any decision. The two heads of state overturned their military chiefs' tentative agreements on strategy on 21 June, and the brief conference ended without resolution. After six months, the British-American alliance still had not agreed on a coalition strategy for an offensive against Germany. They still failed to even agree on a common objective against

Germany in 1942. The root of the disagreement between the Allies still was not discussed. The United States wanted to bring the maximum military power against Germany as quickly as possible. They had the utmost confidence, perhaps too much, in their military. The British, on the other hand, preferred a more indirect approach, and hoped to weaken German strength and morale by attacking on the periphery of the Axis alliance before confronting Hitler's main military force. After Tobruk, British confidence in their military was at a low ebb. The British viewed a cross-channel attack as the final blow conducted only when Germany was on the verge of collapse. Instead of the two sides sharing their concerns and seeking an overarching coalition strategy against Germany, they narrowed their discussion to a simple choice between Gymnast and Sledgehammer in 1942. Time was running out; the Allies had wasted half a year and still lacked a strategy for defeating Germany.

7

Churchill and Roosevelt Give Guidance
July 1942

By July 1942, the British-American alliance had not agreed upon a strategy for the war against Germany. In Russia, the German summer offensive commenced with a series of quick victories that stunned the Allies. German forces in Russia were advancing even faster than they had the previous year. These battlefield developments alarmed the Soviets, as well as many of their American and British supporters, who demanded an immediate second front in western Europe to divert German forces.[1]

After the fall of Tobruk, Rommel continued his offensive in the Middle East and by early July was less than forty miles from Alexandria and a mere eighty miles from Cairo. This debacle hardened British opposition to the American plans for a cross-channel attack in 1942 or 1943. Instead, Churchill and his advisors believed that an American invasion in North Africa would threaten Rommel's rear area and thereby relieve the pressure on the beleaguered Dominion forces fighting in the desert. Thus, North Africa or western Europe became the crux of the strategy debate between the United States and Great Britain.[2]

Churchill had rushed back from Washington on 1 July to face his critics and a possible vote of censure in Parliament. A recent by-election had gone badly for the government, and the House questioned the central direction of the war. The fall of Tobruk shocked both Churchill's supporters and foes. Sir Alexander Cadogan, the permanent undersecretary of state for foreign affairs and a close ally of Churchill, was devastated to learn that Tobruk had fallen. It had previously held out for eight months against Rommel and now had capitulated seemingly overnight. Cadogan quietly questioned the capability of the army and blamed poor generalship for the defeat. His support for Churchill was unwavering but he found the whole affair "most depressing."[3]

After Tobruk, Churchill's foes were more spirited in their disapproval. A Conservative MP, John Wardlaw-Milne, moved for a vote of censure, but conflicting critiques of Churchill's wartime leadership in the Commons left the opposition in disarray and proved easy for the prime minister to counter. The following day, 2 July, it was the opposition Labour Party that questioned the defeat of superior Dominion forces after a mere twenty-six-hour siege. The quick surrender of Tobruk, in contrast to Sebastopol holding out against superior numbers for months, had humiliated the British people, and Churchill bore the responsibility for devising poor strategy, providing inadequate weapons for the troops, and failing to rid the army of its class-conscious prejudice that prevented men of talent from rising to positions of leadership. Aneurin Bevan, the opposition party leader, called for a change in strategy and advocated for a second front in Europe—now. Bevan could not understand why, with the enemy only twenty-one miles away in France, Churchill was sending troops fourteen thousand miles distant to fight in East Asia.[4]

Churchill successfully rebutted his critics and easily won his vote of confidence by a margin of 476–25. Despite this parliamentary victory, according to one observer, the distinguished diplomat Harold Nicolson, there remained a keen sense of unease with Churchill's direction of the war effort, and Bevan's criticisms resonated in the Commons. After defeats in France and at Singapore and Tobruk, Churchill knew that US support was essential for victory in Egypt.[5]

With his critics temporarily silenced, Churchill turned his attention to resolving this strategic military dilemma. The June meeting with Roosevelt and the American chiefs had disappointed him. His purpose for going to Washington was to convince the US president that North Africa was the alternative to a cross-channel attack. He believed that the Tobruk disaster had undercut the prestige of the

British military and consequently the efficacy of his arguments. He wanted Roosevelt to cancel Sledgehammer and undertake Gymnast by 1 September. The 24 June agreement, however, merely called for a further study of both operations and set no specific date for a decision. Churchill had to settle the issue with Roosevelt as soon as possible.[6]

On the evening of 2 July, Churchill met with his War Cabinet to review the British Chiefs of Staff outline of operations through 1942. The chiefs reminded Churchill of his early June guidance that the British would launch Sledgehammer only if its objective was to establish a permanent foothold in France after failure in Russia had broken German morale. The recent German success on the eastern front made such conditions unlikely to occur. Still the chiefs were concerned that no serious preparations for Sledgehammer were currently in progress. They understood and fully supported Churchill's objections to a cross-channel attack in 1942 but preparing for this eventuality had benefits. It kept the Germans uncertain about Allied intentions and prevented the Germans from transferring units, especially air forces, to the Russian front. The chiefs warned the prime minister that the Russians would learn that the British were making no serious preparations for Sledgehammer. If Stalin thought that the British were reneging on the promise to open a second front, the Soviet dictator might go his own, separate way.[7]

Churchill accepted his chiefs' concerns but thought they missed the main point, that is, that Roosevelt still believed, because Churchill had told him so, that if a Russian collapse appeared imminent, Britain would execute Sledgehammer. The only way for Churchill to reconcile his pledge was to propose an alternative operation to Sledgehammer that would use US troops and resonate with Roosevelt. The prime minister knew that Brooke wanted to fight it out in the desert before opening another front. He knew that the Royal Navy did not want to open new sea lines of communication in the Mediterranean to support a new front in Africa. And he also knew that Roosevelt demanded action. Neither national leader was willing to let troops sit idle for the remainder of 1942. On 5 July, Churchill outlined his views on Sledgehammer for the Chiefs of Staff Committee and sought a consensus for action.[8]

According to Churchill, the British-American allies had to decide on Sledgehammer. He reviewed Sledgehammer's disadvantages. All of his senior military leaders opposed the cross-channel attack during 1942, citing a crippling shortage of landing craft and an invasion force composed almost solely of British troops. While the United States talked about contributing, US Army troops scheduled to arrive by September 1942 were untrained in amphibious operations and could not participate in any assault.[9]

Put simply, the prime minister did not believe the British-American coalition was ready to confront the main German army in western Europe. He instead endorsed the peripheral strategy designed to engage the Germans on the margins of their European empire, where they were weaker and could be worn down to the point of collapse before any attempt to return to the European continent. Appreciating Roosevelt's desire for more direct action, he framed his argument against Sledgehammer around its impact on Roundup. A 1942 landing in France would inevitably delay Roundup by several months because it would disrupt amphibious training for the larger operation and inevitably result in the loss of precious landing craft. Even if the Allies gained a successful lodgment in France, protecting the vital beachhead would curtail the strategic bombing campaign against Germany. These factors would delay Roundup, but most significantly, a 1942 operation would end in disaster and prevent any chance of a cross-channel attack the following year. If his advisors agreed with him, then Churchill would notify Roosevelt and then inform the Russians of these conclusions. But he warned the War Cabinet that it must offer President Roosevelt an alternative operation against Germany during 1942 and recommended both Gymnast and Jupiter.[10]

Two days later, during a long and depressing War Cabinet meeting, Churchill again pushed his civilian ministers and military chiefs for a consensus on an operation during 1942. Churchill had difficulty controlling the contentious meeting, as several cabinet ministers criticized the military for opposing all the proposed alternatives for 1942 and yet offering no new operations and vented their uninformed strategic opinions on the war. Churchill grew so frustrated with his chiefs that he recommended advertising in a newspaper for a new alternative operation.[11]

The chiefs still opposed Sledgehammer, Gymnast, and Jupiter. The fall of Tobruk and the recent German successes in Russia left the military no appetite for a cross-channel attack in 1942 or 1943. On Jupiter, they had run out of ways to tell Churchill it was a bad idea. They also disliked Gymnast, but if the heads of state required an offensive before the end of the year, the British military could agree to an American operation in the Middle East. Churchill subsequently cabled Roosevelt that the conditions that would make Sledgehammer a sound and sensible operation were unlikely to occur and that the operation should be cancelled, although limited preparations for the attack should continue in order to deceive the enemy. The War Cabinet agreed that the prime minister propose to the president that the Allies should seek an alternative British-American operation during 1942, either Gymnast for the Americans or northern Norway for the British.[12]

That same day, Major General Eisenhower cabled Marshall an update on British concerns about a cross-channel attack in 1942. Eisenhower had arrived in London two weeks earlier to command the European theater of operations, which was responsible for coordinating with the British on Sledgehammer and planning for Roundup. Eisenhower had departed Washington before the end of the Washington Conference and was unaware of the new requirement to engage the Germans in 1942, and so still thought that Sledgehammer, a contingency, was the sole operation under consideration that year. The British notification that they did not consider it likely that a cross-channel attack in western France would occur during 1942 due to the recent constraints imposed by the prime minister surprised him. Furthermore, the Second Washington Conference's June agreement was imprecise, advocating both Roundup and engaging German ground forces during 1942. If a cross-channel attack in 1942 was impractical, then an alternative, such as Gymnast or Jupiter, needed to be studied and planned for in detail. Eisenhower was unaware that Gymnast was back on the table. His cable asked for Marshall's guidance on responding to the British and, as theater commander, apologized for his ignorance of the latest strategic agreements between the Allies.[13]

The next day, 8 July, Churchill cabled Roosevelt recommending Sledgehammer's cancellation. After three months of seeking a way out of the April promise to launch a cross-channel attack in 1942 if Russia were on the verge of collapse, the prime minister gave the president his unvarnished opinion. The British were not going to sacrifice six divisions in a suicidal mission, no matter what strategic situation developed on the eastern front. The prime minister carefully couched his opposition of Sledgehammer in terms of its negative effect on Roundup, which he supported, but warned that a landing in France in 1942 was premature, would end in disaster, and would delay the large-scale assault in 1943.[14]

Churchill had developed a close personal rapport with the president in the months following the January 1942 Arcadia Conference. Perhaps more than the president's own advisors, he understood Roosevelt's passion for an offensive against Germany somewhere in 1942 and recommended Gymnast, which he alleged was originally Roosevelt's idea, as an alternative to Sledgehammer. According to Churchill's 8 July cable, Gymnast was the credible second front for 1942 because it would satisfy Soviet expectations for a British-American offensive to draw German resources from the eastern front and offered the western Allies the safest operation with the best chance of success in the autumn of 1942. It was not the cross-channel invasion that Stalin and Molotov wanted, but it was the best the Allies could do. Unmentioned in the cable was Churchill's hope that Gymnast would silence demands in Britain and the United States for a second front.[15]

Churchill knew that Roosevelt was under a great deal of pressure to shift US resources to the Pacific and that Sledgehammer's demise would only exacerbate that pressure. The prime minister's acute perception extended beyond the White House. He realized in both the April meetings in London and the June sessions in Washington that Marshall was Britain's best ally in the war against Germany. The US Army chief prevented the diversion of excessive resources to the Pacific theater in favor of a massive buildup of resources in Britain for a cross-channel attack in 1943. After the Tobruk disaster, Marshall had gone out of his way to move tanks, planes, and guns to Libya to help the British. Churchill also recognized that Roosevelt looked to Marshall for military advice on the war with Germany. He sought to find a means to reassure Marshall and the president of his commitment to Roundup in 1943.[16]

Immediately after cabling Roosevelt, the prime minister convened a meeting of the War Cabinet to discuss the command of Operation Roundup. Churchill believed that the supreme commander should be an American, because an American supreme commander would obtain the maximum resources and equipment from the United States. After all, the United States would ultimately provide the most forces, offering twenty-seven divisions compared to twenty-one British divisions. Besides, if the operation did not go well, no one could blame the British. Marshall's gravitas made him the ideal man for the job. Churchill shared his draft cable to the president recommending Marshall's appointment as supreme commander for the 1943 cross-channel attack in France with the War Cabinet. The agreement was unanimous, and Churchill's second cable that day to Roosevelt recommended Marshall's appointment as supreme commander of Bolero and Roundup.[17] A third cable to Roosevelt that day clarified Churchill's second cable and urged the Americans to undertake Gymnast, which he assured the president the Allies could do alongside Roundup.[18]

The War Cabinet in London simultaneously notified Dill in Washington of Sledgehammer's demise and the expectation that the Americans would understand the abrupt shift and support the Gymnast operation. In June, the British chiefs had agreed with the Americans that the North Africa operation was a bad idea. They realized this new position, supporting Gymnast, would come as a complete surprise to their American counterparts. Out of loyalty to the prime minister, however, the British chiefs did not explain their change of minds. Instead, Dill's two-fold mission was to use all his influence with Marshall and the Joint Chiefs of Staff to ensure that the Americans accepted the British decision and to reduce any bad blood between the two allies over the decision.[19]

Roosevelt did not respond immediately to the prime minister's cables. He simply passed on the first cable, cancelling Sledgehammer, to Marshall, without commenting on its contents. When replying to Churchill's military queries, the president normally forwarded them on to either Marshall or King for a response. He would then review his military advisors' recommended reply and edit it as necessary. In this case, the president ordered Marshall to write a proposed response. The president never acknowledged the second cable, concerning the appointment of a supreme commander.

Roosevelt's only communication to the prime minister that day was a brief note that clarified operational codewords. Bolero would designate the preparation and movement of US forces to the European theater and the reception, assembly, transport, training, and storage of equipment therein in support of a cross-channel attack on the continent. Roundup would designate the combined American and British offensive against German forces on the continent in 1943. Interestingly, as late as 8 July Roosevelt still regarded Sledgehammer as a viable, if an emergency, operation.[20]

Two days later, Marshall briefed the Joint Chiefs of Staff on Churchill's cable and his decision to cancel Sledgehammer. The Americans were flabbergasted. Just two weeks earlier the British chiefs had agreed to plan for both Gymnast and Sledgehammer, and together the Allies would select the best alternative. Now, without any consultation, the British had issued their unilateral decision to launch Gymnast. Marshall objected to committing American resources to a theater far from Europe and ending prospects for a cross-channel attack in 1943. He told the JCS that Gymnast was an "expensive and ineffectual" operation but acknowledged that because British support was crucial for future European operations the United States had no choice but to accept the British decision. But he was terribly upset and recommended the Americans drop the Germany First strategy and concentrate American resources on the defeat of Japan. A pivot to the Pacific would be popular in the United States, particularly on the West Coast; in China; and with the Pacific Fleet. He ended with the dubious assertion that next to a cross-channel attack, a pivot to Japan was the best way to help relieve the pressure on Russia.[21]

Admiral King, as might be expected, staunchly supported Marshall's strategic pivot to the Pacific. After the Midway victory, King was anxious to take the offensive against Japan before the Japanese could recover the initiative and continue their advance in the south and southwest Pacific. In late June King had submitted a plan for a 1 August offensive against Guadalcanal in the Solomon Islands. The diversion of resources to the Pacific fit his plans perfectly. The admiral reiterated his opposition to Gymnast because it would pull aircraft carriers from the Pacific, and the transports and escorts required for Gymnast would make it impossible for the US Navy to fulfill its commitments in other theaters.[22]

To conclude the JCS meeting, Marshall read his draft memorandum prepared for the president to reply to Churchill, explaining that the execution of Gymnast would definitely curtail, if not preclude, a cross-channel attack in 1943; was a waste of resources; jeopardized the Allied naval position in the Pacific; and would result in the western Allies' failure to act decisively in any theater during 1942. After the chiefs agreed, Marshall and King sent their signed memorandum to the president.[23]

They recommended that Roosevelt urge Churchill to execute the Bolero plans (Sledgehammer and Roundup) to conduct a cross-channel attack and attempt no alternative operations that might detract from this goal. Any diversion, including Gymnast and Jupiter, would weaken preparations for Roundup in 1943. Abandoning Sledgehammer would stoke Soviet fears of the western Allies reneging on their commitment to the Russians. If the British remained reluctant about the Bolero plans, then the United States should turn its attention to the Pacific and strike decisively against Japan. In other words, the Allies would go on defensive against Germany, except for the strategic bombing campaign, and send all available resources to the Pacific.[24]

Marshall also sent the president a note that outlined his personal views on Churchill's first 8 July cable. It reiterated the same arguments for Bolero and urged the president to turn toward the Pacific if the British persisted with Gymnast. Roosevelt should offer the British a choice; either they completely supported Bolero and the cross-channel attack, or the United States would concentrate its troops and equipment in the Pacific. The proposed ultimatum left the decision to the British.[25]

Marshall then met with Stimson, who backed Marshall and agreed Gymnast was a waste of men and equipment without strategic value. Both men were frustrated. Three times, the two men had discussed Sledgehammer and Gymnast, and each time they thought they had British agreement on Sledgehammer. Stimson hoped that their proposed memorandum would prevent round four of inconclusive and time-consuming negotiations. Why continue with Bolero if the British were unwilling to support it?[26]

The British Joint Mission in Washington worked feverishly to make the British chiefs in London aware of the firestorm in Washington over the prime minister's cable. The Americans saw Gymnast as a sideshow masking the British true intentions to not make a cross-channel attack in either 1942 or 1943. Dill warned Churchill that substituting Gymnast for Sledgehammer was driving the Americans to consider transferring their resources to the Pacific. Dykes told London that Dill was correct.[27]

The prime minister ignored the warnings. Convinced that Dill was overreacting, on 12 July Churchill instructed him to emphasize to the Americans that Gymnast was the "sole means" by which the US could strike Hitler in 1942. The operation would threaten Italy, divert German air forces from the eastern front, and not interfere with Roundup. Churchill told Dill that his decision was final, and if Roosevelt did not want to conduct Gymnast, then the ground forces of both countries would remain idle for the remainder of 1942. If the president insisted on Sledgehammer, let the Americans do it themselves under their own flag.[28]

Roosevelt, however, was unimpressed with Marshall's threat to shift to the Pacific if the British did not agree to Sledgehammer. He phoned Marshall on 12 July from Hyde Park, New York, requesting specifics of the new Pacific strategy, especially what resources, existing or proposed, the JCS would withdraw from the Atlantic theater. What effect would the new strategy have on Russia and the Middle East? The president wanted answers that afternoon.[29]

Roosevelt's request surprised both his chiefs. He had called Marshall and King's bluff because he knew there was no such plan. Indeed, the chiefs weakly confessed they had not yet developed a detailed plan for major offensive operations against Japan. All they could say was that the pivot to the Pacific was the new strategy. The chiefs likewise failed to answer several of the president's specific questions on implications of Bolero's cancellation on resources for the Pacific. They proposed that two-thirds of the fifty-two air force groups scheduled for deployment to Britain would shift to the Pacific, giving the Allies control of the air in that theater. The remaining eighteen groups of the Bolero air forces were still available. No changes occurred among naval forces in the Atlantic, although three amphibious divisions and the paratroop units scheduled for Bolero would immediately divert to the Pacific to garrison the islands captured from the Japanese in yet undetermined numbers. The chiefs admitted a shift to the Pacific would not help in the Middle East but disingenuously suggested it might eliminate the Japanese threat to India. Their conclusion that this new strategy would hinder Allied aid to Russia on the eastern front, the president's top priority, doomed the proposal.[30]

Secretary of War Stimson was the chiefs' champion, because Gymnast ended the possibility of a cross-channel attack during 1942 and 1943. He considered the British to be defeatists who feared directly confronting the Germans on the European continent. Stimson, and, for that matter, the service chiefs, never considered the situation from the British point of view. If Sledgehammer failed, the British public's morale might collapse. To the Americans, Gymnast merely diverted resources and delayed their goal of a 1943 invasion of France. Stimson and Marshall had overreacted, proposing a pivot to the Pacific without evidence to support such a strategy.[31]

Roosevelt was quick to make plain his displeasure with wishful thinking. In a short note to the chiefs, he outlined his objections. The Pacific strategy concentrated against Japan was exactly what the Germans wanted the United States to do after Pearl Harbor because it would give Germany a free hand throughout Europe. The strategy consigned American troops to occupation duties, not combat operations, and would have no major impact on global strategy over the next eighteen months. Finally, the Pacific pivot neither helped the Russians nor addressed the dire situation in the Middle East. Roosevelt signed his message as commander in chief, something he rarely did, to remind to the chiefs that they reported to president, who as commander and chief made the final decisions on strategy.[32]

Stimson, King, and Marshall did not seriously consider the political realities of the alliance. Roosevelt was under heavy pressure to establish a second front to divert German forces from the eastern front and keep Russia in the war. Nor would Roosevelt turn his back on Britain after putting so much emphasis and support into the alliance. In brief, he valued his relationship with Churchill too much to abandon him. The president was facing tough Republican opposition in the mid-term congressional elections that November. Roosevelt worried that the Democrats might lose their majorities in both houses if the American public disapproved of his handling of the war effort. To Roosevelt's thinking, it was imperative for US troops to fight Germans somewhere before the elections occurred. It did not matter where they fought, and if North Africa was the only option, it was fine with him.[33]

Roosevelt was clearly frustrated with his chiefs. Their thinking was rigid and inflexible. Marshall was so fixated on protecting his plan for a 1943 invasion of western Europe that he failed to offer any option to Gymnast other than a poorly thought-out threat to pivot to the Pacific. To a degree, this was Roosevelt's fault. By his own admission, his leadership style was "disingenuous, deceptive, and devious." In this case the president's guidance was so opaque that his subordinates could not discern his intentions. He consistently supported Marshall's plan for the return to the continent in 1943 but, as he pointed out on 21 June, he also wanted to engage Germany in 1942. In Marshall and Stimson's mind these two were mutually exclusive. However, they offered the president no alternative operation for 1942 but Sledgehammer, which Churchill was unwilling to undertake. Roosevelt expected his military advisors to find a way around this seeming inconsistency and recommend an operation against Germany in 1942 that did not undercut Roundup. The pivot to the Pacific was not the answer the president was looking for.[34]

When asked about the Pacific pivot after the war, both Marshall and King distanced themselves from the proposal. Marshall insisted it was only a bluff and that he had no intention of abandoning the British in favor of the Pacific. Stimson likewise said it was a bluff but later admitted that he was embarrassed by his part in recommending to the president the pivot to the Pacific. King was more circumspect, stating that it was not entirely a bluff and that he was "on the fence" on the issue. True, he wanted more resources for the Pacific, but he did not want all the resources. He recognized Russia was on the ropes and understood that Germany was the "number one enemy." The object of his and Marshall's proposal was to force the president to keep pressure on the British for the 1943 cross-channel operation.[35]

Dill, however, took the American threat seriously and accordingly notified Churchill of his disquiet. The British mission in Washington was more sensitive than London about how the British arguments for Gymnast resonated in America. Brigadier Dykes regarded many of the arguments for a North African landing specious at best, disingenuous at worst. Churchill, for example, emphasized that the landing would be unopposed. The American intelligence thought otherwise. The prime minister asserted that the French would remain neutral; the Americans doubted that as well. Churchill stressed that Gymnast would represent a second front to not only the American people but to the Russians as well. The Americans doubted Stalin would agree. He said that Gymnast would not preclude Roundup, and both were possible. The Americans strongly disagreed. But Churchill told Roosevelt that Gymnast could be launched before the mid-term congressional elections in November, and this resonated with Roosevelt, who demanded action.[36]

In London, Churchill worried when Roosevelt did not immediately respond to his 8 July cables. Although outwardly brimming with confidence, Dill's 10 July cable about the pivot to the Pacific concerned both Churchill and the British chiefs sufficiently for them to separately contact Eisenhower to explain their respective rationales for canceling Sledgehammer. They again used the lack of landing craft, the drain on resources for Roundup, and the disastrous impact of a failure as the reasons for their decision. The British told Eisenhower that they were assembling shipping as a deception to convince the Germans of a possible cross-channel attack in 1942. The British chiefs also expressed their anxiety about how Marshall might personally react to Churchill's decision (although Dill already informed the prime minister of his reaction) and were anxious that Eisenhower pass on their high personal and professional regard for Marshall. They anticipated that Marshall would understand their position and agree with their decision. Churchill also used Eisenhower to express his desire that Marshall serve as the supreme commander of the Roundup operation, a source of British anxiety because the Roundup planning was far behind schedule, and they anticipated that Marshall's leadership would reenergize the organization.[37]

The US Army staff harbored doubts about Churchill's offer to appoint Marshall as supreme commander. Maj. Gen. Thomas Handy (who replaced Eisenhower as director of the Operations Division and subsequently became the deputy chief of staff of the army) thought that the British military respected Marshall and believed that he was the right man for the job. They apparently had no ulterior motive for recommending him, but Handy viewed Churchill with skepticism. Churchill may have admired Marshall, yet the prime minister also sought to maintain or expand his control of the overall strategy for the war. Handy saw the appointment as an attempt by Churchill to control Marshall, something that he had heretofore been unable to accomplish. Marshall in London would be dependent on Churchill's support and be subordinate to Churchill on strategic matters. He would no longer be in a position to veto Gymnast or "some other scatteration scheme" of the prime minister's fertile imagination. Handy recommended that Marshall should remain in Washington, where he could exert greater influence on the conduct and direction of the war.[38]

Marshall's 13 July update to Eisenhower mentioned that the president's absence from Washington precluded discussion of Churchill's cable and his Pacific strategy proposal. He encouraged Eisenhower to continue planning for Sledgehammer (acknowledging that it was solely an emergency contingency operation) because it would aid preparations for Roundup and prevent the British from wasting resources on indecisive sideshows. He made no comment on the British recommendation for his appointment as supreme commander.[39]

After a week of waiting, Churchill was worried and frustrated that Roosevelt still had not replied to any of his 8 July cables. On 14 July, Churchill sent Roosevelt another cable designed to elicit a response. Where did Roosevelt stand on Sledgehammer and Gymnast? According to Churchill, the president knew his position on Sledgehammer's impracticability and that the Americans should quickly execute Gymnast. He promised that British would coordinate with the Russians on attempting Jupiter and concluded that preparations for Roundup should proceed "full blast."[40]

In mid-July Churchill as well as Marshall and King awaited the president's reaction to the Pacific strategy. On 14 July, the president notified both chiefs that he was ordering them to London, along with Hopkins, to settle the issue of operations in 1942 once and for all. The following day, 15 July, Roosevelt returned from Hyde Park and met with his chiefs. The secretary of war greeted Roosevelt as soon as the president arrived at the White House and, although lacking a formal appointment, Stimson offered his views on strategy for 1942. Roosevelt mollified his secretary of war with assurances of his commitment to the cross-channel attack. Roosevelt then brusquely told him that he opposed the chiefs' Pacific strategy, likening their actions to "taking up your dishes and going away." Stimson rejoined that after four months of negotiations drastic action was the only way to convince the British to support Bolero and the cross-channel attack. Roosevelt's solution was to send Marshall and King to London to hash out a resolution, and he left Stimson with the impression that he was leaning toward the North Africa operation.[41]

Afterwards the president met alone with Marshall. Roosevelt fully understood Marshall's motivations with the shift to the Pacific but regarded it as "a red herring." The president did not want some future historian writing that the United States proposed to abandon the British. The two men then had a "thumping argument" over Gymnast. Marshall was passionate in his opposition to the North Africa operation, and Roosevelt was enigmatic in stating his position. Subsequently, Marshall mistakenly thought that he convinced Roosevelt of the prohibitive cost of undertaking the North Africa campaign.[42]

Later that evening over dinner, Roosevelt vented his frustration with the chiefs' recommended Pacific strategy to Hopkins and admitted his displeasure with the British insistence that a cross-channel attack in 1942 was impossible. The president acknowledged that the United States had no choice but to accept the British decision for 1942 because they were providing the troops. The Allies, however, could not wait until 1943 to strike against Germany. Without Sledgehammer, they would have to settle for second best, and that was North Africa or the Middle East, not the Pacific. The cross-channel attack remained the primary objective for 1943. Hopkins was to make certain that the British understood the importance that the president attached to Roundup and to report any indications from senior US military leaders in London that the British were lukewarm on the 1943 cross-channel attack as well. Hopkins was also sent as the president's personal representative to coordinate with Churchill and the CCS throughout the meetings. He would continuously update the president on the status of the discussions. Hopkins's main job was

Harry Hopkins confers with Gen. George C. Marshall and Adm. Ernest J. King (courtesy of the George C. Marshall Foundation, Lexington, Virginia, USA)

to preserve the alliance and ensure an agreement was reached that ensured American troops engaged the Germans in 1942. In concert with Roosevelt's leadership style of not telling the right hand what the left hand was doing, Hopkins's reports were independent of and not coordinated with Marshall and King's updates.[43]

That evening, Roosevelt at last tersely responded to Churchill's three 8 July cables, informing the prime minister that he was sending Marshall, King, and Hopkins to London for consultations the following day. He provided no insight into his thinking or position on strategy for 1942.[44]

Just before their departure for London, Roosevelt handed the trio a two-page memorandum titled "Instructions for London Conference—July 1942." This was a written version of his conversation the previous evening and made it clear that he wanted an immediate agreement with the British on joint operational plans for 1942 and a tentative agreement on a 1943 strategy, with preparations for that objective to begin at once. He also added a new requirement—American troops must engage German ground forces sometime during 1942. This proviso dictated the agenda for the upcoming meeting with the British. If the British-American allies ruled out Sledgehammer, they were to find another place where Americans could fight in 1942. The president emphasized the importance of the security of the Middle East and protecting Egypt and the Suez Canal, the Mosul oil wells, the Persian Gulf, and access to Persian oil. The Americans could accomplish this either by sending aid and ground forces to British forces already operating there or landing in Algiers or Morocco to strike at Rommel's backdoor via North Africa. The president gave the chiefs one week to hash out an agreement with the British.[45]

Roosevelt's instructions suggest his increasing interest in Gymnast and regard for the Middle East as an important extension of the European war. An invasion of North Africa would not disrupt the plans for a 1943 cross-channel invasion but would silence his domestic critics clamoring for immediate action against Germany and somewhat fulfill the western Allies' commitment to Stalin for a second front. Lastly, but perhaps most importantly, Gymnast would prevent the British-American coalition from tearing itself apart over a strategy for 1942.[46]

Marshall was not about to allow Gymnast to delay Roundup until 1944. Before departing for London, Marshall cabled Eisenhower to prepare new plans for Sledgehammer that he could present to the British upon his arrival. This was a major change, for just three days earlier Marshall had informed Eisenhower that Sledgehammer was a contingency operation, only to be undertaken if Russia was on the verge of collapse. Now Marshall wanted a "searching analysis" by the American planners in London to recast Sledgehammer as an option to fend off Gymnast and preserve Allied resources for the 1943 cross-channel attack. Marshall also informed Eisenhower of the president's latest instruction that American troops engage German ground forces in 1942.[47]

Dill was also busy, reporting the American mood to London. He warned Churchill that Gymnast had contributed to the growing American ill feeling toward the British. Dill was caught in the unenviable middle yet still tried to retain his objectivity and see both sides' respective perspectives on the issue. The British field marshal was the honest broker who grasped better than anyone the coalition's fragile state in July 1942. He understood the strength of Marshall's feelings for a cross-channel attack in 1943 as well as Churchill's lukewarm attitude toward that operation. Unaware of the president's firm opposition to the pivot to the Pacific, Dill warned the prime minister that unless he convinced the Americans of his support of Bolero, he risked the Americans diverting their resources to the Pacific and leaving Britain to face Germany alone.[48]

Churchill again ignored Dill's warnings. The prime minister expected his eloquence and strategic insights would convince Marshall and King to support his strategy for 1942. No American threats could convince him to undertake Sledgehammer. Let them take their resources to the Pacific. After Singapore and Tobruk, he was not about to risk another catastrophe, the likes of which Sledgehammer had written all over it. As he told the British ambassador in Washington, Lord Halifax, "Just because the Americans can't have a massacre in France this year, they want to sulk and bathe in the Pacific."[49]

Churchill invited Hopkins, Marshall, and King to his country home, without their staff, in hopes of swaying them to support his strategic views and Gymnast over the weekend of 18–19 July. Anticipating such a ploy, Roosevelt cabled the prime minister that he thought it best that the American party go directly to London to confer with the US planners in preparation for the upcoming sessions with the British. He hoped the prime minister would understand. Churchill did, ignored the president's request, and directed the three Americans to come directly to his home.[50]

The US delegation landed in Scotland but was unable to fly on to London because of bad weather over England. Churchill had already dispatched his private train and personal assistant to meet the American visitors and bring them to Chequers, where the group could confer privately for the weekend. Hopkins begged off the prime minister's invitation because the delegation's primary duty was to report to Ambassador Winant in London. As Roosevelt directed, they went to London and conferred with US planners there.[51]

Churchill was irate about losing two days of private discussions with Marshall and King and the delegation's snub of his personal invitation to Chequers. He immediately complained to Hopkins, who retorted that no disrespect was intended since they were simply following the president's express order to meet with Eisenhower's planners in London. To smooth the prime minister's ruffled feathers, Hopkins went to Chequers on Sunday, 19 July, while King and Marshall conferred with the planners. There is no written record of Hopkins's discussions with the prime minister that day. In his report to the president the following day, Hopkins simply noted that Churchill was in "good spirits" and that the situation was cleared up. Since Roosevelt wanted troops in action in 1942, did not believe that undertaking Gymnast would necessarily preclude Roundup, and wanted to quickly reach an agreement on strategy, it is likely Hopkins confidentially informed Churchill of the president's written negotiating instructions to Marshall and King as well as his continued interest in Gymnast.[52]

Hopkins's revelations to Churchill were all the more unusual because the Soviet Union again appeared to be teetering on the verge of collapse. On the eve of the meeting between the British and American chiefs, the Soviets' eastern front was fast deteriorating under the massive German pressure. Secretary of War Stimson worried that the German advance was gaining momentum as they were on the verge of capturing Rostov and advancing toward Stalingrad. He desperately wanted to help the Russians and opposed diverting resources to Gymnast at this critical juncture. Stimson could only encourage Marshall to prevent this from happening.[53]

In London, the British Joint Intelligence Committee (JIC), in a paper for the Chiefs of Staff Committee, estimated on 16 July that even without defeating Russia by the autumn of 1942, the Germans still had sufficient military strength to reinforce their western front against any Allied invasion. The next day British planners accordingly recommended against a cross-channel attack in 1943 (Roundup) and proposed that the Allies proceed with Gymnast.[54]

The British Chiefs of Staff concurred. Brooke was upset that US planners offered no alternatives to Sledgehammer and complained that Marshall was overly inflexible and unwilling to compromise on his plan for an invasion of France in 1943. Brooke opposed any cross-channel attack during 1942 and was weary of repeating his objections to Sledgehammer, which he regarded as a dead letter that had not the "slightest hope" of any British support. His deputy, Major General Kennedy, summed up British military sentiments by declaring that a landing in France was impossible and acknowledging that the main British consideration was to avoid losing the war by making mistakes. This logic led Brooke to advocate an American invasion of North Africa as the better second front option in 1942. In other words, Brooke was restating the approved British peripheral strategy.[55]

On Saturday, 18 July, Churchill summoned his Chiefs of Staff to Chequers to review the arguments pro and con for Sledgehammer and Gymnast. The British agreed that Gymnast was the only feasible course for 1942 and assumed the operation would not interfere with the continued flow of American troops and matériel to Britain.[56]

Marshall and King met the next day with the American planners to develop a proposal that explained the Americans' latest position on Sledgehammer in relation to Roundup before their anticipated showdown with the British. Based on the president's guidance, Marshall had recast the purpose of Sledgehammer from an emergency attack to the establishment of a permanent foothold on the continent to support the main invasion the following spring. Eisenhower's team had examined four landing sites in France and selected Cherbourg because of its deep-water port and its location for a landing within supporting range of British-based fighter aircraft. They also assessed the two British proposed alternatives, Gymnast and Jupiter.[57]

For whatever reasons, the American side persisted in assuming that the British would approve Sledgehammer, but the British side's consistent opposition to the operation left most planning to the Americans, and Eisenhower was having doubts about the revised Sledgehammer's overall goal. The lack of landing craft limited the initial landing force to a single division that had only a fifty-fifty chance of success even with the element of surprise. Getting the remaining five divisions ashore ad seriatim had only a one-in-five chance of succeeding. Although hesitant to recommend a course of action with such abysmal forecasts for success, Eisenhower finally endorsed it by rationalizing that the prize of keeping Russia in the war was worth the risk.[58] This revision was little better than the original Sledgehammer's "sacrifice" of six British divisions.

The Americans saw neither Gymnast nor Jupiter helping Russia. They declared Gymnast a strategically unsound operation that diverted resources from Bolero and likely ended any opportunity for the Allies to conduct a cross-channel invasion of western Europe in 1943. Jupiter was impractical because it required "a large contingent of aircraft carriers," and the US Navy's scheduled offensive in the Solomon Islands in two weeks made any carrier reinforcements impossible. That left a revised Sledgehammer as the best alternative to help Russia during 1942.[59]

The British-American chiefs met for three days, 20–22 July, to work out a coordinated strategy for the remainder of 1942. It was obvious that neither side approached the meeting with an open mind but simply rehashed stale old arguments. Neither side was willing to see the other's point of view, so the allies talked past one another. The Americans understood Sledgehammer's original goal was not to recapture France but to prevent the dispersion of Allied troops and equipment to lesser theaters in 1942. They never appreciated the political and military ramifications the "sacrifice" of six divisions would create in Britain.

For their part, the British loathed Sledgehammer's concept as originally presented in April and hated it even more in July. British antagonism to Sledgehammer masked a visceral opposition to a cross-channel attack in 1943 because both Churchill and Brooke did not think their armies were ready to take on the German army in Europe in the spring of 1943. Nevertheless, they expected the United States to continue to build up its air, sea, and ground forces in Britain. Instead of candidly saying that, they promoted Gymnast as the second front against Germany, which would cause the overextended Germans to withdraw troops from the eastern front and still enable the Allies to conduct both Gymnast and Roundup. The Americans dismissed the argument as wishful thinking.

Churchill opened the Combined Chiefs of Staff meeting on 20 July, doing most of the talking and setting the stage for the discussions. Three issues were on the table. First, should the Allies undertake Sledgehammer or not? If so, what form would it take? Second, what effect would Sledgehammer have on Roundup? Roundup enjoyed British support, but as the prime minister put it, why restrict the location of a second front to a cross-channel landing in France? Why not examine other locations where attacking Germany could help the Russians? Third, the group should re-look Gymnast because it gave the Allies an opportunity to move into French North Africa, and, in conjunction with the British army in Egypt, secure the sea lanes in the Mediterranean for future advances into Sicily and Italy. In effect, Churchill had eloquently aligned the United States with the British peripheral strategy.[60] His pronouncement came as a major shock to the Americans, who finally comprehended that the British opposed any cross-channel invasion of France.

The American and British military chiefs also met informally, but the meeting did not go well. Both sides had staked out their positions, were unwilling to compromise, and were unprepared to offer any new alternatives. Marshall used the analysis from the previous evening to pitch a revised Sledgehammer that he hoped the British would find more palatable. Instead of an emergency or sacrifice landing in France to simply draw German forces from Russia, which the British always detested, the new plan contemplated capturing the port of Cherbourg and establishing a permanent bridgehead on the Cotentin Peninsula in Normandy. This landing in September 1942 would be the first phase of Roundup and would facilitate the main cross-channel invasion the following spring. The British remained unimpressed with this revised plan. Brooke remarked that the bridgehead could not survive the winter, bluntly telling the Americans that the operation was hopeless, would lose six divisions, and that the British disliked Sledgehammer in any form and would not do it. Brooke recommended North Africa only to hear the American response that they would rather send resources to the Pacific than do Gymnast. On that sour note, the first day's meeting ended in an impasse.[61]

Later that evening, Churchill and his War Cabinet reviewed the chiefs' session and coordinated for their next meeting. Churchill found Marshall's proposal to seize and hold Cherbourg intriguing but believed that the Germans would easily bottle up and then destroy this force. Mountbatten deemed the operation feasible but German air superiority over Cherbourg precluded the need for the Germans to withdraw any air units from the eastern front. Churchill agreed and then suggested the Americans report to the president that it was not possible to reach an agreement on Sledgehammer. He was careful, however, to admonish his chiefs "not to show ourselves too ready to raise difficulties." They again agreed that Gymnast was the best course of action for 1942.[62]

On 21 July, the American and British chiefs met for two hours without the prime minister present and accomplished nothing. Their respective positions remained unchanged, with neither side willing to compromise, leaving the alliance without a coalition strategy. Later that evening Churchill met with Hopkins and Anthony Eden, the foreign secretary, behind closed doors. Hopkins, acting as the president's emissary, covertly informed the prime minister that Roosevelt was not firmly committed to Marshall's Sledgehammer plan for 1942. This information allowed the British to hold firm in their opposition to Sledgehammer and would force Marshall to report the stalemate in negotiations back to Washington the following day. The president's use of Hopkins to first leak the negotiating instructions and then signal that he was willing to accept Gymnast was both devious and disingenuous. In this case, the president used Hopkins as his go-between to preserve the British-American coalition and aid Churchill's government without publicly overruling his military chiefs.[63]

The American military chiefs were unaware of the president's decision when Marshall, King, and Admiral Stark met with Eisenhower's planning staff to finalize their revised Sledgehammer plan, which would be launched as soon as possible, but no later than 15 October. Marshall realized he was running out of time because it was already late July and the operation required two months' advance notice. Any later and rough weather in the channel would make a crossing impossible.

Although Marshall demanded quick action, there were skeptics. Stark doubted the revised Sledgehammer's efficacy because of the complexity of an amphibious operation. Eisenhower sympathized with Marshall's desire to quickly strike Germany but counseled delay, doubting that the Allies had enough time to complete preparations for a mid-October invasion. The timing itself was too risky because of unpredictable weather conditions and no guarantee of tactical success. Out of loyalty to Marshall, Eisenhower supported his plan, hoping that he made the right recommendation.[64]

At 11 a.m. the following morning, 22 July, the British-American chiefs heard Marshall's plan for an attack on the Cherbourg salient. The British were unimpressed and emphasized that the disadvantages far outweighed the advantages. Without an Allied consensus on Sledgehammer, the British chiefs recommended the Americans inform Churchill and then Roosevelt of their lack of strategic unity.[65]

Later that afternoon, the prime minister in turn told Hopkins and the Combined Chiefs of Staff that he admired the Americans' offensive spirit and aggressive attitude, but the hazards were still too great to justify the operation. He recommended that Marshall inform his president of the Allies' failure to reach an agreement. As the group was departing, King, reticent for three days, candidly informed Churchill that many of the British arguments against Sledgehammer could also apply to Roundup. Churchill dismissed King's comment and assured the Americans of Britain's firm support for a cross-channel attack in 1943.[66]

Hopkins notified Roosevelt of the deadlock and the British unwillingness to support Sledgehammer. A bitterly disappointed Eisenhower called 22 July the "blackest day in history," although after the war he acknowledged that the revised Sledgehammer was unwise, and the British were correct to oppose it.[67]

The president told Hopkins, Marshall, and King the next day that the decision did not surprise him. (This comment was disingenuous because he had orchestrated this decision through Hopkins's covert dealings with the prime minister.) Sledgehammer's demise opened the door to his directive for an alternative operation where American

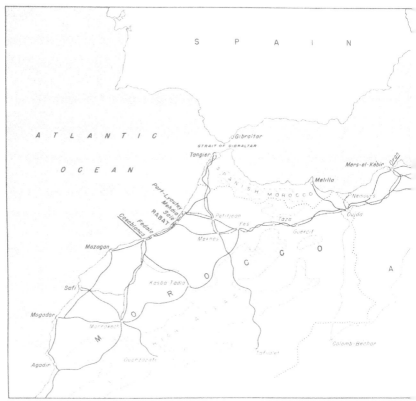

Lines of communication in French North Africa (courtesy of US Army Center of Military History)

ground forces could fight Germans in 1942. He recommended five possibilities: (1) a combined British and US operation in Algeria or Morocco; (2) Gymnast; (3) Jupiter; (4) a reinforcement of the British Eighth Army; or (5) a reinforcement of Iran and the southern supply route to Russia. The president pressed the military leaders to select an option and reach an agreement with the British as soon as possible.[68] Eisenhower's planners disliked all of the alternatives but nominated Gymnast, because its advantages (it would check German expansion in the Middle East) outweighed its disadvantages. The price was the dispersal of resources away from the critical European theater.[69]

On 24 July, the Combined Chiefs of Staff discussed operations during 1942. Marshall proposed that preparations for Roundup

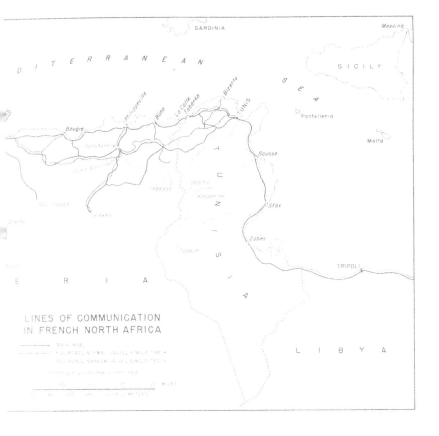

continue on pace as long as any possibility of invasion remained before July 1943. Hereafter Sledgehammer was a deception operation, so long as it did not interfere with Roundup. American ground troops would invade North Africa in 1942 with planning to begin immediately. Marshall notified the group that undertaking Gymnast rendered a cross-channel attack in 1943 impossible and therefore the British-American coalition accepted a defensive encirclement strategy for continental Europe.[70]

Marshall still had not given up all hope for a cross-channel attack in 1943. Although planning for North Africa was to begin immediately, he deferred a final decision on abandoning Roundup and accepting the strategic defensive in Europe until 15 September, pending review of the situation on the Russian front. If a cross-channel attack in 1943 appeared unnecessary or impractical at that time, then the Allies would abandon Roundup and attack North Africa no later than 1 December.[71]

The British got almost everything they wanted in this meeting, although Portal and Brooke took umbrage with describing Gymnast as "defensive," because Roundup might still be possible, and the British were determined to invade the Continent. (However, Brooke was careful not to say when.) Marshall disagreed. Once forces were committed to North Africa there was no possibility of launching a cross-channel attack in 1943, a viewpoint King enthusiastically seconded. As a consequence of the defensive strategy in Europe, Marshall told the British that the United States was diverting fifteen air groups and one infantry division intended for deployment to Britain as part of Bolero to the Pacific theater. The approved document then went to the prime minister for review before sending it to the War Cabinet for final approval.[72]

Brooke told Churchill that he was pleased with the agreement. That evening, both presented the document to the War Cabinet for final approval. Brooke told the War Cabinet that the British chiefs were in complete agreement with the Americans that undertaking Operation Torch (the new codename for Gymnast) would make it unlikely that Roundup would be carried out in 1943. Churchill nevertheless wanted the Bolero buildup in Britain to continue and had admonished Brooke and the chiefs two days earlier at the Chiefs of Staff Committee meeting not to admit that the North Africa operation, though it impinged on Bolero, would negate Roundup. While several War Cabinet members also disliked comments about a defensive strategy in Europe, which Churchill personally disagreed with, both Brooke and Churchill realized that the Americans had made a large concession in abandoning Sledgehammer and agreeing to Gymnast, and they were reluctant to ask them to revisit the wording of the document. The War Cabinet then finalized the document as CCS 94.[73]

Brooke had endured a difficult week, but the British had gotten everything they wanted out of the Americans. The Americans agreed to invade North Africa in 1942 and to postpone a cross-channel invasion at least until 1944. Brooke may have been less sanguine if he fully understood the differing interpretations the British and Americans attached to CCS 94. Both sides agreed that the document cancelled the agreed-upon April strategy of a direct, cross-channel attack. With prospects for the eventuality on hold, the Americans regarded CCS 94 as an opening to funnel more resources to the Pacific. The British believed that the CCS 94 withdrawals were a minor diversion of air and sea reinforcements to the Pacific that left the Germany First strategy unchanged. They expected the Americans to complete the Bolero buildup in the United Kingdom and simultaneously launch Operation Torch. They thought that the Americans had accepted the original peripheral strategy that the British insisted was agreed to at the Arcadia Conference.[74]

Churchill did understand the implications of Marshall's 15 September decision date on Torch and Roundup. He asked Hopkins to contact Roosevelt immediately to confirm the decision for Torch. Hopkins told the president of his belief that the American chiefs were determined to mount the invasion of North Africa but feared that subordinates (at both the Pentagon and War Office at Whitehall) would procrastinate, pending more precise written direction. Hopkins recommended the president set a definite date for the invasion of North Africa. The following day, 25 July, Roosevelt wired King and Marshall of his approval in "principle" of all the proposals (in CCS

94) and underscored that the Americans would invade North Africa not later than 30 October. Churchill was ecstatic when informed of Roosevelt's decision.[75]

Before sending the cable, the president met with Stimson and Marshall's deputy, Lt. Gen. Joseph McNarney, to review its contents, although Roosevelt had already made his decision on an invasion of North Africa by 30 October. During this meeting, Roosevelt voiced disbelief that Torch would preclude Roundup. He told them that he did not understand why the withdrawal of a few troops from Bolero would affect a cross-channel attack in 1943. Perhaps his military advisors were too negative? It was clear to McNarney and Stimson that Roosevelt still thought he could do both. McNarney immediately contacted Marshall to inform him of the president's views. The president's ambiguity left the JCS confused about the status of Roundup. Roosevelt directed a North Africa landing by 30 October, but he also told Stimson he wanted to do Roundup, and he approved the CCS 94 minutes, which included the proviso to postpone a final decision on Torch and Roundup until 15 September. Marshall was in a quandary, because he knew it was impossible to execute Roundup if resources were diverted to North Africa. As a result, Marshall and King believed

Gen. Dwight D. Eisenhower, Allied commander in North Africa (Army Heritage and Education Center Photograph)

Adm. William D. Leahy, USN
(US Naval History and Heritage
Command Photograph, NH 49841)

the 15 September deadline in CCS 94 for a final decision on Roundup remained valid.[76]

The British-American chiefs met in London on the morning of 25 July to finalize command arrangements for Torch and Roundup. They recommended that an American should be the supreme commander for Torch, and Marshall suggested that the same officer command both operations in order to avoid competition for resources between Torch and Roundup. Brooke concurred and proposed that the supreme commander and his staff set up in London. Afterwards, Marshall informed Eisenhower that he would remain in London as the deputy commander for Torch and Roundup until the designation of a supreme commander. The American delegation departed Britain that evening.[77]

On 30 July, the CCS met in Washington to exchange views about operations in 1942. Adm. William Leahy, recently appointed as the chief of staff to the president and ranking member of the JCS, chaired the session. Leahy proposed launching Torch earlier than 30 October and was surprised by his colleagues' lack of consensus on the status of Torch and Roundup. King, for example, thought that Roosevelt and Churchill had yet to agree on the two operations. According to

Marshall, the president still wanted both, and he emphasized that launching Torch cancelled Roundup. He was preparing a paper to explain to the president that the two operations were mutually exclusive. Leahy and Dill thought the president had already decided and preparations for Torch should begin as soon as possible. After the meeting, Leahy sought presidential clarification. Roosevelt was upset with what he regarded as JCS's bickering and summoned the chiefs to his office at 8:30 that evening. He told them directly that as commander in chief, his final decision made Torch the highest priority.[78]

Churchill eagerly sought a total American commitment to Torch. To accomplish this, on 31 July he asked Roosevelt to appoint Marshall as the supreme commander of both Torch and Roundup and recommended Eisenhower serve as the deputy supreme commander. Roosevelt was unresponsive, but the following day Dill notified Churchill that as far as the Americans were concerned, the president's verdict to land in North Africa by 30 October excluded a cross-channel attack in 1943. Everyone was on board for Torch.[79]

Without Churchill's and Roosevelt's direct intervention, it is doubtful the British and American military leaders could have surmounted their strategic deadlock to mount a combined operation. The military meetings in July revealed the strains between the Allied staff and military leaders that obstructed strategy formulation. The political leaders' decision to invade North Africa refocused the Allies on a common objective but had yet to improve cooperation in combined planning. The British-American planners still had to agree on the size of the force, the location, and the timing of Torch. As expected, both sides had their respective opinions, and their tactical discussions would dominate planning throughout the remainder of the summer and early fall of 1942.[80]

Of greater significance, the British-American alliance still lacked a long-range strategy for defeating Germany. Torch ended plans for a direct assault on the continent, but no other strategy replaced it. The relationship between Torch and a future Roundup was open for interpretation by both the British and Americans. In the short run it would be competitive, as resources for the North Africa invasion would drain the buildup for Bolero in the United Kingdom and divert them to the Mediterranean. At the end of July 1942, the British-American military leaders had not put aside national interests, tried to understand their ally's perspective, or agreed on a strategy to defeat Germany. The peripheral-versus-direct-approach strategy debate seemingly defied resolution.[81]

8

Aftermath

The Germany First strategy and the invasion of North Africa were the two most significant decisions the western Allies made during 1942. Germany First, agreed to at the Arcadia Conference in December 1941, served British interests but was based on detailed American military planning and analysis made before the war. It did not result from mutual discussion and compromise by the British-American chiefs and their planning staffs. Instead, American military planners and President Roosevelt believed that defeating the Axis by concentrating the main effort in the European theater best served the interests of the United States. Churchill concurred that Nazi Germany was the greatest threat to British interests. Since the goals of both countries coincided, they reached the Arcadia Agreement without discord. Arcadia's flaw was that neither side attempted to reconcile their divergent national approaches of how to defeat Germany, the American direct approach versus the British peripheral approach.[1]

National goals did not coincide in the decision to invade North Africa. Churchill and Roosevelt had to intervene because the British and American military chiefs were unable and unwilling to compromise and refused to consider each other's perspective on the war. The Combined Chiefs of Staff planners were no closer to an agreement on a military strategy for the war in Europe in July than they were in January. Each side was convinced that its proposed military strategy was the correct one for defeating Germany. The Torch decision only provided a short-term Allied military objective for 1942, and did not resolve, much less provide, the grand strategy for the British-Americans to defeat Germany.[2]

Still in early August, Churchill and Roosevelt were satisfied with the coalition's strategic situation for 1942. Due to their personal mediation, the British-American alliance persevered, and the Allies finally agreed on a combined military operation against Germany that year. Churchill assumed Allied cooperation had coalesced with Roosevelt's 30 July decision for a landing in North Africa. He wrote to Roosevelt that the chiefs had put their disagreements behind them and were now operating at an elevated level of intimacy and efficiency. In his postwar memoirs, Churchill recalled that King and Marshall were disappointed but accepted the decision by the heads of state to cancel Sledgehammer and execute Torch. According to the prime minister, British insights had prevailed and resulted in friendly and cordial relations between the military staffs of both nations. Subsequent events in August and September, however, demonstrated that his optimism on British-American military cooperation was inaccurate, as strategic controversy flared throughout the remainder of 1942.[3]

By August 1942, the relationship between the British and American military was not "special." The decision for Torch exposed how deep the disagreements and lack of trust were between the two allies. From Washington, Brigadier Dykes reported a breakdown within the Combined Chiefs of Staff and the Combined Planning Committees in the weeks following the decision to invade North Africa. He described "a lack of frank discussion on difficult matters." Dykes thought that between April and early July, the planners were able work together harmoniously toward a common goal—the invasion of western Europe. The cancellation of Sledgehammer and Roundup, however, left the British-Americans without a common aim, and each nation interpreted the combined military strategy differently.[4]

As the Combined Chiefs grew further apart, Churchill and Roosevelt placed the North Africa operation on the back burner as both heads of state devoted their attention to unique national objectives and concerns. Churchill was the driving force for North Africa, but when the CCS looked to him to refine this broad coalition strategy and identify objectives and resources for Torch, he was unavailable, having departed for three weeks of talks in Cairo, Moscow, and Tehran. In late July, Churchill was still embarrassed over the loss of Tobruk and frustrated by the lack of progress in the Middle East.

The Eighth Army's month-long battle with Rommel ended in a stalemate, and its commander, General Auchinleck, was unwilling to launch an immediate counteroffensive. Churchill reviewed Auchinleck's estimate with his War Cabinet on 1 August, an appreciation that offensive operations could not resume before the middle of September. Churchill found this unacceptable and told the War Cabinet members that he was departing that evening for the Middle East to shake up the command and promote a counterattack.[5]

Churchill saw the problem in the desert as leadership, and he proposed dramatic changes to the structure of the theater's high command by reorganizing the Middle East Command into two separate organizations: the Near East Command, which would include Egypt, Palestine, and Syria, with headquarters in Cairo; and the Middle East Command, which included Persia and Iraq, with headquarters in Baghdad. He also promptly replaced Auchinleck with Gen. Bernard Montgomery as the commander of the Eighth Army. Such changes, he notified his War Cabinet, would restore confidence in the command and impart a new offensive spirit in the theater.[6]

Then, on 10 August, Churchill departed Cairo for Moscow. He expected to convince the Soviet premier that with Sledgehammer cancelled, Torch was a viable alternative. In brief, Churchill's objective was to explain to Stalin that there would not be a cross-channel attack in 1942. This daunting task, remembered Churchill, was like "carrying a large lump of ice to the North Pole." During their four-day meeting in Moscow, Stalin was visibly upset over the postponement of a second front in the west and underwhelmed by the prime minister's advocacy for Torch. Future British-American troop strengths failed to impress Stalin, despite the prime minister's commitment to Roundup and a second front in 1943. The Soviet premier demanded immediate action during 1942, but Churchill held firm. Stalin then presented an aide memoire to Churchill that argued conditions in France favored an immediate assault because the best German troops were in Russia, while those in France were of inferior quality. Besides, the British-Americans might face worse conditions in 1943. Averell Harriman, who represented Roosevelt on this visit, agreed that the situation on the eastern front was tenuous and that Stalin personally feared that Stalingrad would not hold. Nevertheless, Harriman told the president that Churchill did an excellent job of delivering the unwelcome news, and although Stalin was disappointed, the Big Three alliance remained intact.[7]

Churchill's solution to Stalin's "bitter pill" was to follow through on Torch and defeat Rommel. He also promised the Soviet premier increased military assistance via the Murmansk convoys and the Trans-Siberian Railway supply routes to help them fight the Germans. On 16 August the two leaders issued a joint communiqué, reaffirming the close relationship among the Soviet Union, Great Britain, and the United States.[8]

Churchill next flew to Tehran to meet with the shah of Iran to discuss improvements to the Trans-Iranian Railway that would increase the flow of war matériel to the Soviet Union. The existing railway was insufficient to meet Russian needs. Fortunately, Harriman, a railway expert, had traveled with Churchill to Tehran and put his expertise to work by analyzing the rail network. Based on Harriman's counsel, Roosevelt agreed that the US Army would manage the rail system with American troops and expected to double the flow of supplies to Russia to six thousand tons daily by the end of the year.[9]

With the Trans-Iranian Railway issue settled, Churchill returned to Cairo to implement his recently proposed organizational changes to the Middle East and Near East Commands. He spent two days at the desert front with the new Eighth Army commander, General Montgomery, who informed the prime minister that the time to assimilate new troops and American-made Sherman tanks meant that his planned offensive would occur during mid-September. The delayed timing disappointed Churchill, but Montgomery's confidence and bold plan of attack still impressed him. Churchill's lengthy absence in Cairo, Moscow, and Tehran, however, had precluded his participation in Torch planning during an especially acrimonious time between the British and American planning staffs.[10]

While still in Egypt, Churchill had approved the British assault, scheduled for August, of the German-occupied port of Dieppe in northern France. Ostensibly, the raid's purpose was to test German coastal defenses, capture a port, destroy infrastructure, relieve some pressure on the eastern front by damaging the German air force, and gather intelligence. The unstated reason, following the British rejection of Sledgehammer, was to reassure both the Russians and Americans of British resolve to return to the continent. Churchill also expected that the daring raid would demonstrate the prowess of British arms to Roosevelt, particularly after the recent military debacles in the Middle East. Unfortunately, Dieppe was a disaster, with more than half the British and Canadian troops involved killed or captured. A Canadian historian described Dieppe as "a lesson on how not to mount an amphibious assault." As Churchill returned to London, Dieppe was yet another personal embarrassment for the prime minister and a propaganda coup for Germany.[11]

Meanwhile, Roosevelt also had shifted his attention from North Africa to the South Pacific. Both Admiral King and General MacArthur resented the lack of American resources earmarked for the Pacific compared to those destined for the Germany First strategy. Together they agreed to seize the initiative in the Pacific before the Allies undertook a major operation against Germany. To keep the main supply route between the US West Coast and Australia open, they would neutralize the major Japanese naval and air base at Rabaul, New Britain. The Joint Chiefs of Staff concurred. In early July, MacArthur's forces would seize advance bases on Papua New Guinea's north coast, then move along the coast toward the base. Simultaneously the US Navy and Marines would capture Guadalcanal and Tulagi in the Solomons and build air bases to strike at Rabaul. This coordinated advance would neutralize Rabaul and secure the sea routes to Australia, not to mention additional men and equipment for the south and southwest Pacific.

The Japanese, however, struck first in New Guinea and threatened to capture Port Moresby. With MacArthur's offensive delayed, the American navy independently launched its Solomons campaign, with US Marine landings at Guadalcanal and Tulagi on 7 August. Admiral King anticipated a quick operation that the navy could conduct on slim resources.[12]

AFTERMATH

US Marine Corps M2A4 Stuart light tank is hoisted from USS Alchiba (AK-23) into an LCM (2) landing craft off the Guadalcanal invasion beaches on the first day of landings there, 7 August 1942 (Navy History and Heritage Command, 80-G-10973, now in the collections of the National Archives)

Guadalcanal put the president in a dilemma. Torch was America's primary offensive operation for 1942, but after the catastrophe at Pearl Harbor and defeat in the Philippines, he could not afford another disaster in the Pacific.

Army and navy planners in the Pacific had hoped to postpone the offensive in the Solomons until they concentrated more powerful assault forces. King refused, preferring celerity over a more methodical approach. Planning was amateurish, equipment in short supply, maps flawed, and training for an amphibious assault inadequate. Just two days after the American landings, a Japanese naval force surprised and sank four Allied heavy cruisers and damaged another, along with two destroyers in waters near Guadalcanal. This naval debacle cost one thousand American sailors and was one of the worst naval defeats in US history. Afterwards, the Guadalcanal Campaign degenerated into a six-month battle of attrition. The drain on ships, men, and equipment far exceeded King's roseate expectations, and throughout the summer and fall of 1942 the admiral and the navy called for more resources. Such unintended consequences shifted Roosevelt's attention from North Africa to Guadalcanal.[13]

The president was also concerned with civil-military relations in the United States. He had decided for Torch against the military advice of his senior generals and admirals, in effect supporting British policy over his military advisors' recommendations. His action was rooted in political rather than purely military reasons.[14]

Secretary of War Stimson was especially perturbed both by the president's decision to override his advisors as well as to abandon a cross-channel attack in favor of what Stimson saw as a "dangerous dispersion and a possible disaster" in North Africa. The president notified Hopkins and Marshall of his Gymnast decision and on 25 July met with Stimson. The two had a frank discussion that ended with a bet on whose point of view was correct. Stimson accepted that Roosevelt had made up his mind, and his job was to loyally support the commander in chief. However, he went on record with a memorandum for the president that outlined his opposition to Gymnast.[15]

Stimson's memo annoyed Roosevelt, who in turn dictated his own memo that refuted the secretary's arguments. According to Roosevelt, Stimson failed to understand the need to have American ground troops engage the Germans in 1942. Stimson's note was also contradictory and failed to meet the president's 1942 objectives, without offering an alternative. Roosevelt concluded that he was unwilling to sit idle for another year and offer no help to the Russians in 1942. Perhaps fearful that leaks of discord among senior officials might reach the press, Roosevelt placed both memos in his files for future historical reference.[16]

Despite the president's efforts, on 6 August press reports appeared that the president was making strategic decisions contrary to the advice of his senior military advisors. Reporters claimed that Churchill and Roosevelt were running the war and ignoring the input from the military. Roosevelt lost his temper and called a cabinet meeting on 7 August designed to kill the rumors that he was not listening to his military advisors. He vociferously denied ignoring military advice, comments Stimson found disingenuous. He thought the president was deluding himself. He especially begrudged Roosevelt choosing Churchill's proposals over his.[17]

Stimson stewed over the cabinet meeting for two days before meeting with Marshall. He asked Marshall if he would undertake Torch if he were president or a dictator. Marshall told the secretary that if the final decision were his, he would not do it. Stimson thanked him for his honesty and departed to draft another candid memorandum for record for the president outlining his opposition to Torch.[18]

The next day, Stimson showed Marshall his intemperate memo. Beyond setting the record straight on the decision for Torch, Stimson peppered his memo with derogatory comments about the president's relations with his military advisors in the recent strategic discussions. He intimated that the president's memory was failing and summarized the discussions of June and July where Roosevelt shifted his instructions from support of a cross-channel attack in 1943 to a requirement for engaging German forces somewhere in Europe in 1942. The secretary emphasized that Roosevelt's interference in the negotiations delayed the cross-channel attack until at least 1944. Marshall was aghast at Stimson's comments and asked him not to send them, because it would alienate the president and make Marshall appear to be lacking the moral courage to confront Roosevelt face-to-face with his personal objections.[19]

Marshall insisted that Roosevelt knew what he was doing in the cabinet meeting. The president instead wanted to keep the press ignorant of the discord between the British-American planning staffs. Marshall also understood that the president did not want the US public to know of his disagreement with his military advisors or his decision to back the British position. He dismissed slurs that the president had a memory problem.[20]

Stimson accepted Marshall's advice and did not send the inflammatory note to the president. However, Stimson was still angry when he met with Secretary of State Cordell Hull the next day to update him on the president's recent decisions on Torch. Secretary of the

Navy Knox also attended. Stimson vented his frustration over the cancellation of the cross-channel attack and its replacement with the North African operation. He complained about Churchill's overriding influence on the president and criticized the accuracy of the president's comments in the recent cabinet meeting. Stimson was surprised by Knox's response. Knox agreed that Churchill's eloquence exerted disproportionate influence on Roosevelt's decision but contrary to Stimson remarked that he worried more about executing Sledgehammer than Torch. Knox found Torch far less risky and was more uneasy about the Solomons campaign than objections to the upcoming North Africa campaign.[21]

Nevertheless, many army and navy planners shared Stimson's resentment of the planning process, an attitude that manifested itself in the combined planning sessions in August and early September. Brigadier Dykes, the British secretary to the CCS, perceived less American support for Torch. On 3 August, Brig. Gen. Walter Bedell Smith, the American secretary to the CCS, told Dykes that the Americans were frustrated because Torch was postponing the cross-channel attack until 1944. The following day, Maj. Gen. Thomas Handy remarked about his unease over Torch's success. Two days later both King and Leahy publicly expressed the navy's doubts about Torch during a CCS meeting. There was an extremely fractious planning meeting on 7 August, during which the American side openly expressed a lack of support for Torch and claimed that CCS 94 had changed the basic strategic concept of Germany First.[22]

The next day a frustrated Dill complained to Marshall about the American planners' negativity and their lack of support for Torch, passing on the British perception that indifferent American planners were not giving Torch the priority and enthusiasm it deserved. He warned Marshall that unless everyone got behind the agreed-upon operation, it would fail. Dill also questioned the extent that CCS 94 revised the grand strategy agreement (WW-1) from Arcadia. Here the contention was over the diversion of resources to the Pacific to support the Solomons campaign.[23]

For whatever reason, the British expected that the Americans would continue to buildup forces in Britain as part of Bolero *and* fully support the requirements for Torch. After all, Torch fit in the guidelines of the grand strategy, which dictated "tightening and closing the ring around Germany" by bombardment, blockade, and subversive activities while allocating only the minimum forces necessary to safeguard vital interests in the Pacific.[24]

Marshall's 14 August response caught Dill off guard. The two men had forged a unique bond and friendship that figured heavily in unifying the Combined Chiefs of Staff. Both shared information openly and took pains to understand the other's perspective. Thus, Marshall's pointed admonishment to Dill that the Americans were engaged in planning and conducting multiple operations whose implications they had to consider came as a nasty surprise. Marshall also addressed the relationship between the grand strategy agreement at Arcadia and CCS 94, and he defended the withdrawal of fifteen air groups originally scheduled for deployment to the United Kingdom to the Pacific, as well as the diversion of heavy and medium bombers from Britain to the African theater. As far as Marshall was concerned, the US commitment to Torch, and the subsequent postponement of Roundup until at least 1944, constituted the acceptance of a defensive encircling strategy in continental Europe. The grand strategy agreement at Arcadia was an overall guide, subject to modifications by subsequent agreements and developments elsewhere. His sharply worded conclusion reminded Dill that American military planners fully supported the president's decisions as their commander in chief.[25]

Marshall's irritation reflected two issues. First, there was no hope for a quick campaign in the Solomons. The navy's prestige was at stake, and King used CCS 94 as a tool to insist on more resources for the Pacific. Second, Marshall personally had fought hard against Torch and his planners supported him. After the president's decision, he should have taken a more active role in rooting out negative attitudes among his planning staff. Instead, his note to Dill brimmed with the same resentment.[26]

The British and Americans still held widely divergent strategic views. The Torch decision provided a British-American military objective for 1942 but did not resolve the broader question of what the overarching grand strategy for defeating Germany was. Was it to be the peripheral approach of the British or the direct approach of the Americans? Torch fit into the British strategic view, but not the Americans', who were slow to adjust.[27]

Without constant pressure from Churchill or Roosevelt, CCS discussions more or less collapsed. In the seven months of discussions about Gymnast, the British and American planners had never agreed on the objective for the operation. Both nations had widely different opinions on the size, direction, and timing of the operation. More importantly, they were far apart in their views of where to direct the main effort.[28]

The Americans saw danger inherent in the North African operation. They worried about French opposition to the landings, about the Spanish reaction, and about the possibility of a German counterstroke

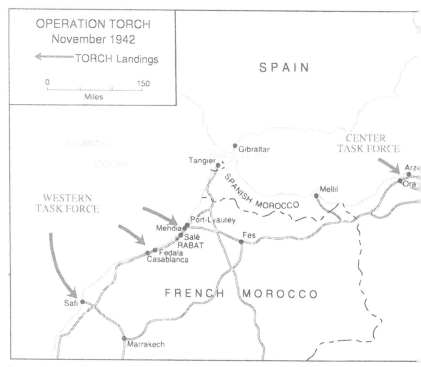

Operation Torch, November 1942 (courtesy of US Army Center of Military History)

against Gibraltar. Axis-occupied Gibraltar would seal access to the Mediterranean and cut vital support to the Allied landing force from the Atlantic. Thus, the Americans envisioned a conservative operation to capture Casablanca on the Atlantic coast of French Morocco (outside the Mediterranean). Troops would seize the port, highway, and railroad as auxiliary lines of communication and then secure the approaches to Gibraltar. The Americans were also prepared to simultaneously land at Oran, a major Mediterranean port in French Algeria about 240 nautical miles east of Gibraltar. It was a tentative and risk adverse approach but offered the United States the best chance for success in its first independent foray against the Germans.[29]

The British envisioned a much bolder strategy. The Casablanca landing was unnecessary because the Spanish would not intervene. They proposed three or four simultaneous landings in the eastern

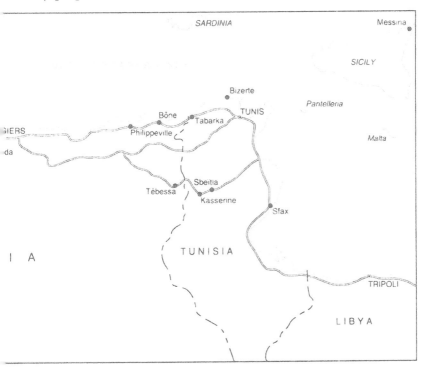

Mediterranean to gain complete control of French Algeria and, in coordination with the British Eighth Army in Egypt, seize Tunisia before the Germans could reinforce the region. The daring strategy, they believed, would impress the French garrison in Morocco and Algeria and dissuade the Spanish from allowing the Germans free passage through their country to attack Gibraltar.[30]

The British and American planning staffs wasted most of August arguing for their respective positions without compromise. This so-called Transatlantic Essay Contest left Eisenhower, responsible for executing strategy, in the middle. Dill attempted to explain the American position to the British in London in early August. According to Dill, the Americans realized that they were not yet highly trained and wanted to ensure that there was "no question of failure." Such a "mentality makes for delay." Dykes agreed and the same day wrote that the Americans had "cold feet" over Torch because they were beginning to recognize their inexperience. The stalemate continued.[31]

The diverse objectives demonstrated the British-Americans' continued lack of coordination and cooperation. The irony of this situation was not lost on the planners. In July, the Americans were advocating Sledgehammer, a bold and daring strategy with significant risk, while the British, whose troops would have conducted the operation, balked. A month later the British were advocating an audacious plan to secure objectives in the eastern Mediterranean, with American troops facing significant risk. Each side believed, and pointed out repeatedly, that their counterparts were conservative with their own troops but aggressive with those of their allies. Tensions and tempers in London and Washington rose throughout August as neither side would compromise.[32]

Guadalcanal exacerbated the problems American and British planners faced. In mid-August Japanese reinforcements landed on Guadalcanal, and as fighting in the Solomons showed no sign of diminishing, the British became increasingly concerned over American resources sent to the Pacific. The British based their aggressive plan for multiple Mediterranean landings on expectations that the United States would provide large numbers of transport and escort vessels. Aircraft carriers were essential to protect the convoys and landing sites. King retorted that he had no carriers available for Torch and was unable to say when carriers might be ready. During CCS meetings, British officers found King difficult and "cantankerous." They believed that his attitude and uncooperativeness represented a shift from the Germany First strategy and opposition to Torch. Dykes described King as making "it clear that there is a fundamental difference of opinion on grand strategy."[33]

Eisenhower notified the Combined Chiefs of Staff on 23 August of his doubts that the Torch expedition as planned was strong enough to overcome theater opposition. There were two major risks: first, determined resistance from the French would prevent the Allies from occupying Tunisia, thereby allowing the Axis to quickly reinforce the region; second, a Spanish army move into Gibraltar would sever the Allied lines of communication. The central problem was the lack of naval support. Despite weeks of negotiations, his naval advisors doubted that sufficient escorts and covering forces were available. The British-American navies both repeatedly emphasized other global commitments and the threat of potential losses to German submarine and air attacks. Eisenhower told the CCS that he believed that simultaneous assaults on both Casablanca and on objectives in French Algeria were possible only if the governments of both nations committed to provide the naval resources.[34]

On 25 August, Marshall notified Eisenhower that King had flatly stated that he was unable to provide the naval escorts required to undertake the additional landings proposed by the British in the Mediterranean. Smith believed that King could send transports and escort vessels but was overly fixated on Guadalcanal. Dykes then realized that once again the military alone could never resolve the problem and that Churchill and Roosevelt would have to get involved in the planning.[35]

Churchill had just returned from Cairo and Moscow and labeled the planning for Torch disappointing. His discovery of the serious divergences that had emerged between the American and British staffs in three short weeks over the scope of the plan to assault and capture French North Africa was a "bombshell." The British were prepared to take considerable risks to capture Tunisia before the

Germans could occupy it, while the Americans feared that Germans would open the door into the Mediterranean for the Americans and then slam it shut by having Spain occupy Gibraltar.[36]

British planners deemed US offers of simultaneous landings at Casablanca and Oran unacceptable and reported so to Churchill in a tone official British history described as "apocalyptic gloom." British planners thought that the conservative American approach would permit the Germans to seize Tunisia, along with most of French Algeria and the French fleet anchored there. This would close the Mediterranean, and Malta and Egypt would in turn fall to the Axis. They recommended scrapping the operation rather than executing it on such a limited scope.[37]

Churchill agreed with the British position that capturing Tunisia before the Axis could occupy it was the key objective in North Africa, but he was willing to consider the American position before dismissing it out of hand. On 25 August he met with Eisenhower, who outlined both positions and explained that the lack of naval support was limiting the operation. Churchill quickly grasped the situation and explained that the Allies should attack on a broad front in the Mediterranean with overwhelming force. Churchill brought Admiral Pound to the conference and instructed him to make every accessible Royal Navy ship available for Torch, even if that meant Pound had to strip the Indian Ocean of all warships, transports, and escort vessels for the Mediterranean operation.[38]

The prime minister then contacted Roosevelt to broker a solution. Churchill had promised Stalin action and was determined that Torch was that action. The two heads of state corresponded with each other for two weeks about the size and location of the landing sites for the operation. Churchill thought a landing at Casablanca unnecessary and recommended that the Americans skip it, instead sailing directly into the Mediterranean and landing at Oran and Algiers. Roosevelt, however, referred all correspondence on Torch, including Churchill's, to Marshall. The president would not unilaterally dictate the specifics of how his army and navy conducted the operation. Marshall's adamancy that Casablanca was necessary to ensure that the Americans' first operation against Germany did not end in a catastrophe convinced Roosevelt. Churchill eventually compromised: the Allies would simultaneously land at Casablanca, Oran, and Algiers if there were sufficient naval transports and escorts for the operation. He politely recommended to Roosevelt that the US Navy try to find more internal resources for Torch.[39]

Roosevelt accepted Churchill's proposals with the quid pro quo that US troops would conduct all three initial landings. The president also wanted the United States to take over negotiations with French military and political leaders in Morocco and Algeria. Churchill agreed, and the two leaders finalized the objectives and forces for Torch. Despite the agreement by the heads of state, Eisenhower and his planners were still "completely in the dark" about the assets the US Navy would provide for Torch. During a brief meeting at the White House with Admiral King on 4 September, the president acknowledged his sympathies over King's difficulties in the Solomons, but demanded the US Navy provide the required resources for Torch. King acquiesced and provided fifty-seven ships for the operation, including one aircraft carrier, two auxiliary carriers, three battleships, five cruisers, and forty destroyers.[40]

After the war, Ismay acknowledged that "the Combined Chiefs of Staff might have continued their arguments until doomsday had it not been for the personal intervention of the President and Prime Minister." However, once the heads of state had settled the objectives, size, location, and naval support for Torch, the planners could finally move forward on organizing, training, and assembling forces. In just two short months Eisenhower and his staff performed a minor miracle by pulling the operation together. Eisenhower's planning staff for Torch was unique because it completely integrated British and American intelligence sources, notably the sharing of Ultra intercepts, the deciphered German and Italian army, navy, and air force communications. The operational use of decoded Axis signals enabled the planners to anticipate German responses to an invasion. By early October Eisenhower was reasonably certain that the Germans would not move into Spain to cut off his forces in the Mediterranean. The intercepts also revealed that German forces were tied down on the eastern front with Russian resistance at Stalingrad.

North Africa invasion, November 1942 (US National Archives, SC 163437)

In such circumstances, the Germans felt that the operations in the desert were a drain on resources and more feared a possible Allied invasion of Norway or western Europe. According to Ultra decrypts, no Axis reinforcements to the Mediterranean were likely, and any Vichy French resistance to the invasion would be light. This information, which proved accurate, was a balm to tensions on the new Allied staff.[41]

On the eve of the Torch invasion, General Montgomery, after two months of preparations, finally commenced his offensive against Rommel on 23 October. Churchill desperately wanted a victory to prove to Roosevelt that Britain still possessed a formidable military and was a dependable ally. After a long string of defeats, capped by the recent Dieppe fiasco, he needed Montgomery to succeed at El Alamein and restore the prestige of the British Army. By 4 November, Montgomery had broken through the German lines and forced the Axis troops into full retreat. As Churchill celebrated the British Army's first decisive victory against German troops, Allied ships were already en route from the United States and Britain to North Africa for Torch.[42]

Eisenhower and his combined Allied staff had assembled more than one hundred thousand Allied troops (mostly American) and five hundred British and American warships, transports, supply vessels, and landing craft for the largest amphibious invasion undertaken to that point in history. Landings occurred at all three locations on 8 November, and four days later all three major objectives—Oran, Algiers, and Casablanca—were in American hands. The British assessment had been correct: French resistance collapsed quickly, and neutral Spain made no move toward Gibraltar.[43]

In terms of Allied grand strategy, however, Torch was merely a "stop-gap" measure, because once completed the two allies would have to decide on how Torch fit into an overall strategy to defeat Germany. Churchill had already started when he met with Eisenhower on 21 September and said that he was astonished "that Torch eliminates any opportunity for a 1943 Roundup." Eisenhower, the original author of Roundup, had little sympathy for Churchill's disingenuous remark. The prime minister complained about fewer US deployments to Britain for Bolero because of the Torch operation. He also feared that Bolero's resources were being siphoned to the Pacific. Eisenhower astutely noted, in a letter to Marshall, that Churchill was unwilling to admit that Torch had so strained American and British resources that the British-American alliance would remain in 1943, as they were in 1942, unable to meet Stalin's expectations for a second front in western Europe.[44]

The undeterred prime minister contacted Roosevelt the following day and again expressed his surprise that Torch precluded Roundup and reported his promise to Stalin of a second front in 1943. As usual Churchill requested more US military aid, especially bombers, for the strategic bombing campaign, and more ground divisions, to defend Britain against a possible invasion, tie down German forces in France, and take advantage of a potential German collapse. But he also wanted to mass forces in Britain prepared for deployment to the Mediterranean against the "soft underbelly of the Axis," Sardinia, Sicily, and Italy. For the first time he broached a follow-on peripheral advance in the Mediterranean after Torch.[45]

Churchill followed up on this recommendation to the president by directing the British Chiefs of Staff Committee to plan for future

Mediterranean campaigns. He anticipated a quick victory in French Algeria, followed by the occupation of Tunisia, to eliminate the Axis threat in French North Africa and provide airbases for attacks against southern Italy. On 4 October, Churchill informed Roosevelt that the Allies were producing too many tanks when more escort ships, vessels, and airplanes were needed. In other words, Churchill again sought to control wartime production to provide logistics support for his peripheral strategy against Germany.[46]

Roosevelt forwarded the message to Marshall and King for reply. Both saw Churchill's note as an attempt to commit the United States to a British strategy. The Americans were building a massive force for a cross-channel attack in France in 1944, and yet the British wanted ships and planes for their peripheral Mediterranean strategy. In brief, there was no grand strategy to defeat Germany. Roosevelt sided with his chiefs and curtly rejected Churchill's premises, recommending that the prime minister address any future production issues directly to the Combined Chiefs of Staff.[47]

Torch's rapid success brought its own problems, because the British-American allies had no strategy for what to do next. Torch killed Roundup, and Churchill had promised Stalin an attack on the continent in 1943. He was loath to tell Stalin that the western Allies could do nothing in Europe until 1944. In late November he asked the president to send Marshall and King to London for strategic discussions.[48]

Roosevelt replied to Churchill on 26 November that he would not send Marshall and King to London for a strategy session because any future strategy discussion had to include the Soviets. On Roundup, he bluntly told Churchill that in July the CCS made it clear that undertaking Torch did preclude a cross-channel attack in 1943. The United States remained committed to a cross-channel assault in 1944, but the North African and Pacific theaters took priority.[49]

Stalin did agree on a conference among the Big Three leaders to coordinate a grand strategy for defeating Germany. However, he repeatedly pressed Churchill that autumn for the promised second front in Europe in 1943. Churchill realized that a cross-channel attack in 1943 was out of the question but kept its possibility alive for purposes of negotiation with Stalin. Churchill insisted that he did not mislead Stalin and had done all that could be done to launch a second front. He believed that the German forces in Tunisia might have been used to reinforce the eastern front. This was disingenuous at best. Churchill's postwar memoirs asserted that the decision to postpone the invasion of France by a year was the correct one, and he took credit for the success of the 1944 cross-channel invasion.[50]

Throughout 1942 then, the British-American alliance remained a work in progress. American and British planners on the CCS argued for eight months over a grand strategy, forcing Churchill and Roosevelt to intervene and eventually approve Torch. As soon as the national leaders moved to other issues, parochialism once more subsumed CCS planning, The two heads of state again had to intervene to resolve differences and forge compromises. But this did nothing to resolve the overarching issue of a grand strategy to defeat Germany. The British foresaw a Mediterranean strategy running through Tunisia, Sicily, and Italy. The Americans were less structured and could not agree among themselves on the appropriate grand strategy for 1943. Marshall still hoped to withdraw troops and equipment from the Mediterranean and build up forces in Britain for a preliminary invasion of western Europe during 1943, followed by a main attack in 1944, while MacArthur and King wanted more resources for their Pacific campaigns. As it turned out, the troops and equipment earmarked for Guadalcanal and North Africa made it impossible for the Allies to conduct a major cross-channel attack in 1943. The US Joint Chiefs of Staff (JCS) were again unable to provide the president with a unified strategic proposal for defeating Germany.[51]

Without a consensus among the Combined Chiefs of Staff, the British-American allies would continue to conduct the war without an agreed-upon grand strategy for defeating Germany. Churchill and Roosevelt realized that the war against Germany could not continue on an ad hoc basis. The western Allies required a common, agreed-upon strategy.

The strategic debates of 1942 would prove the genesis for bitter recriminations, mistrust, and future disagreements on grand strategy. The relationship between the British and American chiefs was strained. Both sides continued to view strategy through the prism of national prerogatives. The British believed that they had diverted a potentially disastrous attack on the continent with their strategic perception and insight. They felt they had skillfully avoided being pushed into a premature suicide attack on the continent by both the Americans and Soviets. The British were suspicious of the resources the Americans dedicated to the Pacific and questioned the US commitment to the Germany First strategy. The British also resented the failure to win a decisive victory in North Africa due to the timidity of the American JCS in rejecting their advice to land further east in Algeria, which they believed would have resulted in an overwhelming Allied victory. The JCS, on the other hand, believed the British were duplicitous in agreeing to a cross-channel attack they had no intention of undertaking and then manipulating the president into overriding their advice and agreeing to divert resources from a decisive objective to a politically inspired but militarily unimportant operation in North Africa. Despite the protests of Churchill and the British chiefs of staff to the contrary, the JCS knew this decision had delayed the cross-channel attack until 1944. The Americans were suspicious that the British opposed a landing in France and that their primary goal was to put it off as long as possible, or even avoid it completely.[52]

Dykes astutely identified the problem in his diary: the Allies still lacked a common aim. The British-Americans had to agree on a clearly defined coalition strategy that planners in both uniforms agreed upon and interpreted the same way. According to Dykes, each side had to appreciate their counterpart's point of view before they could frankly reconcile their differing national perspectives. A common goal, he thought, would enable both sides to work together and "travel the same road and not take divergent courses." To win the war and develop the special relationship Churchill made so much of in his memoirs, the British-Americans had to resolve their differing perspectives on grand strategy that plagued the alliance during 1942.[53]

As the year ended, the two heads of state agreed to another meeting of the Combined Chiefs of Staff in January 1943 to discuss strategy. The Allies needed a long-term strategy for defeating Germany, and Roosevelt and Churchill could not continue to referee disagreements between their respective staffs. The Joint Chiefs of Staff needed to improve their internal coordination. The US Army and Navy still offered military advice to the president on the basis of their inter-service rivalries and personal and professional prejudices. They would have to overcome these in order to provide sound military advice to America's civilian leader and present a united front in dealing with their British counterparts. Only when the American military could speak with one voice could the two nations have a meaningful discussion on resources and strategy. If the two sides could then walk across the table and try to see the other's perspective, the Combined Chiefs of Staff would finally develop a sound foundation for creating a common grand strategy to defeat Germany. This was their challenge for 1943.

Meeting of Allied leaders, 1943. Front row: Mackenzie King, Franklin Roosevelt, and Winston Churchill. Back row: Gen. Henry Arnold, Air Marshal Charles Portal, Gen. Alan Brooke, Adm. Ernest King, Field Marshal John Dill, Gen. George Marshall, Adm. Dudley Pound, and Adm. William Leahy (courtesy of the George C. Marshall Foundation, Lexington, Virginia, USA)

NOTES

Abbreviations

AHEC	US Army Heritage and Education Center, Carlisle, PA
FDR Library	Franklin Delano Roosevelt Librar and Museum, Hyde Park, New York, http://www.fdrlibrary.marist.edu/archives/collections/franklin
LAC	Library and Archives Canada, Ottawa, Canada, https://library-archives.canada.ca
LOC	Library of Congress, Washington, DC Marshall Papers George C. Marshall Papers, George C. Marshall Library, Lexington, VA
NARA	National Archives and Research Archives, College Park, MD
TNA	The National Archives, Kew, Richmond, Surrey, TW9 4DU, United Kingdom, www.nationalarchives.gov.uk

Introduction

1. Winston S. Churchill, "Sinews of Peace" speech at Westminster College, Fulton, Missouri, 5 March 1946, https://www.nationalchurchillmuseum.org/sinews-of-peace-iron-curtain-speech.html.

2. John Charmley, *Churchill's Grand Alliance: The Anglo-American Special Relationship, 1940–57* (New York: Harcourt, Brace, 1995), 7.

3. David Reynolds, *In Command of History* (New York: Random House, 2005), 39; Matthew Phelan, "The History of 'History is Written by the Victors,'" *Slate*, 26 November 2019, https://slate.com/culture/2019/11/history-is-written-by-the-victors-quote-origin.html.

4. Reynolds, *In Command of History*, 41–42.

5. Reynolds, 530–31. For the State Department's use of Churchill's memoirs, see Fredrick Aandahl, William Franklin, and William Slany, eds.,

Foreign Relations of the United States: The Conferences at Washington, 1941–1942, and Casablanca, 1943 (Washington, DC: US Government Printing Office, 1958), https://history.state.gov/historicaldocuments/frus1941-43.

6. First quotation in Reynolds, *In Command of History*, 324; second quotation in William Slim, "Higher Command in War," address to Command and General Staff College on 8 April 1952, in *Military Review*, May–June 2020, 58.

7. William Johnsen, *The Origins of the Grand Alliance: Anglo-American Military Collaboration from the Panay Incident to Pearl Harbor* (Lexington: University of Kentucky Press), 26.

8. David Dimbleby and David Reynolds, *An Ocean Apart: The Relationship between Britain and America in the Twentieth Century* (London: Hodder and Stoughton, 1988), 61.

9. Quotation from Johnsen, *Origins of the Grand Alliance*, 29. In his memoirs Pershing gives a slightly less dramatic explanation. John Pershing, *My Experiences in the World War*, vol. 2 (Charleston, SC: Arcadia Press, 2019), 232–33.

10. Quotation in Dimbleby and Reynolds, *Ocean Apart*, 60; Gregory Florence, *Courting a Reluctant Ally: An Evaluation of US/UK Naval Intelligence Cooperation, 1935–1941*, (Center for Strategic Intelligence Research, January 2004), 17.

11. "Random Notes" to Joint History Office, Ernest J. King papers, box 35, LOC.

12. Quotation from Florence, *Courting a Reluctant Ally*, 17; Dimbleby and Reynolds, *Ocean Apart*, 79.

13. Samuel Eliot Morrison, *The Two-Ocean War* (New York: Little, Brown, 1963), 6; Florence, *Courting a Reluctant Ally*, 18.

14. Dimbleby and Reynolds, *Ocean Apart*, 78–79.

15. Correlli Barnett, *The Collapse of British Power* (London: Faber and Faber, 1972), 7–8.

16. Barnett, 589.

17. Barnett, 591; Winston S. Churchill, *Their Finest Hour* (Boston: Houghton Mifflin, 1949), 414.

18. Churchill, *Finest Hour*, 415.

19. Churchill, 416.

20. Lend Lease Agreement, 23 February 1942, Franklin D. Roosevelt, President's Secretary's File, Confidential Files, box 12, FDR Library; quotations in Robert Sherwood, *Roosevelt and Hopkins: An Intimate History* (New York: Harper and Brothers, 1948), 264–65; Charmley, *Churchill's Grand Alliance*, 24.

21. First quotation from Churchill speech, 10 November 1941, in Martin Gilbert, *The Churchill War Papers*, vol. 3, *The Ever-Widening War, 1941* (New York: Norton, 2000), 1427; second quotation from Winston S. Churchill to Kingsley Wood, 20 March 1941, in Gilbert, *Churchill War Papers*, vol. 3, 372; Barnett, *Collapse of British Power*, 591.

22. Memorandum of conversation between Maynard Keynes and Dean Acheson, "Temporary British-American Lease-Lend Agreement," 28 July 1941, Franklin D. Roosevelt, President's Secretary's Files, Confidential Files, box 12, FDR Library.
23. Winston S. Churchill to Lord Halifax, May 1943, in Martin Gilbert, *Winston S. Churchill*, vol. 7, *Road to Victory, 1941–1945* (Hillsdale, MI: Hillsdale University Press, 1986), 410.
24. Churchill, *Finest Hour*, 569.
25. Sherwood, *Roosevelt and Hopkins*, 270–71.
26. Winston S. Churchill, *The Grand Alliance* (Boston: Houghton Mifflin, 1950), 137.
27. Mark Stoler, *The Politics of the Second Front: American Military Planning and Diplomacy in Coalition Warfare, 1941–1943* (Westport, CT: Greenwood, 1977), 4; Johnsen, *Origins of the Grand Alliance*, 41; John F. Shortal, *Code Name Arcadia* (College Station: Texas A&M Press, 2021), 26.
28. Shortal, *Code Name Arcadia*, 27.
29. Quotation from Winston S. Churchill to A. V. Alexander and Admiral Pound, 17 February 1941, in Gilbert, *Churchill War Papers*, vol. 3, 235; Shortal, *Code Name Arcadia*, 29.
30. James Ramsay Montagu Butler, *Grand Strategy*, vol. 3, *June 1941–August 1942*, part 2 (London: Her Majesty's Stationery Office, 1964), 127–29.
31. Ernest King to Joint History Office, "Notes on Chapter 1," Ernest J. King papers, box 35, LOC.
32. Christopher Thorne, *Allies of a Kind: The United States, Britain and the War against Japan, 1941–1945* (New York: Oxford University Press, 1978), 97–98.
33. Thorne, 98–99.
34. Slim, "Higher Command in War," 58.

Chapter One

1. Churchill, *Grand Alliance*, 608; Stimson diary, 8 December 1941, reel 7, vol. 36, Marshall Papers (original in Yale University Library, New Haven, CT).
2. Stimson diary, 8 December 1941, reel 7, vol. 36, Marshall Papers; Churchill, *Grand Alliance*, 608.
3. Henry L. Stimson to Franklin Roosevelt, 12 November 1941 and 19 February 1942, Franklin D. Roosevelt, President's Secretary's Files, Confidential Files, box 12, FDR Library; Stimson diary, 8 and 9 December 1941, reel 7, vol. 36, Marshall Papers.
4. First quotation from Churchill to Roosevelt, cable, 9 December 1941, in Churchill, *Grand Alliance*, 609; second quotation from Roosevelt to Churchill, draft cable (not sent), 10 December 1941, in Franklin D. Roosevelt, Map Room Papers, box 1, FDR Library; Warren F. Kimball, ed., *Churchill and Roosevelt: The Complete Correspondence*, vol. 1, *Alliance Emerging, October 1933–November 1942* (Princeton: Princeton University Press, 1984), 284.

5. First quotation in Churchill to Roosevelt, cable, 10 December 1941, Franklin D. Roosevelt, Map Room Files, box 1, FDR Library; second quotation in Roosevelt to Churchill, cable, 10 December 1941, Franklin D. Roosevelt, Map Room Files, box 1, FDR Library.

6. Churchill, *Grand Alliance*, 625–26.

7. First quotation from Lord Moran, *Churchill: Taken from the Diaries of Lord Moran; The Struggle for Survival, 1945–1960* (Boston: Houghton Mifflin, 1966), 21; second quotation from James Lacey, *The Washington War: FDR's Inner Circle and the Politics of Power That Won World War II* (New York: Bantom Books, 2019), 200.

8. Stimson diary, 18 December 1941, reel 7, vol. 36, Marshall Papers.

9. Joseph Stilwell to Winifred Stilwell, 27 December 1941, in Theodore White, ed., *The Stilwell Papers* (New York: Da Capo, 1975), 15.

10. Ian Jacob diary, 23 December 1941, in Charles Richardson, *From Churchill's Secret Circle to the BBC: The Biography of Lieutenant General Sir Ian Jacob GBE CB DL* (London: Brassey's, 1991), 89.

11. Richardson, *From Churchill's Secret Circle to the BBC*, 90–91, 97.

12. First quotation from Gen. Thomas T. Handy interview by Lt. Col. Edward M. Knopf Jr., 41, Senior Officer Debriefing Program, US Army Military Research Collection, US Army Military History Institute, AHEC; second quotation from Thomas Buell, *Master of Sea Power: A Biography of Fleet Admiral Ernest J. King* (Boston: Little, Brown, 1980), 163.

13. Churchill, *Grand Alliance*, 663.

14. "Record of Staff Conferences held on 19 December 1941, at 1230 p.m.," CAB 99/17, TNA; "Meeting of the United States and British Chiefs of Staff, 10:30 a.m.," 24 December 1941, document 52, in Aandahl, Franklin, and Slany, *Foreign Relations of the United States*.

15. "Memorandum by British Chiefs of Staff," 24 December 1941, document 114, in Aandahl, Franklin, and Slany, *Foreign Relations of the United States*.

16. Interview, Col. Lawrence Guyer and Admiral Stark, 14 May 1947, in Lawrence Guyer, "The War against Germany," chapter 2, 75, record group 218, entry UD 299, box 6, stack 190, row 2, NARA. This is an unpublished manuscript produced by the Joint History Office in the late 1940s. It was never finished, and the only known copy is at NARA. It has an excellent collection of documents attached to it.

17. Mark Stoler, *George C. Marshall: Soldier-Statesman of the American Century* (Boston: Twayne, 1989), 93; Shortal, *Code Name Arcadia*, 64.

18. Guyer, "The War against Germany," chapter 2, p. 66; "Memorandum by the Chief of Staff, United States Army (Marshall)," 23 December 1941, document 47, in Aandahl, Franklin, and Slany, *Foreign Relations of the United States*.

19. Winston S. Churchill to Clementine Churchill, 21 December 1941, in Gilbert, *Churchill War Papers*, vol. 3, 1664.

20. "Record of a Staff Conference held on 18 December 1941, at 11 a.m.," War Cabinet and Chiefs of Staff Committee, Records of the Proceedings at the Washington War Conference, December 1941–January 1942, CAB-99/17, Records of the Cabinet, War Cabinet and Cabinet: Commonwealth International Conferences: Minutes and Papers, "Arcadia" Record of Proceedings at Washington Conference 1941–1942, TNA; Guyer, "The War against Germany," chapter 2, pp. 116–17; "Memorandum by the Chief of Staff, United States Army (Marshall)," 23 December 1941, document 47, in Aandahl, Franklin, and Slany, *Foreign Relations of the United States*; "Memorandum by Lieutenant General Arnold," 23 December 1941, document 48, in Aandahl, Franklin, and Slany, *Foreign Relations of the United States*.

21. Quotation in Guyer, "The War against Germany," chapter 2, p. 72; Maurice Matloff and Edwin Snell, *Strategic Planning for Coalition Warfare, 1941–1942* (Washington, DC: US Army Center of Military History, 1999), 104.

22. Guyer, "The War against Germany," chapter 2, pp. 73–78.

23. Churchill, *Grand Alliance*, 705.

24. Dykes diary, 24 December 1941, in *Establishing the Anglo-American Alliance: The Second World War Diaries of Brigadier Vivian Dykes*, ed. Alex Danchev (London: Brassey's, 1990), 77; quotation in Richardson, *From Churchill's Secret Circle to the BBC*, 97.

25. "The Secretary of the British Chiefs of Staff (Hollis) to the Secretary, War Department General Staff (Smith)," 24 December 1941, document 146, in Aandahl, Franklin, and Slany, *Foreign Relations of the United States*.

26. Churchill, *Grand Strategy*, 669.

27. Stimson diary, 25 December 1941, reel 7, vol. 36, Marshall Papers.

28. Brig. Gen. Dwight Eisenhower, "Notes Taken at the Joint Conference of Chiefs of Staff on Afternoon, December 25," dated 28 December 1941, in Records of the War Department and General Staffs, record group 165, War Plans Division General Correspondence, 1920–1941, box 234, #4402–136, NARA; "Meeting of the United States and British Chiefs of Staff, 4 p.m.," 25 December 1941, document 54, in Aandahl, Franklin, and Slany, *Foreign Relations of the United States*; Robinett diary, 25 December 1941, box 20, Marshall Papers; Stoler, *George C. Marshall*, 91; Shortal, *Code Name Arcadia*, 80.

29. "Meeting of United States and British Chiefs of Staff, 3 p.m.," 27 December 1941, document 67, in Aandahl, Franklin, and Slany, *Foreign Relations of the United States*; Sherwood, *Roosevelt and Hopkins*, 457–58.

30. Forrest Pogue interview with George C. Marshall, 5 October 1956, in *George C. Marshall: Interviews and Reminiscences for Forrest Pogue*, ed. Larry Bland (Lexington, VA: George C. Marshall Foundation, 1996), 601.

31. Winston S. Churchill to Clement Atlee, 27 December 1941, in Gilbert, *Churchill War Papers*, vol. 3, 1696.

32. "Revised Memorandum by the British Chiefs of Staff," 13 January 1942, document 120, in Aandahl, Franklin, and Slany, *Foreign Relations of the United States*.

33. "Revised Memorandum by the British Chiefs of Staff," 13 January 1942.
34. First quotation in Winston Churchill to Franklin Roosevelt, 7 February 1942, in Franklin Roosevelt, Papers as President: 1933–1945, Franklin D. Roosevelt, Map Room Papers, box 2, Winston Churchill to Franklin Roosevelt, January–February 1942, FDR Library; second quotation in Churchill, *Grand Alliance*, 686–87.
35. Butler, *Grand Strategy*, vol. 3, part 2, 318.
36. Butler, *Grand Strategy*, vol. 3, part 2, 388–89; Dykes diary, 3–6 January 1942, in Danchev, *Establishing the Anglo-American Alliance*, 84–86.
37. Louis Lochner, ed., *The Goebbels Diaries, 1942–1943* (New York: Doubleday, 1948), 29, 179; Arthur Herman, *Freedom's Forge* (New York: Random House, 2012), 13.
38. Guyer, "The War against Germany," chapter 2, p. 69.
39. "Meeting of the United States and British Chiefs of Staff, 3 p.m.," 27 December 1941, document 67, in Aandahl, Franklin, and Slany, *Foreign Relations of the United States*; quotation in "United States Minutes," 5:30 p.m., 4 January 1942, document 96, in Aandahl, Franklin, and Slany, *Foreign Relations of the United States*; Guyer, "The War against Germany," chapter 2, p. 150.
40. Brooke diary, 24 and 25 December 1941, in *War Diaries, 1939–1945: Field Marshal Lord Alanbrooke*, ed. Alex Danchev and Daniel Todman (Berkeley: University of California Press, 2001), 214.
41. "Minutes by Major Sexton," 4:30 p.m., 26 December 1941, document 58, in Aandahl, Franklin, and Slany, *Foreign Relations of the United States*.
42. Eisenhower diary, 12 January 1942, in *The Eisenhower Diaries*, ed. Robert Ferrell (New York: W. W. Norton, 1981), 43.
43. Guyer, "The War against Germany," chapter 2, pp. 96–98; "Meeting of Roosevelt and Churchill with Their Military advisors, 5:30 p.m.," 14 January 1942, document 112, in Aandahl, Franklin, and Slany, *Foreign Relations of the United States*
44. Guyer, "The War against Germany," chapter 2, pp. 120–22.
45. Churchill, *Grand Alliance*, 705–6.
46. First quotation in Sir Charles Wilson diary, 14 January 1942, in Moran, *Churchill*, 24; second and third quotations in Churchill discussion with War Cabinet, 17 January 1942, in Gilbert, *Winston S. Churchill*, vol. 7, 43; fourth quotation in King George VI diary, 19 January 1942, in Gilbert, *Winston S. Churchill*, vol. 7, 44.
47. Matloff and Snell, *Strategic Planning for Coalition Warfare*, 98.
48. Forrest Pogue, *George C. Marshall: Ordeal and Hope, 1939–1942* (New York: Viking, 1967), 265.

Chapter Two

1. J. M. A. Gwyer, *Grand Strategy*, vol. 3, *June 1941–August 1942*, part 1 (London: Her Majesty's Stationery Office, 1964), 360.

2. Winston Churchill, *Hinge of Fate* (Boston: Houghton Mifflin, 1951), 4.
3. Churchill, 61; Moran, *Churchill*, 26; William Manchester and Paul Reed, *The Last Lion: Winston Spencer Churchill, Defender of the Realm, 1940–1965* (New York: Little, Brown, 2012), 470–71.
4. Winston Churchill, address to House of Commons, 27 January 1942, in Martin Gilbert, *The Churchill Documents*, vol. 17, *Testing Times, 1942* (Hillsdale, MI: Hillsdale College Press, 2014), 174.
5. Churchill address to House of Commons, 27 January 1942, 174–75.
6. Churchill address to House of Commons, 27 January 1942, 157–58.
7. Churchill address to House of Commons, 27 January 1942, 154–61.
8. Churchill address to House of Commons, 27 January 1942, 168.
9. Churchill address to House of Commons, 27 January 1942, 175–76.
10. First quotation in Lord Beaverbrook to Harry Hopkins, 2 February 1942, in Churchill Address to House of Commons, 27 January 1942, 210; second quotation in Franklin Roosevelt to Winston Churchill, 30 January 1942, in Kimball, *Churchill and Roosevelt*, vol. 1, 337; third quotation in Sherwood, *Roosevelt and Hopkins*, 494.
11. Barnett, *Collapse of British Power*, 272–77.
12. Barnett, 275–81 (quotation on 276); Stanley Woodburn Kirby, *The War against Japan*, vol. 1, *The Loss of Singapore* (Uckfield: Naval and Military Press, 2004), 2.
13. Thorne, *Allies of a Kind*, 3, 35.
14. Raymond Callahan, "The Illusion of Security: Singapore 1919–1942," *Journal of Contemporary History* 9, no. 2 (April 1974): 79–80, 92.
15. Callahan, 81–84.
16. Daniel Todman, *Britain's War: Into Battle, 1937–1941* (Oxford: Oxford University Press, 2016), 100–101; Raymond Callahan, *The Worst Disaster* (Newark: University of Delaware Press, 1977), 29.
17. Winston Churchill to Gen. Hastings Ismay for the Chiefs of Staff Committee, 19 January 1942, in Gilbert, *Churchill Documents*, vol. 17, 106.
18. Moran, *Churchill*, 27.
19. Winston Churchill to Capt. Henry Margesson, Gen. Sir Alan Brooke, and Brendan Bracken, 31 January 1942, in Gilbert, *Churchill Documents*, vol. 17, 205.
20. First quotation in Winston Churchill to Gen. Hastings Ismay for the Chiefs of Staff Committee, 19 January 1942, in Gilbert, *Churchill Documents*, vol. 17, 108; second quotation in Winston Churchill to Gen. Archibald Wavell, 20 January 1942, in Gilbert, *Churchill Documents*, vol. 17, 112; Callahan, "The Illusion of Security," 89.
21. Winston Churchill to Gen. Archibald Wavell, 10 February 1942, in Gilbert, *Churchill Documents*, vol. 17, 236; Callahan, "The Illusion of Security," 90.
22. Kirby, *War against Japan*, vol. 1, 415, 473; quotation in Butler, *Grand Strategy*, vol. 3, part 2, 463.

23. Kirby, *War against Japan*, vol. 1, 472–73; Callahan, *The Worst Disaster*, 273.
24. Kirby, *War against Japan*, vol. 1, p. 471.
25. Harold Nicholson diary, 12 February 1942, in Gilbert, *Churchill Documents*, vol. 17, 242.
26. Churchill, *Hinge of Fate*, 50.
27. Gen. Alan Brooke diary, 2 February 1942, in Danchev and Todman, *War Diaries*, 226.
28. Nigel Hamilton, *The Mantle of Command: FDR at War, 1941–1942* (Boston: Houghton Mifflin, 2014), 209.
29. General Brooke diary, 11 and 18 February 1942, in Danchev and Todman, *War Diaries*, 228–31.
30. General Brooke diary, 31 March 1942, in Danchev and Todman, *War Diaries*, 243; Arthur Bryant, *The Turn of the Tide, 1939–1943: A History of the War Years Based on the Diaries of Field Marshall Lord Alanbrooke, Chief of the Imperial General Staff* (Garden City, NY: Doubleday, 1957), 269.
31. John Kennedy, *The Business of War: The War Narrative of Major General Sir John Kennedy G. S. M. G., K. C. V. O., C. B., M. C.* (New York: William Morrow, 1958), 198; quotation in Max Hastings, *Winston's War: Churchill, 1940–1945* (New York: Alfred A. Knopf, 2010), 213.
32. Gen. Archibald Wavell to Winston Churchill, 18 February 1942, in Gilbert, *Churchill Documents*, vol. 17, 282.
33. Raymond Callahan, *Triumph at Imphal-Kohima: How the Indian Army Finally Stopped the Japanese Juggernaut* (Lawrence: University Press of Kansas, 2017), 58; Stanley Woodburn Kirby, *The War against Japan*, vol. 2, *India's Most Dangerous Hour* (Uckfield: Naval and Military Press, 2004), 47.
34. Quote in Hastings, *Winston's War*, 220; Callahan, *Triumph at Imphal-Kohima*, 58; Todman, *Britain's War: Into Battle*, 219; Kennedy, *Business of War*, 199; Edward Aldrich, *The Partnership: George C. Marshall, Henry Stimson, and the Extraordinary Collaboration That Won World War II* (Guilford, CT: Stackpole Books, 2022), 296.
35. Gilbert, *Winston S. Churchill*, vol. 7, 36.
36. Winston S. Churchill, broadcast, 15 February 1942, in Gilbert, *Churchill Documents*, vol. 17, 255.
37. Sherwood, *Roosevelt and Hopkins*, 501.
38. First quotation in Kimball, *Churchill and Roosevelt*, vol. 1, 362; second quotation in Franklin Roosevelt to Winston Churchill, 19 February 1942, in Gilbert, *Churchill Documents*, vol. 17, 285.
39. Louis Morton, *The Fall of the Philippines* (Washington, DC: US Government Printing Office, 1953), 471–72.
40. Morton, 61–64.
41. Ronald Spector, *Eagle against the Sun* (New York: Vintage, 1985), 56–57; R. Ernest Dupuy and Trevor Dupuy, *Encyclopedia of Military History* (New

York: Harper Row, 1970), 1130–31; John Whitman, *Bataan: Our Last Ditch* (New York: Hippocrene Books, 1990), 106.

42. Whitman, *Bataan*, 125–26.

43. Ricardo Trota Jose, "July 4, 1946: The Philippines Gained Independence from the United States," National World War II Museum, 2 July 2021, https://www.nationalww2museum.org/war/articles/july-4-1946-philippines-independence.

44. Henry Stimson and McGeorge Bundy, *On Active Services in Peace and War* (New York: Harper and Brothers, 1947), 395.

45. Henry L. Stimson diary, 8 February 1942, reel 7, vol. 37, Marshall Papers.

46. Stimson diary, 8 February 1942.

47. Franklin Roosevelt to Pres. Manuel Quezon, 9 February 1942, in Stimson diary, 9 February 1942, reel 7, vol. 37, Marshall Papers.

48. Franklin Roosevelt to Gen. Douglas MacArthur, 9 February 1942, in Stimson diary, 9 February 1942, reel 7, vol. 37, Marshall Papers.

49. President Quezon to President Roosevelt, 12 February 1942, and General MacArthur to President Roosevelt, 11 February 1942, in Stimson diary, 13 February 1942, reel 7, vol. 37, Marshall Papers.

50. Stimson diary, 9 February 1942, and Stimson message to General MacArthur, 12 February 1942, in Stimson diary, 13 February 1942, reel 7, vol. 37, Marshall Papers; Pogue, *George C. Marshall*, 248.

51. Whitman, *Bataan*, 15, 29.

52. Hamilton, *Mantle of Command*, 205; D. Clayton James, *The Years of MacArthur*, vol. 2, *1941–1945* (New York: Houghton Mifflin, 1975), 65; Kimball, *Churchill and Roosevelt*, vol. 1, 373.

53. Franklin Roosevelt to Winston Churchill, 25 February 1942, Franklin D. Roosevelt, Papers as President: Map Room Papers, 1941–1945, series 1, box 2, FDR Library.

54. Kirby, *War against Japan*, vol. 1, 263–64; Ronald Lewin, *The Chief: Field Marshal Lord Wavell, Commander-in-Chief and Viceroy, 1939–1947* (New York: Farrar, Straus, Giroux, 1980), 161.

55. Louis Morton, *Strategy and Command: The First Two Years* (Washington, DC: US Army Center of Military History, 1985), 174.

56. Quotation in Winston S. Churchill to John Curtin, 20 February 1942, in Gilbert, *Churchill Documents*, vol. 17, 289; James MacGregor Burns, *Roosevelt: The Soldier of Freedom* (New York: Harcourt Brace Jovanovich, 1970), 186.

57. Prime Minister John Curtin to Prime Minister Winston Churchill, cablegram, 23 February 1942, https://recordsearch.naa.gov.au/SearchNRetrieve/Interface/DetailsReports/SeriesDetail.aspx?series_no=M1415.

58. Grace Hayes, *The History of the Joint Chiefs of Staff in World War II: The War against Japan* (Annapolis, MD: Naval Institute Press, 1982), 121; quotation in Thorne, *Allies of a Kind*, 253.

59. Combined Chiefs of Staff, minutes of a meeting held in Room 340,

Public Health Building, on Tuesday, February 17, 1942, at 3:00 p.m. (C.C.S. 5th meeting), Conference Minutes of Meetings of the Combined Chiefs of Staff—Post-Arcadia, Franklin D. Roosevelt, Papers as President: Map Room Papers, 1941–1945, box 25, FDR Library.

60. Combined Chiefs of Staff, minutes of a meeting held in Room 340, Public Health Building, on Monday, February 23, 1942, at 3:00 p.m. (C.C.S. 8th meeting), Conference Minutes of Meetings of the Combined Chiefs of Staff—Post-Arcadia, Franklin D. Roosevelt, Papers as President: Map Room Papers, 1941–1945, box 25, FDR Library; Morton, *Strategy and Command*, 177.

61. Hayes, *History of the Joint Chiefs of Staff*, 87; Morton, *Strategy and Command*, 179; Gwyer, *Grand Strategy*, vol. 3, part 1, 381.

62. First quotation in Brooke diary, 22 February 1942, in Danchev and Todman, *War Diaries*, 232; final quotation in Arthur Butler, *The Turn of the Tide* (New York: Doubleday, 1957), 254.

63. Pogue, *George C. Marshall*, 304.

64. Combined Chiefs of Staff, minutes of a meeting held in Room 340, Public Health Building, on Monday, February 23, 1942, at 3:00 p.m. (C.C.S. 8th meeting), Conference Minutes of Meetings of the Combined Chiefs of Staff—Post-Arcadia, Franklin D. Roosevelt, Papers as President: Map Room Papers, 1941–1945, box 25, FDR Library.

65. Eisenhower diary, 17 and 23 February 1942, in Ferrell, *Eisenhower Diaries*, 48–49.

66. Hayes, *History of the Joint Chiefs of Staff*, 104.

67. Hayes, 106–7.

68. Guyer, "The War against Germany," chapter 2, "The Period of Arcadia, December 1941–February 1942," p. 175; Winston Churchill to Lord Leathers, Lord Cherwell, and Sir Edward Bridges, 28 February 1942, in Gilbert, *Churchill Documents*, vol. 17, 330.

69. Stimson diary, 14 and 19 February 1942, reel 7, vol. 37, Marshall Papers.

70. Stimson diary, 24 February 1942, reel 7, vol. 37, Marshall papers; Larry I. Bland and Sharon Ritenour Stevens, eds., *The Papers of George Catlett Marshall*, vol. 3, *"The Right Man for the Job," December 7, 1941–May 31, 1943* (Baltimore: Johns Hopkins University Press, 1991), 157.

Chapter Three

1. Clayton R. Newell, *Burma, 1942* (Washington, DC: US Army Center of Military History, ND), 3, 6, https://history.army.mil/brochures/burma42/burma42.htm.

2. Newell, 5.

3. Newell, 5.

4. Kirby, *War against Japan*, vol. 2, 80–82; Callahan, *Triumph at Imphal-Kohima*, 25–27.

5. Kirby, *War against Japan*, vol. 2, 100.

6. Kirby, 102; Herbert Feis, *The China Tangle: The American Effort in China from Pearl Harbor to the Marshall Mission* (Princeton: Princeton University Press, 1953), 30.
7. Quotation in Stilwell diary, 6 March 1942, in White, ed., *The Stilwell Papers*, 50, 54; Feis, *China Tangle*, 16; Newell, *Burma*, 14; Kirby, *War against Japan*, vol. 2, 154; Bland and Stevens, *Papers of George Catlett Marshall*, vol. 3, 141.
8. Winston Churchill to Franklin Roosevelt, 17 March 1942, in Kimball, *Churchill and Roosevelt*, vol. 1, 418.
9. Stimson diary, 19 March 1942, reel 7, vol. 38, Marshall Papers; quotation in Franklin Roosevelt to Winston Churchill, 19 March 1942, in Kimball, *Churchill and Roosevelt*, vol. 1, 422–23.
10. George C. Marshall, "Memorandum for Field Marshall Sir John Dill," 19 March 1942, in Bland and Stevens, *Papers of George Catlett Marshall*, vol. 3, 140–41.
11. Kirby, *War against Japan*, vol. 2, 156.
12. Winston Churchill to Franklin Roosevelt, 5 March 1942, in Kimball, *Churchill and Roosevelt*, vol. 1, 379–81.
13. Churchill to Roosevelt, 5 March 1942, 381–82.
14. Churchill to Roosevelt, 5 March 1942, 381–83.
15. Stimson diary, 5 March 1942, reel 7, vol. 38, Marshall Papers.
16. Stimson diary, 5 March 1942; Guyer, "The War against Germany," chapter 3, p. 14.
17. Stimson diary, 6 March 1942, reel 7, vol. 38, Marshall Papers.
18. Guyer, "The War against Germany," chapter 3, "Development of Strategy between March and July 1942," pp. 1–2.
19. Quotation in Guyer, chapter 3, p. 6; Stimson diary, 7 March 1942, reel 7, vol. 38, Marshall Papers.
20. Combined Chiefs of Staff, 10th meeting, minutes of meeting held in Room 240, Public Health Building, on Saturday, March 7, 1942, at 3:30 p.m., Franklin D. Roosevelt, Papers as President: Map Room Papers, 1941–1945, box 25, FDR Library; quotation in Franklin Roosevelt to Winston Churchill, 7 March 1942, in Kimball, *Churchill and Roosevelt*, vol. 1, 390–93.
21. Combined Chiefs of Staff, 10th meeting, minutes of meeting held in Room 240, Public Health Building, on Saturday, March 7, 1942, at 3:30 p.m., Franklin D. Roosevelt, Papers as President: Map Room Papers, 1941–1945, box 25, FDR Library; quotation in Combined Chiefs of Staff, 11th meeting, minutes of meeting held in Room 240, Public Health Building, on Tuesday, March 10, 1942, at 2:30 p.m., Franklin D. Roosevelt, Papers as President: Map Room Papers, 1941–1945, box 25, FDR Library; Franklin Roosevelt to Winston Churchill, 7 March 1942, in Kimball, *Churchill and Roosevelt*, vol. 1, 389–93.
22. Quotation in Stimson diary, 8 March 1942, reel 7, vol. 38, Marshall Papers; Combined Chiefs of Staff, 12th meeting, minutes of meeting held in Room 240, Public Health Building, on Tuesday, March 17, 1942, at 2:30 p.m.,

Franklin D. Roosevelt, Papers as President: Map Room Papers, 1941–1945, box 25, FDR Library.

23. Winston Churchill to Franklin Roosevelt, 17 March 1942, in Kimball, *Churchill and Roosevelt*, vol. 1, 409, 411–14; quotation from General Brooke diary, 10 March 1942, in Danchev and Todman, *War Diaries*, 238; Guyer, "The War against Germany," chapter 3, p. 9.

24. Guyer, "The War against Germany," chapter 3, pp. 7–8.

25. Quotations in Franklin Roosevelt to Winston Churchill, 9 March 1942, in Kimball, *Churchill and Roosevelt*, vol. 1, 399; Guyer, "The War against Germany," chapter 3, p. 9.

26. Winston Churchill to Field Marshal Sir John Dill, 14 March 1942, in Gilbert, *Churchill Documents*, vol. 17, 390.

27. Dykes diary, 15 March 1942, in Danchev, *Establishing the Anglo-American Alliance*, 115.

28. First quotation in Winston Churchill to Franklin Roosevelt, 17 March 1942, in Gilbert, *Churchill Documents*, vol. 17, 401; second quotation in Winston Churchill to Franklin Roosevelt, 14 March 1942, Kimball, *Churchill and Roosevelt*, vol. 1, 404; Franklin Roosevelt to Winston Churchill, 16 March 1942, in Kimball, *Churchill and Roosevelt*, vol. 1, 406.

29. First quotation in Stimson diary, 17 March 1942, reel 7, vol. 38, Marshall Papers; second quotation in Eisenhower diary, 23 February 1942, in Ferrell, *Eisenhower Diaries*, 49; Hayes, *History of the Joint Chiefs of Staff*, 112; Kimball, *Churchill and Roosevelt*, vol. 1, 415, 425; Guyer, "The War against Germany," p. 11.

30. Quotation in Eisenhower diary, 19 March 1942, in Ferrell, *Eisenhower Diaries*, 52; Hayes, *History of the Joint Chiefs of Staff*, 113; Guyer, "The War against Germany," chapter 3, p. 12.

31. First quotation in Churchill, *Hinge of Fate*, 199; second quotation in Franklin Roosevelt to Winston Churchill, 7 March 1942, in Kimball, *Churchill and Roosevelt*, vol. 1, 392; Combined Chiefs of Staff, 5th meeting, minutes of meeting held in Room 240, Public Health Building, on Tuesday, February 17, 1942, at 3:00 p.m., in Franklin D. Roosevelt, Papers as President: Map Room Papers, 1941–1945, box 25, FDR Library; Hayes, *History of the Joint Chiefs of Staff*, 105.

32. Gilbert, *Winston S. Churchill*, vol. 7, 68–69; Churchill, *Hinge of Fate*, 123, 126, 199.

33. JCS 23, "Strategic Deployment of the Land, Sea, and Air Forces of the United States," 14 March 1942, in Guyer, "The War against Germany," chapter 3, p. 12.

34. JCS 23, "Strategic Deployment of the Land, Sea, and Air Forces of the United States," 14 March 1942.

35. First quotation in "Summary of a Plan, 14 March 1942, By the Joint United States Strategic Committee for the Invasion of Europe," in Guyer, "The War against Germany," chapter 3, appendix A; final quotation in JCS 23, "Strategic Deployment of the Land, Sea, and Air Forces of the United

States," 14 March 1942, in Guyer, "The War against Germany," chapter 3, p. 13; Hayes, *History of the Joint Chiefs of Staff*, 114.

36. Quotation in cable from the military attaché in Cairo to War Department, 5 March 1942, also reviewed by Harry Hopkins, in Franklin D. Roosevelt, Papers as President: President's Secretary's Files, box 49, FDR Library; David Roll, *The Hopkins Touch: Harry Hopkins and the Forging of the Alliance to Defeat Hitler* (Oxford: Oxford University Press, 2013), 184.

37. Roll, *Hopkins Touch*, 184; quotation in Sherwood, *Roosevelt and Hopkins*, 519.

38. Guyer, "The War against Germany," chapter 3, p. 13.

39. "Summary of British Plan, 24 December 1941, For Operation Round-Up, A Cross-Channel Return to the Continent," in Guyer, "The War against Germany," appendix B, i–iv; Gordon Harrison, *Cross-Channel Attack* (Washington, DC: US Army Center of Military History, 2007), 8.

40. First quotation in Andrew Roberts, *Masters and Commanders: How Four Titans Won the War in the West, 1941–1945* (New York: Harper, 2009), 126; second quotation in Kennedy, *Business of War*, 210; Dykes diary, 16 March 1942, in Danchev, *Establishing the Anglo-American Alliance*, 116.

41. Quotation in Franklin Roosevelt to Winston Churchill, 18 March 1942, in Gilbert, *Churchill Documents*, vol. 17, 411; Brooke diary, 17 March 1942, in Danchev and Todman, *War Diaries*, 240; Kennedy, *Business of War*, 210.

42. Combined Chiefs of Staff, 13th Meeting, minutes of meeting held in Room 240, Public Health Building, on Tuesday, March 24, 1942, at 2:30 p.m., in Franklin D. Roosevelt, Papers as President: Map Room Papers, 1941–1945, box 25, FDR Library.

43. Stimson diary, 23 March 1942, reel 7, vol. 38, Marshall Papers.

44. Elting Morison, *Turmoil and Tradition: A Study of the Life and Times of Henry L. Stimson* (New York: History Book Club, 2003), 416–17.

45. Stimson diary, 20 March 1942, reel 7, vol. 38, Marshall Papers; Alfred Chandler and Stephen Ambrose, eds., *The Papers of Dwight Davis Eisenhower: The War Years*, vol. 1 (Baltimore: Johns Hopkins University Press, 1970), 207.

46. Dwight Eisenhower to George Marshall, 25 March 1942, in Chandler and Ambrose, *Papers of Dwight David Eisenhower*, vol. 1, 205–6.

47. Eisenhower to Marshall, 25 March 1942, 205–6.

48. Eisenhower to Marshall, 25 March 1942, 205–6.

49. Quotation in Stimson and Bundy, *On Active Services in Peace and War*, 416–17.

50. Quote in Stimson diary, 27 March 1942, reel 7, vol. 38, Marshall Papers; Chandler and Ambrose, *Papers of Dwight David Eisenhower*, vol. 1, 207; Roberts, *Masters and Commanders*, 128.

51. Dwight D. Eisenhower to George C. Marshall, 30 March 1942, in Chandler and Ambrose, *Papers of Dwight David Eisenhower*, vol. 1, 219; Hayes, *History of the Joint Chiefs of Staff*, 116; Lacey, *Washington War*, 245; Matloff and Snell, *Strategic Planning for Coalition Warfare*, 211.

52. Kirby, *War against Japan*, vol. 2, 115–16.

53. Quotation in Franklin Roosevelt to Winston Churchill, draft note, 25 February 1942, in Kimball, *Churchill and Roosevelt*, vol. 1, 401; Callahan, *Triumph at Imphal-Kohima*, 36–37; John Charmley, *Churchill: The End of Glory* (London: Hodder and Stoughton, 1993), 497; Kimball, *Churchill and Roosevelt*, vol. 1, 373, 388, 400, 402.

Chapter Four

1. Harrison, *Cross-Channel Attack*, 16; Matloff and Snell, *Strategic Planning for Coalition Warfare*, 182–84.

2. Gen. Henry Arnold, memorandum for record, 1 April 1942, in Henry Arnold Papers, reel 205, LOC.

3. Stimson diary, 1 April 1942, reel 7, vol. 38, Marshall Papers; Gen. Henry Arnold, memorandum for record, 1 April 1942, in Henry Arnold Papers, reel 205, LOC; "Summary of General Marshall's Plan 'Operations in Western Europe,'" Presented in London, April 1942," in Guyer, "The War against Germany," chapter 3, "Development of Strategy between March and July 1942," appendix C.

4. Matloff and Snell, *Strategic Planning for Coalition Warfare*, 185; "Summary of General Marshall's Plan' Operations in Western Europe,'" Presented in London, April 1942," in Guyer, "The War Against Germany," chapter 3, appendix C.

5. Matloff and Snell, *Strategic Planning for Coalition Warfare*, 185–86; "Summary of General Marshall's Plan 'Operations in Western Europe,'" Presented in London, April 1942," in Guyer, "The War against Germany," chapter 3, appendix C.

6. Pogue, *George C. Marshall*, 305.

7. Gen. Henry Arnold, memorandum for record, 1 April 1942, in Henry Arnold Papers, reel 205, LOC.

8. Matloff and Snell, *Strategic Planning for Coalition Warfare*, 186–87; "Summary of General Marshall's Plan 'Operations in Western Europe,'" Presented in London, April 1942," in Guyer, "The War against Germany," chapter 3, appendix C; "General Marshall's Plan: Operations in Western Europe," in Butler, *Grand Strategy*, vol. 3, part 2, appendix 3.

9. Gen. Henry Arnold, memorandum for record, 1 April 1942, in Henry Arnold Papers, reel 205, LOC; quotation from King's 29 March 1942 letter in Matloff and Snell, *Strategic Planning for Coalition Warfare*, 211.

10. Gen. Henry Arnold, memorandum for record, 1 April 1942, in Henry Arnold Papers, reel 205, LOC.

11. First quotation in Franklin Roosevelt to Winston Churchill, 2 April 1942, in Kimball, *Churchill and Roosevelt*, vol. 1, 437; second quotation in Franklin Roosevelt to Winston Churchill, 3 April 1942, in Kimball, *Churchill and Roosevelt*, vol. 1, 441.

12. Stimson diary, 2 April 1942, reel 7, vol. 38, Marshall Papers.

13. Dykes diary, 3 April 1942, in Danchev, *Establishing the Anglo-American Alliance*, 122.

14. Danchev, *Establishing the Anglo-American Alliance*, 13–14; quotation in Roberts, *Masters and Commanders*, 132; D. K. R. Crosswell, *Beetle: The Life of General Walter Bedell Smith* (Lexington: University of Kentucky Press, 2010), 272.

15. Dykes diary, 1 and 3 April 1942, in Danchev, *Establishing the Anglo-American Alliance*, 122; Crosswell, *Beetle*, 255, 258.

16. "Operation Sledgehammer, Joint Memorandum by Commander-in-Chief Home Forces, Air Officer Commander-in-Chief Fighter Command, and Chief of Combined Operations," War Cabinet Chiefs of Staff Committee, "Operation Sledgehammer," 7 April 1942, CAB 80/62, TNA.

17. "Operation Sledgehammer, Joint Memorandum."

18. "Operation Sledgehammer, Joint Memorandum."

19. First quotation in Butler, *Grand Strategy*, vol. 3, part 2, 573; second quotation in Roberts, *Masters and Commanders*, 133; third quotation in Brooke diary, 8 April 1942, in Danchev and Todman, *War Diaries*, 245.

20. Kirby, *War against Japan*, vol. 2, 118; Spector, *Eagle against the Sun*, 152; Hedley P. Wilmott, *Empires in the Balance: Japanese and Allied Pacific Strategies to April 1942* (Annapolis, MD: Naval Institute Press, 1982), 444–45.

21. Spector, *Eagle against the Sun*, 152; Wilmott, *Empires in the Balance*, 444–45.

22. Brooke diary, 6 and 7 April 1942, in Danchev and Todman, *War Diaries*, 245.

23. Winston Churchill to Franklin Roosevelt, 7 April 1942, and Franklin Roosevelt to Harry Hopkins, 8 April 1942, in Kimball, *Churchill and Roosevelt*, vol. 1, 442–43.

24. "Possible Dispatch of Six Fighter Squadrons from Middle East to India," War Cabinet Chiefs of Staff Committee, 8 April 1942, CAB 80/62, TNA.

25. Sherwood, *Roosevelt and Hopkins*, 523; Crosswell, *Beetle*, 258.

26. Sherwood, *Roosevelt and Hopkins*, 523.

27. Quotation in Brooke diary, 8 April 1942, in Danchev and Todman, *War Diaries*, 246; Sherwood, *Roosevelt and Hopkins*, 523.

28. War Cabinet Chiefs of Staff Committee Meeting, 9 April 1942, "Meeting with General Marshall," CAB 79-56-23, TNA.

29. War Cabinet Chiefs of Staff Committee Meeting, 9 April 1942; Albert Wedemeyer, *Wedemeyer Reports* (New York: Henry Holt, 1958), 135.

30. Brooke diary, 8 April and 31 March 1942, in Danchev and Todman, *War Diaries*, 243, 246.

31. Brooke diary, 9, 14, and 15 April 1942, in Danchev and Todman, *War Diaries*, 246–49; Aldrich, *Partnership*, 295.

32. Sherwood, *Roosevelt and Hopkins*, 524–25.

33. Sherwood, 526.
34. Winston Churchill to Franklin Roosevelt, 11 April 1942, and Franklin Roosevelt to Winston Churchill, 11 April 1942, in Kimball, *Churchill and Roosevelt*, vol. 1, 444, 446.
35. Quotations in Stimson diary, 22 April 1942, reel 7, vol. 38, Marshall Papers; Sherwood, *Churchill and Roosevelt*, 530–31.
36. Winston Churchill to Franklin Roosevelt, 12 April 1942, in Kimball, *Churchill and Roosevelt*, vol. 1, 448; Churchill, *Hinge of Fate*, 316.
37. Brooke diary, 13 April 1942, in Danchev and Todman, *War Diaries*, 247; "Comments on General Marshall's Memorandum," War Cabinet Chiefs of Staff Committee, 13 April 1942, CAB 80/62, TNA.
38. War Cabinet Chiefs of Staff Committee, "Operation Sledgehammer," 14 April 1942, and "Comments on General Marshall's Memorandum," 13 April 1942, presented on 14 April 1942, CAB 80/62, TNA.
39. George C. Marshall to Joseph McNarney, 13 April 1942, in Bland and Stevens, *Papers of George Catlett Marshall*, vol. 3, 160–61; Stimson diary, 13 April 1942, reel 7, vol. 38, Marshall Papers.
40. War Cabinet, Defence Committee, "Minutes of Meeting held on Tuesday, 14th April 1942, at 10p.m.," CAB 69/4, TNA.
41. War Cabinet, "Minutes of Meeting held on Tuesday, 14th April 1942, at 10p.m."
42. War Cabinet, "Minutes of Meeting held on Tuesday, 14th April 1942, at 10p.m."
43. War Cabinet, "Minutes of Meeting held on Tuesday, 14th April 1942, at 10p.m."
44. War Cabinet, "Minutes of Meeting held on Tuesday, 14th April 1942, at 10p.m."
45. First quotation in George C. Marshall to Henry L. Stimson, 15 April 1942, in Bland and Stevens, *Papers of George Catlett Marshall*, vol. 3, 162; second quotation in Winston Churchill to Franklin D. Roosevelt, 17 April 1942, Kimball, *Churchill and Roosevelt*, vol. 1, 459; third quotation in Sherwood, *Roosevelt and Hopkins*, 533.
46. Moran, *Churchill*, 38–39.
47. Averell Harriman recollection, 21 April 1942, in Gilbert, *Churchill Documents*, vol. 17, 545.
48. Brooke diary, 14 and 16 April 1942, in Danchev and Todman, *War Diaries*, 248, 250; Aldrich. *Partnership*, 295; General Lord Hastings Ismay, *The Memoirs of General Lord Ismay* (New York: Viking, 1960), 249–50.
49. Ismay, *The Memoirs of General Lord Ismay*, 249–50.
50. Churchill, *Hinge of Fate*, 322–25.
51. Mackenzie King diary, 15 April 1942, Diaries of William Lyon Mackenzie King, item 24029, LAC, https://library-archives.canada.ca/eng/collection/research-help/politics-government-law/Pages/diaries-william-lyon-mackenzie-king.aspx.

52. Mackenzie King diary, 15 April 1942, item 24030, LAC.
53. Mackenzie King diary, 24 April 1942, LAC.
54. Mackenzie King diary, 16 April 1942, LAC; Winston Churchill to Franklin Roosevelt, 15 April 1942, in Kimball, *Churchill and Roosevelt*, vol. 1, 452–54.
55. Franklin Roosevelt to Winston Churchill, 16 April 1942, in Kimball, *Churchill and Roosevelt*, vol. 1, 452, 455.
56. Henry Miller, *The Reminiscences of Rear Admiral Henry L. Miller, USN (Ret)* (Annapolis, MD: US Naval Institute Press, 1973), 34–41.
57. Kirby, *War against Japan*, vol. 2, 225–26.

Chapter Five

1. Combined Chiefs of Staff, minutes of meeting held in Room 240, Combined Chiefs of Staff Building (this was the new designation of the Public Health Building for the duration of the war), on Tuesday, April 28, 1942, at 2:30 p.m., Franklin D. Roosevelt, Papers as President: Map Room Papers, 1941–1945, FDR Library; Guyer, "The War against Germany," chapter 3, "Development of Strategy between March and July 1942," p. 25.
2. Memorandum for the Joint Chiefs of Staff, 1 May 1942, signed by the president's naval aide, Capt. John McCrea, and George C. Marshall, memorandum for the president, 4 May 1942, Franklin D. Roosevelt, Papers as President: Safe Files, box 4, FDR Library.
3. George C. Marshall, memorandum for the president, 3 May 1942, in Franklin D. Roosevelt, Papers as President: Safe Files, box 4, FDR Library.
4. General Wainwright to General Marshall, telegram, 4 May 1942, Franklin D. Roosevelt, Papers as President: FDR Significant Documents, FDR 44, FDR Library.
5. Admiral King, memorandum to the Joint Chiefs of Staff, "Subject: J.C.S.- Defense of Island Bases in the Pacific," 4 May 1942, in Franklin D. Roosevelt, Papers as President: Safe Files, box 4, FDR Library: Guyer, "The War against Germany," chapter 3, p. 26.
6. George C. Marshall to Franklin Roosevelt, memorandum for the president, "The Pacific Theater versus 'Bolero,'" 6 May 1942, Franklin D. Roosevelt, Papers as President: Safe Files, box 4, FDR Library.
7. Franklin Roosevelt to General George C. Marshall, 6 May 1942, Franklin D. Roosevelt, Papers as President: Safe Files, box 4, FDR Library.
8. Franklin Roosevelt, memorandum to secretary of war, secretary of the navy, Harry Hopkins, Admiral King, chief of staff, and General Arnold, 6 May 1942, Franklin D. Roosevelt, Papers as President: President's Secretary File, box 83, FDR Library.
9. Roosevelt, memorandum to secretary of war, secretary of the navy, Harry Hopkins, Admiral King, chief of staff, and General Arnold, 6 May 1942.
10. Roll, *Hopkins Touch*, 195.
11. Samuel Eliot Morison, *Coral Sea, Midway and Submarine Actions, May 1942–August 1942* (Annapolis, MD: Naval Institute Press, 2010), 4–5; Ian Toll,

Pacific Crucible: War at Sea in the Pacific, 1941–1942 (New York: W. W. Norton, 2012), 329, 344.

12. Toll, *Pacific Crucible*, 344, 370–71.

13. War Cabinet and Chiefs of Staff Committee meeting, 7 May 1942, Subject: "Operation 'Sledgehammer,'" CAB 80/62, Records of the Cabinet: War Cabinet and Cabinet: Chiefs of Staff Committee: memorandum, TNA.

14. Ian C. B. Dear and Michael R. D. Foot, eds., *The Oxford Companion to World War II*. (London: Oxford University Press, 1995), 649–50.

15. War Cabinet: Conclusions, 10 Downing Street, 21 May 1942, in Gilbert, *Churchill Documents*, vol. 17, 693.

16. Minutes of War Cabinet Meeting, 10 Downing Street, 22 May 1942, in Gilbert, *Churchill Documents*, vol. 17, 697–702.

17. Minutes of War Cabinet Meeting, 697–702.

18. Minutes of War Cabinet Meeting, 697–702.

19. Minutes of War Cabinet Meeting, 697–702.

20. Winston Churchill to Franklin Roosevelt, 27 May 1942, in Franklin D. Roosevelt Library, Papers as President: Map Room Papers, box 2, FDR Library.

21. Franklin Roosevelt to Winston Churchill, 27 May 1942, in Franklin D. Roosevelt Library, Papers as President: Map Room Papers, box 2, FDR Library.

22. Winston Churchill to Franklin Roosevelt, 28 May 1942, in Franklin D. Roosevelt Library, Papers as President: Map Room Papers, box 2, FDR Library.

23. "Memorandum of Conference Held at the White House, by Mr. Samuel H. Cross, Interpreter," Saturday, 30 May 1942, 11 a.m., document 471, in *Foreign Relations of the United States: Diplomatic Papers, 1942, Europe*, vol. 3, ed. G. Bernard Noble and E. Perkins (Washington, DC: Government Printing Office, 1961), https://history.state.gov/historicaldocuments/frus1942v03.

24. Sherwood, *Roosevelt and Hopkins*, 563; Burns, *Roosevelt: The Soldier of Freedom*, 233.

25. "Memorandum of Conference Held at the White House, by Mr. Samuel H. Cross, Interpreter," Monday, 1 June 1942, 10:30 a.m., document 472, in Noble and Perkins, *Foreign Relations of the United States*.

26. Franklin Roosevelt to Winston Churchill, 31 May 1942, in Franklin D. Roosevelt Library, Papers as President: Map Room Papers, box 2, FDR Library.

27. "Press Release Issued by the White House, 11 June 1942," document 483, in Noble and Perkins, *Foreign Relations of the United States*.

28. Gilbert, *Winston S. Churchill*, vol. 7, 113.

29. Burns, *Roosevelt: The Soldier of Freedom*, 234–35; quotation in Churchill, *Hinge of Fate*, 342.

30. Brooke diary, 13 June 1942, in Danchev and Todman, *War Diaries*, 265; Burns, *Roosevelt: The Soldier of Freedom*, 235.

Chapter Six

1. "Enemy Situation and Operations," 28 May 1942 to 11 June 1942, Franklin D. Roosevelt, Papers as President: Map Room Papers, 1941–1945, box 67, FDR Library; Guyer, "The War against Germany," chapter 3, "Development of Strategy between March and July 1942," p. 46.

2. Morison, *Coral Sea, Midway and Submarine Actions*, 75; Spector, *Eagle against the Sun*, 167–68.

3. Toll, *Pacific Crucible*, 280, 379–80.

4. Spector, *Eagle against the Sun*, 167–68.

5. Toll, *Pacific Crucible*, 476–79, 489; Morison, *Coral Sea, Midway and Submarine Actions*, 78–79.

6. Sherwood, *Roosevelt and Hopkins*, 580; Toll, *Pacific Crucible*, 489; Kirby, *War against Japan*, vol. 2, 233.

7. Franklin Roosevelt to Winston Churchill, 7 June 1942, and Winston Churchill to Admiral of the Fleet Sir Dudley Pound, 10 June 1942, in Gilbert, *Churchill Documents*, vol. 17, 759–60, 768; John Connell, *Wavell: Supreme Commander* (London: Collins, 1969), 230.

8. First quotation in Michael Smith, *The Emperor's Codes* (New York: Arcade, 2011), 153; second quotation in interview with General of the Army George C. Marshall by Col. Lawrence Guyer and Col. C. H. Donnelly of the Historical Section, Joint Chiefs of Staff, 11 February 1949, Marshall Papers.

9. Churchill, *Hinge of Fate*, 253.

10. Sherwood, *Roosevelt and Hopkins*, 556; Crosswell, *Beetle*, 262.

11. "Report by Lord Louis Mountbatten, 4 June 1942, as to the Progress of Planning and Training for Continental Operations," in Guyer, "The War against Germany," chapter 3, appendix D, p. 46.

12. Forrest Pogue interview with Rear Adm. Viscount Mountbatten of Burma, former commander of Combined Operations, at 16 Chester Street, London, 18 February 1947, Pogue Interviews, AHEC; Buell, *Master of Sea Power*, 205–6.

13. Pogue interview with Mountbatten, 18 February 1947, Pogue Inteviews, AHEC; quotation in Pogue, *George C. Marshall*, 331; Buell, *Master of Sea Power*, 206; Charles MacDonald, *The Mighty Endeavor: American Armed Forces in the European Theater in World War II* (New York: Oxford University Press, 1969), 63.

14. Pogue interview with Mountbatten, 18 February 1947, Pogue Interviews, AHEC; Pogue, *George C. Marshall*, 331; Buell, *Master of Sea Power*, 206.

15. Adm. Louis Mountbatten to Franklin Roosevelt, 15 June 1942, Marshall Papers.

16. Pogue interview with Mountbatten, 18 February 1947, Pogue Inteviews, AHEC; Mountbatten to Roosevelt, 15 June 1942; Sherwood, *Roosevelt and Hopkins*, 582.

17. Mountbatten to Roosevelt, 15 June 1942; Sherwood, *Roosevelt and Hopkins*, 582.

18. Warren Kimball, *The Juggler: Franklin Roosevelt as Wartime Statesman* (Princeton: Princeton University Press, 1991), 7, 16; Burns, *Roosevelt: The Soldier of Freedom*, 342–43; Robert Kagan, *The Ghost at the Feast: America and the Collapse of World Order, 1900–1941* (New York: Alfred A. Knopf, 2023), 413–14.

19. Quotation in Brooke diary, 13 June 1942, in Danchev and Todman, *War Diaries*, 256; Guyer, "The War against Germany," chapter 3, p. 46; Butler, *Grand Strategy*, vol. 3, part 2, 622.

20. Churchill, *Hinge of Fate*, 348.

21. "War Cabinet: Confidential Annex," 11 June 1942, in Gilbert, *Churchill Documents*, vol. 17, 772.

22. "War Cabinet: Confidential Annex," 772.

23. "War Cabinet: Confidential Annex," 772.

24. "War Cabinet: Confidential Annex," 772; "Aide Memoir, Operation Jupiter," 7 June 1942, annex to War Cabinet, Chiefs of Staff Committee, minutes of meeting on Monday, 8 June 1942, at 10:30 a.m., CAB 79-21-22, TNA.

25. "War Cabinet: Confidential Annex," 773; "Operation Jackpot," 9 June 1942, annex to War Cabinet, Chiefs of Staff Committee, minutes of meeting on Wednesday, 10 June 1942, at 10:30 a.m., CAB 79-21-22, TNA.

26. "Operation Viceroy," 9 June 1942, annex to War Cabinet, Chiefs of Staff Committee, minutes of meeting on Wednesday, 10 June 1942, at 10:30 a.m., CAB 79-21-22, TNA.

27. Winston S. Churchill, memorandum, "Operation Round-up," 15 June 1942, in Gilbert, *Churchill Documents*, vol. 17, 793–95; Churchill, *Hinge of Fate*, 353–55.

28. Butler, *Grand Strategy*, vol. 3, part 2, 623; Reynolds, *In Command of History*, 314.

29. Winston Churchill to Franklin Roosevelt, 13 June 1942, and Franklin Roosevelt to Winston Churchill, 13 June 1942, in Kimball, *Churchill and Roosevelt*, vol. 1, 510.

30. Winston Churchill to Gen. Hastings Ismay for the Chiefs of Staff Committee, 13 June 1942, in Gilbert, *Churchill Documents*, vol. 17, 781–84; Churchill, *Hinge of Fate*, 355.

31. Churchill, *Hinge of Fate*, 355–56; Sherwood, *Roosevelt and Hopkins*, 583.

32. Stimson diary, 17 June 1942, reel 7, vol. 39, Marshall Papers.

33. Stimson diary, 17 June 1942; Matloff and Snell, *Strategic Planning for Coalition Warfare*, 235–36.

34. MacKenzie King diary, Diaries of William Lyon MacKenzie King, 19 June 1942, LAC.

35. Stimson diary, 19 June 1942, reel 7, vol. 39, Marshall Papers.

36. Henry Stimson to Franklin Roosevelt, 19 June 1942, in Stimson diary, 19 June 1942.

37. Stimson to Roosevelt, 19 June 1942, in Stimson diary, 19 June 1942.

38. "Meeting of the Combined Chiefs of Staff, 12:30 p.m.," Friday, 19 June 1942, document 263, in Aandahl, Franklin, and Slaney, *Foreign Relations of the United States*.
39. "Meeting of the Combined Chiefs of Staff, 12:30 p.m.," Friday, 19 June 1942.
40. "Informal meeting of American and British military leaders, 2 p.m.," 19 June 1942, document 264, in Aandahl, Franklin, and Slaney, *Foreign Relations of the United States*; "Minutes of an Informal Meeting between General Marshall and Members of His Staff Representing the United States War Department and Sir John Dill, General A. Brooke and General Ismay. 2:00 PM, 19 June 1942. General Marshall's Office," in Chandler and Ambrose, *Papers of Dwight David Eisenhower*, vol. 1, 346–48; Brooke diary, 19 June 1942, in Danchev and Todman, *War Diaries*, 267; Lacey, *Washington War*, 263.
41. "Meeting of the Combined Chiefs of Staff, 11 a.m.," 20 June 1942, document 266, in Aandahl, Franklin, and Slaney, *Foreign Relations of the United States*.
42. "Meeting of the Combined Chiefs of Staff, 11 a.m.," 20 June 1942.
43. "Meeting of the Combined Chiefs of Staff, 11 a.m.," 20 June 1942.
44. "Meeting of the Combined Chiefs of Staff, 11 a.m.," 20 June 1942; quotation in Brooke diary, 20 June 1942, in Danchev and Todman, *War Diaries*, 267–68.
45. "Prime Minister Churchill to President Roosevelt," 20 June 1942, document 293, in Aandahl, Franklin, and Slaney, *Foreign Relations of the United States*.
46. "The President's Naval Aide (McCrea) to the Chief of Staff, United States Army (Marshall) and the Chief of Naval Operations (King)," 20 June 1942, document 294, in Aandahl, Franklin, and Slaney, *Foreign Relations of the United States*.
47. Butler, *Grand Strategy*, vol. 3, part 2, 627; Pogue, *George C. Marshall*, 333–34.
48. "Report by the Combined Chiefs of Staff," 21 June 1942, document 296, in Aandahl, Franklin, and Slaney, *Foreign Relations of the United States*; quotation in Brooke diary, 21 June 1942, in Danchev and Todman, *War Diaries*, 268; Guyer, "The War against Germany," chapter 3, p. 52; Butler, *Grand Strategy*, vol. 3, part 2, 627.
49. Stimson diary, 21 June 1942, reel 7, vol. 39, Marshall Papers; "Editorial Note," 21 June 1942, document 269, in Aandahl, Franklin, and Slaney, *Foreign Relations of the United States*; Sherwood, *Roosevelt and Hopkins*, 592; Guyer, "The War against Germany," chapter 3, p. 53; Lacey, *Washington War*, 264; Mark Stoler, *Allies in War: Britain and America against the Axis Powers, 1940–1945* (London: Hodder Arnold, 2005), 68; Daniel Todman, *Britain's War: A New World, 1942–1947* (New York: Oxford University Press, 2020), 213.
50. Brooke diary, 21 June 1942, in Danchev and Todman, *War Diaries*, 269; quotation in Churchill, *Hinge of Fate*, 383.

51. Quotation in Brooke diary, 21 June 1942, in Danchev and Todman, *War Diaries*, 269; "Memorandum by Prime Minister Churchill's Chief Staff Officer (Ismay)," 21 June 1942, document 270, in Aandahl, Franklin, and Slaney, *Foreign Relations of the United States*.

52. Dykes diary, 20 June 1942, in Danchev, *Establishing the Anglo-American Alliance*, 159; "Memorandum by Prime Minister's Chief Staff Officer (Ismay)," 21 June 1942, document 270, in Aandahl, Franklin, and Slaney, *Foreign Relations of the United States*; "Memorandum by the Secretary, War Department General Staff (Smith) to the Chief of Staff, United States Army (Marshall)," document 298, in Aandahl, Franklin, and Slaney, *Foreign Relations of the United States*; quotation in "Note by the Secretariat of the Combined Chiefs of Staff," 24 June 1942, document 304, in Aandahl, Franklin, and Slaney, *Foreign Relations of the United States* .

53. Butler, *Grand Strategy*, vol. 3, part 2, 627–28; Guyer, "The War against Germany," chapter 3, pp. 55–56; "Editorial Note," 21 June 1942, document 269, in Aandahl, Franklin, and Slaney, *Foreign Relations of the United States*; Pogue, *George C. Marshall*, 333–34.

54. Crosswell, *Beetle*, 267; Roll, *Hopkins Touch*, 204.

55. Interview with General of the Army George C. Marshall by Col. Lawrence Guyer and Col. C. H. Donnelly of the Historical Section, Joint Chiefs of Staff, 11 February 1949, Marshall Papers; Crosswell, *Beetle*, 267.

56. Stimson diary, 22 June 1942, reel 7, vol. 39, Marshall Papers; Churchill, *Hinge of Fate*, 385; Matloff and Snell, *Strategic Planning for Coalition Warfare*, 245.

57. Memorandum for the president, "American Forces in the Middle East," 23 June 1942, in Bland and Stevens, *Papers of George Catlett Marshall*, vol. 3, 248–49.

58. Jon Meacham, *Franklin and Roosevelt: An Intimate Portrait of an Epic Friendship* (New York: Random House, 2002), 187.

59. "Roosevelt-Churchill Meeting, 11:10 a.m.," 22 June 1942, document 273, in Aandahl, Franklin, and Slaney, *Foreign Relations of the United States*; Stimson diary, 22 June 1942, reel 7, vol. 39, Marshall Papers.

60. Stimson diary, 22 June 1942, reel 7, vol. 39, Marshall Papers; "Roosevelt-Churchill meeting, 11:10 a.m.," 22 June 1942.

61. "Roosevelt-Churchill conversation, 1:02 p.m.," 22 June 1942, document 275, in Aandahl, Franklin, and Slaney, *Foreign Relations of the United States*; OPD History Unit File, item 3, 8 June 1942, in Chandler and Ambrose, *Papers of Dwight David Eisenhower*, vol. 1, 333; OPD History Unit File, item 3, 11 June 1942, in Chandler and Ambrose, *Papers of Dwight David Eisenhower*, vol. 1, 337; Butler, *Grand Strategy*, vol. 3, part 2, 623.

62. Moran, *Churchill*, 42.

63. Stimson diary, 23, 24, 25 June 1942, reel 7, vol. 39, Marshall Papers.

64. First quotation in Ismay, *Memoirs of General Lord Ismay*, 257; second quotation in Brooke diary, 24 June 1942, in Danchev and Todman, *War

Diaries, 271; third quotation in Churchill, *Hinge of Fate*, 386; Stimson diary, 23, 24, 25 June 1942, reel 7, vol. 39, Marshall Papers.

65. Winston S. Churchill to Henry L. Stimson, 25 June 1942, in Gilbert, *Churchill Documents*, vol. 17, 107; Roberts, *Masters and Commanders*, 149.

66. Gerald Pawle, *The War and Colonel Warden: Based on the Recollections of Commander C. R. Thompson, C. M. G., O. B. E., R. N. (RET.), Personal Assistant to the Prime Minister 1940–1945* (New York: Alfred A. Knopf, 1963), 171.

67. "Meeting of the Combined Chiefs of Staff, 9:30 a.m.," 25 June 1942, document 284, in Aandahl, Franklin, and Slaney, *Foreign Relations of the United States*.

68. Mackenzie King diary, Diaries of William Lyon MacKenzie King, 25 June 1942, LAC.

69. King diary, 25 June 1942; meeting of the Pacific War Council, 12:30 p.m., "Memorandum by the President's Naval Aide (McCrea)," 25 June 1942, document 287, in Aandahl, Franklin, and Slaney, *Foreign Relations of the United States*.

70. Brooke diary, 26 June 1942, in Danchev and Todman, *War Diaries*, 272–73.

Chapter Seven

1. Vincent J. Esposito, *The West Point Atlas of American Wars*, vol. 2, *1900–1953* (New York: Praeger, 1972), section 2, pp. 30–32.

2. Gilbert, *Winston S. Churchill*, vol. 7, 137; Hayes, *History of the Joint Chiefs of Staff*, 141–42.

3. Cadogan diary, 21 June 1942, in *The Diaries of Sir Alexander Cadogan, 1938–1945*, ed. David Dilks (New York: G. P. Putnam's Sons, 1972), 458, 460.

4. Harold Nicholson diary, 1 July 1942, in Gilbert, *Churchill Documents*, vol. 17, 837–38; House of Commons debate, 2 July 1942, in Gilbert, *Churchill Documents*, vol. 17, 846–50; Gilbert, *Winston S. Churchill*, vol. 7, 137.

5. Harold Nicholson diary, 2 July 1942, in Gilbert, *Churchill Documents*, vol. 17, 910.

6. Moran, *Churchill*, 48; "Note by the Secretariat of the Combined Chiefs of Staff," 24 June 1942, document 304, in Aandahl, Franklin, and Slaney, *Foreign Relations of the United States*.

7. Chiefs of Staff, memorandum to prime minister, 2 July 1942, in Gilbert, *Churchill Documents*, vol. 17, 911.

8. Winston Churchill to Gen. Hastings Ismay, for the Chiefs of Staff Committee, 5 July 1942, in Gilbert, *Churchill Documents*, vol. 17, 922.

9. Churchill to Ismay, for the Chiefs of Staff Committee, 5 July 1942, 922.

10. Churchill to Ismay, for the Chiefs of Staff Committee, 5 July 1942, 922–23.

11. War Cabinet: Confidential Annex, 7 July 1942, in Gilbert, *Churchill Documents*, vol. 17, 931–32; Sir Alexander Cadogan diary, 7 July 1942, in Gilbert, *Churchill Documents*, vol. 17, 933; Brooke diary, 7 July 1942, in Danchev and Todman, *War Diaries*, 277.

12. War Cabinet: Confidential Annex, 7 July 1942, 931–32.
13. Dwight Eisenhower to George C. Marshall, 30 June and 7 July 1954, in Chandler and Ambrose, *Papers of Dwight David Eisenhower*, vol. 1, 366–67, 373–75.
14. Winston Churchill to Pres. Franklin D. Roosevelt, 8 July 1942, in Gilbert, *Churchill Documents*, vol. 17, 934.
15. Churchill to Roosevelt, 8 July 1942, 934.
16. From former naval person for the president, 8 July 1942, in Kimball, *Churchill and Roosevelt*, vol. 1, 523.
17. War Cabinet: Confidential Annex, 8 July 1942, and Churchill to Roosevelt, 8 July 1942, in Gilbert, *Churchill Documents*, vol. 17, 933–35.
18. Churchill to Roosevelt, 8 July 1942, 936.
19. Bland and Stevens, *Papers of George Catlett Marshall*, vol. 3, 269.
20. Franklin Roosevelt to Winston Churchill, 8 July 1942, in Kimball, *Churchill and Roosevelt*, vol. 1, 522–23.
21. Joint US Chiefs of Staff, 24th meeting, 10 July 1942, minutes of meeting held in Room 240, the Combined Chiefs of Staff building, on Friday, 10 July 1942, at 14:00, Records of the War Department General and Special Staffs, record group 165, American-British-Canadian Correspondence, entry 421, box 184, NARA; Chandler and Ambrose, *Papers of Dwight Davis Eisenhower*, vol. 1, 379.
22. Joint US Chiefs of Staff, 24th meeting, 10 July 1942, minutes; Guyer, "The War against Germany," chapter 3, "Development of Strategy between March and July 1942," p. 59.
23. Marshall and King, memorandum to the president, 10 July 1942, in Bland and Stevens, *Papers of George Catlett Marshall*, vol. 3, 269–70; Guyer, "The War against Germany," chapter 3, "Development of Strategy between March and July 1942," p. 60.
24. Marshall and King, memorandum to the president, 10 July 1942, 269–70; Guyer, "The War against Germany," chapter 3, p. 59.
25. George C. Marshall, memorandum for the president, "Latest British Proposals Relative to Bolero and Gymnast," 10 July 1942, in Bland and Stevens, *Papers of George Catlett Marshall*, vol. 3, 271.
26. Stimson diary, 10 July 1942, reel 7, vol. 39, Marshall Papers.
27. Stimson diary, 12 July 1942, reel 7, vol. 39, Marshall Papers; Dykes diary, 12 July 1942, in Danchev, *Establishing the Anglo-American Alliance*, 166–67.
28. Winston S. Churchill to Field Marshal Sir John Dill, 12 July 1942, in Gilbert, *Churchill Documents*, vol. 17, 945–46.
29. Memorandum for the president, "Subject: Pacific Operation," 12 July 1942, in Stimson diary, 12 July 1942, reel 7, vol. 39, Marshall Papers; Col. John R. Deane, memorandum for Admiral King, 12 July 1942, in Bland and Stevens, *Papers of George Catlett Marshall*, vol. 3, 272.
30. Memorandum for the president, "Subject: Pacific Operation," 12 July 1942, in Stimson diary, 12 July 1942, reel 7, vol. 39, Marshall Papers.
31. Stimson diary, 12 July 1942, reel 7, vol. 39, Marshall Papers.

32. FDR-76: FDR's draft memorandum to General Marshall, Admiral King, and General Arnold, pencil on blue paper, Small Collections: John L. McCrea Papers, FDR Library; File: drafts of FDR Memos to General Marshall, July 1942, Franklin D. Roosevelt, Papers as President: Significant Document Collection, FDR Library.

33. Buell, *Master of Sea Power*, 208.

34. Kimball, *Juggler*, 7.

35. Col. G. Donnelly interview with Adm. Ernest King, 23 March 1949, Ernest J. King Papers, LOC; Forrest Pogue, interview with George C. Marshall, 5 October 1956, in Bland, *George C. Marshall*, 602; Stimson and Bundy, *On Active Services in Peace and War*, 425; Hayes, *History of the Joint Chiefs of Staff*, 151.

36. Dykes diary, 12, 13, and 14 July 1942, in Danchev, *Establishing the Anglo-American Alliance*, 129, 167–68.

37. Dwight Eisenhower to George Catlett Marshall, 11 July 1942, in Chandler and Ambrose, *Papers of Dwight David Eisenhower*, vol. 1, 370–71.

38. Maj. Gen. Thomas Handy, "Memorandum for the Chief of Staff, 'Supreme Command,' 14 July 1942," Records of the War Department General and Special Staffs, record group 165, Miscellaneous Executive Office Files, entry 422, box 53, NARA.

39. George C. Marshall to Lt. Gen. Dwight Eisenhower, 13 July 1942, in Bland and Stevens, *Papers of George Catlett Marshall*, vol. 3, 273–74; Chandler and Ambrose, *Papers of Dwight David Eisenhower*, vol. 1, 381.

40. Winston S. Churchill to Pres. Franklin D. Roosevelt, 14 July 1942, in Gilbert, *Churchill Documents*, vol. 17, 956.

41. Stimson diary, 15 July 1942, reel 7, vol. 39, Marshall Papers.

42. Stimson diary, 15 July 1942; George C. Marshall, memorandum for Admiral King, 15 July 1942, in Bland and Stevens, *Papers of George Catlett Marshall*, vol. 3, 276.

43. Sherwood, *Roosevelt and Hopkins*, 602–3; Kimball, *Juggler*, 8, 73.

44. Franklin Roosevelt to Winston Churchill, 15 July 1942, and Winston Churchill to Franklin Roosevelt, 16 July 1942, in Kimball, *Churchill and Roosevelt*, vol. 1, 534–35.

45. "Memorandum for: Hon. Harry Hopkins, General Marshall, Admiral King. Subject: Instructions for London Conference—1942," 16 July 1942, in Sherwood, *Roosevelt and Hopkins*, 603–5.

46. Mark Stoler, *Allies and Adversaries: The Joint Chiefs of Staff, The Grand Alliance, and U.S. Strategy in World War II* (Chapel Hill: University of North Carolina Press, 2000), 86.

47. George C. Marshall to Dwight Eisenhower, Subject: Operations for This Year, 16 July 1942, Marshall Pentagon Papers, Marshall Papers; George C. Marshall to Dwight Eisenhower, 13 July 1942, cited in Chandler and Ambrose, *Papers of Dwight David Eisenhower*, vol. 1, 391.

48. Field Marshall Dill to Winston Churchill, 15 July 1942, in Wedemeyer, *Wedemeyer Reports*, 165–67; Gilbert, *Winston S. Churchill*, vol. 7, 148.

49. Dykes diary, 15 July 1942, in Danchev, *Establishing the Anglo-American Alliance*, 129.
50. Franklin Roosevelt to Winston Churchill, 16 July 1942, in Kimball, *Churchill and Roosevelt*, vol. 1, 536.
51. Pawle, *War and Colonel Warden*, 181; Sherwood, *Roosevelt and Hopkins*, 607.
52. Pawle, *War and Colonel Warden*, 181; Sherwood, *Roosevelt and Hopkins*, 607–8; Kimball, *Churchill and Roosevelt*, vol. 1, 536; Roll, *Hopkins Touch*, 213.
53. Stimson diary, 17 July 1942, reel 7, vol. 39, Marshall Papers.
54. Francis Harry Hinsley, *British Intelligence in the Second World War: Its Influence on Strategy and Operations*, vol. 2 (London: Her Majesty's Stationery Office, 1981), 101; Gilbert, *Winston S. Churchill*, vol. 7, 149.
55. Brooke diary, 17 July 1942, in Danchev and Todman, *War Diaries*, 281; Kennedy, *Business of War*, 257.
56. Brooke diary, 18 July 1942, in Danchev and Todman, *War Diaries*, 282; Chiefs of Staff Committee: Minutes, 18 July 1942, in Gilbert, *Churchill Documents*, vol. 17, 971–72; Gilbert, *Winston S. Churchill*, vol. 7, 150.
57. Eisenhower and the planners met with King and Marshall to review, edit, and revise this document on 19, 20, and 21 July. Eisenhower, memorandum, "Conclusions as to Practicality of Sledgehammer," 17 July 1942, and Eisenhower, memorandum to George C. Marshall and Ernest Joseph King, 19 and 21 July 1942, in Chandler and Ambrose, *Papers of Dwight David Eisenhower*, vol. 1, 388–96, 402–5.
58. Eisenhower, memorandum, "Conclusions as to Practicality of Sledgehammer," 388–96.
59. Eisenhower, memorandum, "Conclusions as to Practicality of Sledgehammer," 388–96.
60. Minutes of the Combined Chiefs of Staff Conference held at No. 10 Downing Street, S.W.I., on Monday, 20 July 1942, at 12:30 p.m., CAB 99/19, TNA.
61. Brooke diary, 20 July 1942, in Danchev and Todman, *War Diaries*, 282; Roll, *Hopkins Touch*, 213–14.
62. War Cabinet: Confidential Annex, 20 July 1942, 5:30 p.m., in Gilbert, *Churchill Documents*, vol. 17, 975–78.
63. Brooke diary, 21 July 1942, in Danchev and Todman, *War Diaries*, 283; Roll, *Hopkins Touch*, 214, 222.
64. Eisenhower diary, 22 July 1942, in Ferrell, *Eisenhower Diaries*, 72–73; Buell, *Master of Sea Power*, 211.
65. War Cabinet Minutes, Confidential Annex, 22 July 1942, CAB 65/31/6, TNA; Brooke diary, 22 July 1942, in Danchev and Todman, *War Diaries*, 283–84.
66. Minutes of the Combined Chiefs of Staff Conference, held at No. 10 Downing Street, S.W.I., on Wednesday, 22 July 1942, at 3:00p.m., CAB 99/19, TNA.

67. Dykes diary, 22 July 1942, in Danchev, *Establishing the Anglo-American Alliance*, 178–79; Butcher diary, 22 July 1942, in *My Three Years with Eisenhower*, by Harry Butcher (New York: Simon and Schuster, 1946), 29; Dwight Eisenhower, *Crusade in Europe* (Garden City, NY: Doubleday, 1949), 71.

68. Sherwood, *Roosevelt and Hopkins*, 610.

69. Memorandum for George Catlett Marshall, "Survey of Strategic Situation," 23 July 1942, in Chandler and Ambrose, *Papers of Dwight David Eisenhower*, vol. 1, 407–13; Pogue interview with George C. Marshall, 28 September 1956, in Bland and Stevens, *Papers of George Catlett Marshall*, vol. 3, 278.

70. Combined Chiefs of Staff, minutes of meeting held in Conference Room B, War Cabinet Offices, Great George Street, London, on Friday, 24 July 1942, at 12 noon, and Combined Chiefs of Staff, operations in 1942/43, memorandum by the Combined Chiefs of Staff, 24 July 1942 (CCS 94), CAB 99/21, TNA.

71. Combined Chiefs of Staff, minutes of meeting held in Conference Room B, on Friday, 24 July 1942.

72. Combined Chiefs of Staff, minutes of meeting held in Conference Room B, on Friday, 24 July 1942, at 12 noon.

73. Brooke diary, 24 July 1942, in Danchev and Todman, *War Diaries*, 284–85; Winston Churchill to Hastings Ismay for the Chiefs of Staff Committee, 23 July 1942, in Gilbert, *Churchill Documents*, vol. 17, 986–87; Michael Howard, *Grand Strategy*, vol. 4 (London: Her Majesty's Stationery Office, 1970), xxiv.

74. Brooke diary, 24 July 1942, in Danchev and Todman, *War Diaries*, 284–85; Admiral King, comments on chapter 6 of the Joint History Office Study *The War Against Japan*, 22 June 1949, in the Ernest J. King Papers, LOC; Stoler, *Allies and Adversaries*, 90; "Memorandum by the United States and British Chiefs of Staff," 31 December 1941, document 115, in Aandahl, Franklin, and Slaney, *Foreign Relations of the United States*.

75. Sherwood, *Roosevelt and Hopkins*, 611; Stoler, *Allies and Adversaries*, 90; Matloff and Snell, *Strategic Planning for Coalition Warfare*, 282.

76. Matloff and Snell, *Strategic Planning for Coalition Warfare*, 282; Guyer, "The War against Germany," chapter 3, "Development of Strategy between March and July 1942," p. 73; Chandler and Ambrose, *Papers of Dwight David Eisenhower*, vol. 1, 418.

77. Combined Chiefs of Staff, minutes of meeting held in Conference Room B, War Cabinet Offices, London, on Saturday, 25 July 1942, at 10:30 a.m., CAB 99/21, TNA; Chandler and Ambrose, *Papers of Dwight David Eisenhower*, vol. 1, 418–19.

78. Extract from minutes, CCS 34th meeting, 30 July 1942, item 3, Records of the War Department General and Special Staffs, record group 165, American-British-Canadian Correspondence, entry 421, box 321, NARA; Guyer, "The War against Germany," chapter 3, "Development of Strategy between March and July 1942," pp. 73–76; Winston Churchill to Franklin D.

Roosevelt, 30 July 1942, in Gilbert, *Churchill Documents*, vol. 17, 1018; Matloff and Snell, *Strategic Planning for Coalition Warfare*, 282–83; Dykes diary, 30 July 1942, in Danchev, *Establishing the Anglo-American Alliance*, 183.

79. Winston Churchill to Franklin Roosevelt, 31 July 1942, in Gilbert, *Churchill Documents*, vol. 17, 1022; Field Marshal John Dill to Winston Churchill, 1 August 1942, in Churchill, *Hinge of Fate*, 450–51.

80. Leo Meyer, "The Decision to Invade North Africa (Torch)," in *Command Decisions*, ed. Kent Roberts Greenfield (Washington, DC: US Army Center of Military History, 1960), 188.

81. Harrison, *Cross-Channel Attack*, 32–33.

Chapter Eight

1. Louis Morton, "Germany First: The Basic Concept of Allied Strategy in World War II," in Greenfield, *Command Decisions*, 11.

2. Meyer, "The Decision to Invade North Africa (Torch)," in Greenfield, *Command Decisions*, 175.

3. Winston Churchill to Franklin Roosevelt, 27 July 1942, in Gilbert, *Churchill Documents*, vol. 17, 1002–3; Churchill, *Hinge of Fate*, 447.

4. Dykes diary, 3 September 1942, in Danchev, *Establishing the Anglo-American Alliance*, 198–99.

5. Winston Churchill to Gen. Claude Auchinleck, 27 July 1942, and War Cabinet: Confidential Report, 1 August 1942, in Gilbert, *Churchill Documents*, vol. 17, 1006, 1026; Howard, *Grand Strategy*, vol. 4, 51.

6. Churchill, *Hinge of Fate*, 458–61; Winston Churchill to Clement Atlee, 6 August 1942, in Gilbert, *Churchill Documents*, vol. 17, 1041–42.

7. Quotation in Churchill, *Hinge of Fate*, 475, 478–79; Josef Stalin to Winston S. Churchill, aide memoire, 13 August 1942, and Josef Stalin to Winston S. Churchill, 14 August 1942, in Gilbert, *Churchill Documents*, vol. 17, 1069, 1077–78; Averell Harriman to Franklin Roosevelt, 14 August 1942, in the W. Averell Harriman Papers, box 162, LOC.

8. Winston S. Churchill to Clement Atlee, 16 August 1942, and Winston Churchill to members of the War Cabinet and Pres. Franklin Roosevelt, 16 August 1942, in Gilbert, *Churchill Documents*, vol. 17, 1084–88.

9. Winston Churchill to Franklin Roosevelt, 22 August 1942, in Churchill, *Hinge of Fate*, 513.

10. Churchill, *Hinge of Fate*, 515–17.

11. Hinsley, *British Intelligence in the Second World War*, vol. 2, 695–704; quotation in J. L Granatstein and Dean F. Oliver, *The Oxford Companion to Canadian Military History* (Don Mills, Ontario: Oxford University Press, 2011), 152.

12. Howard, *Grand Strategy*, vol. 4, 87–88; Spector, *Eagle against the Sun*, 186–87.

13. Buell, *Master of Sea Power*, 219–24; Burns, *Roosevelt: The Soldier of Freedom*, 283–84.

NOTES TO PAGES 192–199

14. Rick Atkinson, *An Army at Dawn: The War in North Africa, 1942–1943* (New York: Henry Holt, 2002), 16.

15. Stimson diary, 25 July 1942, and "Memorandum for the President, My Views as to the Proposals in Message 625," 25 July 1942, reel 7, vol. 39, Marshall Papers.

16. "Memorandum to Go with Memorandum from the Secretary of War, Dated 25 July 1942, in Relation to Proposals in Message 625 from Marshall and King in London," 29 July 1942, in Franklin D. Roosevelt, Papers as President; President's Secretary's Files, 1933–1945, Safe Files, series 1, box 4, Marshall, 15 April 42–44, FDR Library.

17. Stimson diary, 7 August 1942, reel 7, vol. 40, Marshall Papers; Morison, *Turmoil and Tradition*, 426.

18. Stimson diary, 9 August 1942, reel 7, vol. 40, Marshall Papers.

19. Stimson diary, 10 August 1942, reel 7, vol. 40, Marshall Papers.

20. Stimson diary, 10 August 1942.

21. Stimson diary, 11 August 1942, reel 7, vol. 40, Marshall Papers.

22. Dykes diary 3, 4, 6, and 7 August 1942, in Danchev, *Establishing the Anglo-American Alliance*, 185–86.

23. Field Marshal Sir John Dill to George C. Marshall, 8 August 1942, in Bland and Stevens, *Papers of George Catlett Marshall*, vol. 3, 303–4.

24. Field Marshal Sir John Dill to George C. Marshall, 8 August 1942, in Bland and Stevens, *Papers of George Catlett Marshall*, vol. 3, 303–4; "Memorandum by the United States and British Chiefs of Staff," 31 December 1941, document 115, in Aandahl, Franklin, and Slaney, *Foreign Relations of the United States*; Matloff and Snell, *Strategic Planning for Coalition Warfare*, 295–96.

25. George C. Marshall to Field Marshal Sir John Dill, 14 August 1942, in Bland and Stevens, *Papers of George Catlett Marshall*, vol. 3, 302–3.

26. Dykes diary, 10, 12 and 14 August 1942, in Danchev, *Establishing the Anglo-American Alliance*, 187–89.

27. Matloff and Snell, *Strategic Planning for Coalition Warfare*, 296–97.

28. Meyer, "The Decision to Invade North Africa (Torch)," in Greenfield, *Command Decisions*, 188.

29. Harry Butcher diary, 31 July 1942, in Butcher, *My Three Years with Eisenhower*, 37; Crosswell, *Beetle*, 279; Howard, *Grand Strategy*, vol. 4, 112; Meyer, "The Decision to Invade North Africa (Torch)," in Greenfield, *Command Decisions*, 188.

30. Dwight Eisenhower to George C. Marshall, 1 August 1942, in Chandler and Ambrose, *Papers of Dwight David Eisenhower*, vol. 1, 433; Meyer, "The Decision to Invade North Africa (Torch)," in Greenfield, *Command Decisions*, 189.

31. Quotation in Dykes diary, 6 August 1942, in Danchev, *Establishing the Anglo-American Alliance*, 186; Butcher diary, 2 September 1942, in Butcher, *My Three Years with Eisenhower*, 82–83; Howard, *Grand Strategy*, vol. 4, 120.

32. Howard, *Grand Strategy*, vol. 4, 127.

33. Quotation in Dykes diary, 22 August 1942, in Danchev, *Establishing*

the Anglo-American Alliance, 192; Bland and Stevens, *Papers of George Catlett Marshall*, vol. 3, 319; Meyer, "The Decision to Invade North Africa (Torch)," in Greenfield, *Command Decisions*, 190.

34. Dwight Eisenhower to the Combined Chiefs of Staff, 23 August 1942, in Chandler and Ambrose, *Papers of Dwight David Eisenhower*, vol. 1, 488–89.

35. George C. Marshall to Lt. Gen. Dwight D. Eisenhower, 25 August 1942, in Bland and Stevens, *Papers of George Catlett Marshall*, vol. 3, 318; Dykes diary, 25 August 1942, in Danchev, *Establishing the Anglo-American Alliance*, 193.

36. Churchill, *Hinge of Fate*, 529; Howard, *Grand Strategy*, vol. 4, 124.

37. Howard, *Grand Strategy*, vol. 4, 125.

38. Dwight Eisenhower to George C. Marshall, 26 August 1942, in Chandler and Ambrose, *Papers of Dwight David Eisenhower*, vol. 1, 499–501.

39. Winston Churchill to Franklin Roosevelt, 27 and 30 August and 1 September 1942, in Gilbert, *Churchill Documents*, vol. 17, 1124–25, 1133–35, 1140; Franklin Roosevelt to Winston Churchill, 30 August 1942, in Gilbert, *Churchill Documents*, vol. 17, 1131–32.

40. Dykes diary, 3–4 September 1942, in Danchev, *Establishing the Anglo-American Alliance*, 199; Franklin Roosevelt to Winston Churchill, 3 September 1942, in Gilbert, *Churchill Documents*, vol. 17, 1147–49; Franklin Roosevelt to Winston Churchill, 4 September 1942, in Kimball, *Churchill and Roosevelt*, vol. 1, 591; Crosswell, *Beetle*, 283.

41. Quotation from Ismay, *Memoirs of General Lord Ismay*, 262; Hinsley, *British Intelligence in the Second World War*, vol. 2, 465, 473–74, 478.

42. Churchill, *Hinge of Fate*, 589–603; Howard, *Grand Strategy*, vol. 4, 206.

43. Dykes diary, 7–11 November 1942, in Danchev, *Establishing the Anglo-American Alliance*, 223–25; Howard, *Grand Strategy*, vol. 4, 136; John Whiteclay Chambers, ed., *American Military History* (New York: Oxford University Press, 1999), 506.

44. Quotation in Dwight Eisenhower to George C. Marshall, 21 September 1942, in Chandler and Ambrose, *Papers of Dwight David Eisenhower*, vol. 1, 570–72; Howard, *Grand Strategy*, vol. 4, 195; Matloff and Snell, *Strategic Planning for Coalition Warfare*, 325–27.

45. Winston Churchill to Franklin Roosevelt, 22 September 1942, in Gilbert, *Churchill Documents*, vol. 17, 1224–26; Howard, *Grand Strategy*, vol. 4, 208.

46. Winston Churchill to Gen. Hastings Ismay for the Chiefs of Staff Committee, 28 September 1942, and Winston Churchill to Franklin Roosevelt, 4 October 1942, in Gilbert, *Churchill Documents*, vol. 17, 1236, 1247–48; Kimball, *Churchill and Roosevelt*, vol. 1, 614.

47. Franklin Roosevelt to Winston Churchill, 12 October 1942, in Kimball, *Churchill and Roosevelt*, vol. 1, 631–32.

48. Winston S. Churchill to Gen. Hastings Ismay, 18 November 1942, and Winston S. Churchill to Franklin Roosevelt, 24 November 1942, in Gilbert, *Churchill Documents*, vol. 17, 1419–20, 1432–33.

49. Franklin Roosevelt to Winston Churchill, 26 November 1942, in Gilbert, *Churchill Documents*, vol. 17, 1142–43; Matloff and Snell, *Strategic Planning for Coalition Warfare*, 327.

50. Churchill, *Hinge of Fate*, 659; Josef Stalin to Winston Churchill, 27 November 1942 and 6 December 1942, in Gilbert, *Churchill Documents*, vol. 17, 1446–47, 1488–89.

51. Howard, *Grand Strategy*, vol. 4, 219–21, 242–43; Forrest Pogue interview with George C. Marshall, 5 October 1956, in Bland, *George C. Marshall*, 601–2.

52. Stoler, *Allies in War*, 71; Ismay, *The Memoirs of General Lord Ismay*, 297–98.

53. Dykes diary, 3 September 1942, in Danchev, *Establishing the Anglo-American Alliance*, 199.

SELECT BIBLIOGRAPHY

Aandahl, Fredrick, William M. Franklin, and William Slany, eds. *Foreign Relations of the United States: The Conferences at Washington, 1941–1942, and Casablanca, 1943*. Washington, DC: US Government Printing Office, 1958. https://history.state.gov/historicaldocuments/frus1941-43.

Aldrich, Edward. *The Partnership: George Marshall, Henry Stimson, and the Extraordinary Collaboration That Won World War II*. Guilford, CT: Stackpole Books, 2022.

Ambrose, Stephen. *Eisenhower: Soldier, General of the Army, President-Elect, 1890–1952*. New York: Touchstone Books, 1983.

Arnold, Henry. *American Airpower Comes of Age: General Henry H. "Hap" Arnold's World War II Diaries*. Edited by John Huston. Maxwell Air Force Base, AL: Air University Press, 2002.

———. *Global Mission*. New York: Harper and Brothers, 1949.

Atkinson, Rick. *An Army at Dawn: The War in North Africa, 1942–1943*. New York: Henry Holt, 2002.

Barnett, Correlli. *The Audit of War: The Illusion and Reality of Britain as a Great Nation*. London: Faber and Faber, 2011.

———. *The Collapse of British Power*. London: Faber and Faber, 1972.

———. *The Desert Generals*. New York: Viking, 1961.

Bland, Larry, ed. *George C. Marshall: Interviews and Reminiscences for Forrest C. Pogue*. Lexington, VA: George C. Marshall Foundation, 1996.

Bland, Larry, and Sharon Ritenour Stevens, eds. *The Papers of George Catlett Marshall*. Vol. 3, "The Right Man for the Job," December 7, 1942–May 31, 1943. Baltimore, MD: Johns Hopkins University Press, 1991.

Brand, H. W. *Traitor to His Class: The Privileged Life and Radical Presidency of Franklin Delano Roosevelt*. New York: Doubleday, 2008.

Bryant, Arthur. *The Turn of the Tide, 1939–1943: A History of the War Years Based on the Diaries of Field Marshal Lord Alanbrooke, Chief of the Imperial General Staff*. Garden City, NY: Doubleday, 1957.

Buell, Thomas. *Master of Sea Power: A Biography of Admiral of the Fleet Ernest J. King*. Boston: Little, Brown, 1980.

Burns, James MacGregor. *Roosevelt: The Soldier of Freedom*. New York: Harcourt Brace Jovanovich, 1970.

Butcher, Harry. *My Three Years with Eisenhower: The Personal Diary of Captain Harry C. Butcher, USNR Naval Aide to General Eisenhower, 1942 to 1945.* New York: Simon and Schuster, 1946.
Butler, James Ramsay Montagu. *Grand Strategy.* Vol. 3, *June 1941–August 1942*, part 2. London: Her Majesty's Stationery Office, 1964.
Callahan, Raymond. *Churchill and His Generals.* Lawrence: University Press of Kansas, 2007.
———. *Triumph at Imphal-Kohima: How the Indian Army Finally Stopped the Japanese Juggernaut.* Lawrence: University Press of Kansas, 2017.
———. *The Worst Disaster: The Fall of Singapore.* Newark: University of Delaware Press, 1977.
Callahan, Raymond, and Daniel Marston. *The 1945 Burma Campaign and the Transformation of the British Indian Army.* Lawrence: University Press of Kansas, 2020.
Chandler, Alfred, and Stephen Ambrose, eds. *The Papers of Dwight David Eisenhower: The War Years.* Vol. 1. Baltimore: Johns Hopkins University Press, 1988.
Charmley, John. *Churchill's Grand Alliance: The Anglo-American Special Relationship, 1940–57.* New York: Harcourt, Brace, 1995.
———. *Churchill: The End of Glory.* London: Hodder and Stoughton, 1993.
Churchill, Winston. *Closing the Ring.* Boston: Houghton Mifflin, 1951.
———. *The Grand Alliance.* Boston: Houghton Mifflin, 1950.
———. *The Hinge of Fate.* Boston: Houghton Mifflin, 1951.
———. *Their Finest Hour.* Boston: Houghton Mifflin, 1949.
Cline, Ray. *Washington Command Post: The Operations Division.* Washington, DC: US Army Center of Military History, 1990.
Connell, John. *Wavell: Supreme Commander, 1941–1943.* London: Collins, 1969.
Conroy, James. *The Devils Will Get No Rest: FDR, Churchill, and the Plan That Won the War.* New York: Simon and Schuster, 2023.
Coville, John. *Winston Churchill and His Inner Circle.* New York: Wyndham Books, 1981.
Crosswell, D. K. R. *Beetle: The Life of General Walter Bedell Smith.* Lexington: University of Kentucky Press, 2010.
Dallek, Robert. *Franklin D. Roosevelt: A Political Life.* New York: Viking, 2017.
Danchev, Alex. *Establishing the Anglo-American Alliance: The Second World War Diaries of Brigadier Vivian Dykes.* London: Brassey's, 1991.
———. *Very Special Relationship: Field Marshal Sir John Dill and the Anglo-American Alliance, 1941–44.* London: Brassey's, 1986.
Danchev, Alex, and Daniel Todman, eds. *War Diaries, 1939–1945: Field Marshal Lord Alanbrooke.* Berkeley: University of California Press, 2001.
Davis, Vernon. *The History of the Joint Chiefs of Staff in World War II.* Washington, DC: United States Department of Defense, 1972.
D'Este, Carlo. *Warlord: A Life of Winston Churchill at War, 1874–1945.* New York: Harper, 2008.

Dilks, David, ed. *The Diaries of Sir Alexander Cadogan, 1938–1945*. New York: G. P. Putnam's Sons, 1972.
Dimbleby, David, and David Reynolds. *An Ocean Apart: The Relationship between Britain and America in the Twentieth Century*. London: Hodder and Stoughton, 1988.
Dower, John. *War without Mercy: Race and Power in the Pacific War*. New York: Pantheon Books, 1986.
Drea, Edward. *Japan's Imperial Army: Its Rise and Fall, 1853–1945*. Lawrence: University Press of Kansas, 2009.
Eisenhower, Dwight. *Crusade in Europe*. Garden City, NY: Doubleday, 1949.
Esposito, Vincent. *The West Point Atlas of American Wars*. Vol. 2, *1900–1953*. New York: Praeger, 1972.
Farrell, Brian. *The Defense and Fall of Singapore, 1940–1942*. Singapore: Monsoon Books, 2017.
Feis, Herbert. *The China Tangle: The American Effort in China from Pearl Harbor to the Marshall Mission*. Princeton: Princeton University Press, 1953.
———. *Churchill–Roosevelt–Stalin: The War They Waged and the Peace They Sought*. Princeton: Princeton University Press, 1967.
Ferreiro, Larrie. *Churchill's American Arsenal: The Partnership behind the Innovations That Won World War Two*. New York: Oxford University Press, 2023.
Ferrell, Robert, ed. *The Eisenhower Diaries*. New York: W. W. Norton, 1981.
Fraser, David. *Alanbrooke*. New York: Athenaeum, 1982.
Gilbert, Martin. *Churchill: A Life*. New York: Henry Holt, 1991.
———. *The Churchill Documents*. Vol. 17, *Testing Times, 1942*. Hillsdale, MI: Hillsdale College Press, 2014.
———. *The Churchill War Papers*, Vol. 3, *The Ever-Widening War, 1941*. New York: W. W. Norton, 2000.
———. *Winston S. Churchill*. Vol. 7, *Road to Victory, 1941–1945*. Hillsdale, MI: Hillsdale College Press, 1986.
Granatstein, J. L., and Dean Oliver. *The Oxford Companion to Canadian Military History*. Don Mills, Ontario: Oxford University Press, 2011.
Greenfield, Kent Roberts, ed. *Command Decisions*. Washington, DC: US Army Center of Military History, 1990.
Guyer, Lawrence. "History of the Joint Chiefs of Staff: The War against Germany and Her Satellites." Unpublished manuscript, record group 218, entry UD 299, box 6, stack 190, row 2, National Archives and Research Archives, College Park, MD.
Gwyer, J. M. A. *Grand Strategy*. Vol. 3, *June 1941–August 1942*, part 1. London: Her Majesty's Stationery Office, 1964.
Hamilton, Nigel. *The Mantle of Command: FDR at War, 1941–1942*. Boston: Houghton Mifflin, 2014.
Harries, Merion, and Susie Harries. *Soldiers of the Sun: The Rise and Fall of the Imperial Japanese Army*. New York: Random House, 1991.

Harriman, Averell, and Elie Abel. *Special Envoy to Churchill and Stalin, 1941–1946*. New York: Random House, 1975.

Harrison, Gordon: *Cross-Channel Attack*. Washington, DC: US Army Center of Military History, 2007.

Hassett, William. *Off the Record with FDR, 1942–1945*. New York: Enigma Books, 2016.

Hastings, Max. *Winston's War: Churchill, 1940–1945*. New York: Alfred A. Knopf, 2010.

Hayes, Grace. *The History of the Joint Chiefs of Staff in World War II: The War against Japan*. Annapolis, MD: Naval Institute Press, 1982.

Heinrichs, Waldo. *Threshold of War: Franklin D. Roosevelt and American Entry into World War II*. New York: Oxford University Press, 1988.

Heinrichs, Waldo, and Mark Gallicchio. *Implacable Foes: The War in the Pacific, 1944–1945*. New York: Oxford University Press, 2017.

Herman, Arthur. *Freedom's Forge*. New York: Random House, 2012.

Hinsley, Francis Harry. *British Intelligence in the Second World War: Its Influence on Strategy and Operations*. Vol. 2. London: Her Majesty's Stationery Office, 1981.

Howard, Michael. *Grand Strategy*. Vol. 4, *August 1942–September 1943*. London: Her Majesty's Stationery Office, 1970.

Howe, George. *Northwest Africa: Seizing the Initiative in the West*. Washington, DC: US Army Center for Military History, 2002.

Huston, John. *American Airpower Comes of Age: General Henry H. "Hap" Arnold World War II Diaries*. Vol. 1. Maxwell Air Force Base: Air University Press, 2002.

Iriye, Akira. *Across the Pacific: An Inner History of American-East Asian Relations*. New York: Harcourt Brace Jovanovich, 1967.

Ismay, General Lord Hastings. *The Memoirs of General Lord Ismay*. New York: Viking, 1960.

James, D. Clayton. *The Years of MacArthur*. Vol. 2, *1941–1945*. New York: Houghton Mifflin, 1975.

Johnsen, William. *The Origins of the Grand Alliance: Anglo-American Military Collaboration from the Panay Incident to Pearl Harbor*. Lexington: University of Kentucky Press, 2016.

Jordan, Jonathan. *American Warlords: How Roosevelt's High Command Led America to Victory in World War II*. New York: Nal Caliber, 2016.

Kagan, Robert. *The Ghost at the Feast: America and the Collapse of World Order, 1900–1941*. New York: Alfred A. Knopf, 2023.

Keegan, John. *Churchill's Generals*. New York: William Morrow, 1991.

Kennedy, David. *Freedom from Fear: The American People in Depression and War, 1929–1945*. New York: Oxford University Press, 1999.

Kennedy, John. *The Business of War: The War Narrative of Major General Sir John Kennedy G. S. M. G., K. C. V. O., K. B. E., C. B., M. C*. New York: William Morrow, 1958.

Kimball, Warren, ed. *Churchill and Roosevelt: The Complete Correspondence.* Vol. 1, *Alliance Emerging, October 1933–November 1942.* Princeton: Princeton Legacy Library, 2008.

———. *The Juggler: Franklin Roosevelt as Wartime Statesman.* Princeton: Princeton University Press, 1991.

King, Ernest J., and Walter Muir Whitehill. *Fleet Admiral King: A Naval Record.* New York: W. W. Norton, 1952.

Kirby, Stanley Woodburn. *The War against Japan.* Vol. 2, *India's Most Dangerous Hour.* Uckfield: Naval and Military Press, 2004.

———. *The War against Japan.* Vol. 1, *The Loss of Singapore.* Uckfield: Naval and Military Press, 2004.

Lacey, James. *The Washington War: FDR's Inner Circle and the Politics of Power That Won World War II.* New York: Bantom Books, 2019.

Larrabee, Eric. *Commander in Chief: Franklin Delano Roosevelt, His Lieutenants, and Their War.* New York: Harper and Row, 1987.

Leahy, William. *I Was There.* New York: Whittlesey House, 1950.

Leasor, James. *War at the Top: Based on the Experiences of General Sir Leslie Hollis K. C. B., K. B. E.* London: Michael Joseph, 1959.

Leighton, Richard, and Robert W. Coakley. *Global Logistics and Strategy, 1940–1943.* Washington, DC: US Army Center of Military History, 1995.

Lewin, Ronald. *The Chief: Field Marshal Lord Wavell, Commander-in-Chief and Viceroy, 1939–1947.* New York: Farrar, Straus, Giroux, 1980.

Lochner, Louis, ed. *The Goebbels Diaries, 1942–1943.* New York: Doubleday, 1948.

MacDonald, Charles. *The Mighty Endeavor: American Armed Forces in the European Theater in World War II.* New York: Oxford University Press, 1969.

Manchester, William, and Paul Reid. *The Last Lion: Winston Spencer Churchill, Defender of the Realm, 1940–1965.* New York: Little, Brown, 2012.

Matloff, Maurice, and Edwin Snell. *Strategic Planning for Coalition Warfare, 1941–1942.* Washington, DC: US Army Center of Military History, 1999.

McCarthy, Dudley. *South-West Pacific Area—First Year: Kokoda to Wau.*

McCrea, John. *Captain McCrea's War: The World War II Memoir of Franklin D. Roosevelt's Naval Aide and USS Iowa's First Commanding Officer.* New York: Skyhorse, 2016.

Meacham, Jon. *Franklin and Winston: An Intimate Portrait of an Epic Friendship.* New York: Random House, 2003.

Miller, Henry. *The Reminiscences of Rear Admiral Henry L. Miller, USN (Ret).* Annapolis, MD: US Naval Institute, 1973.

Miller, Merle. *Ike the Soldier: As They Knew Him.* New York: G. P. Putnam's Sons, 1987.

Montgomery, Bernard Law. *The Memoirs of Field Marshal the Viscount Montgomery of Alamein.* London: Collins, 1958.

Moran (Charles Wilson), Lord. *Churchill: Taken from the Diaries of Lord*

Moran; *The Struggle for Survival, 1945–1960*. Boston: Houghton Mifflin, 1966.

Morison, Elting. *Turmoil and Tradition: A Study of the Life and Times of Henry L. Stimson*. New York: History Book Club, 2003.

Morison, Samuel Eliot. *Coral Sea, Midway and Submarine Actions, May 1942–August 1942*. Annapolis, Maryland: Naval Institute Press, 2010.

———. *The Two Ocean War: A History of the United States Navy in the Second World War*. New York: Little, Brown, 1963.

Morton, Louis. *The Fall of the Philippines*. Washington, DC: US Army Center of Military History, 1985.

———. *Strategy and Command: The First Two Years*. Washington, DC: U.S. Government Printing Office, 1962.

Noble, G. Bernard, and E. R. Perkins, eds. *Foreign Relations of the United States: Diplomatic Papers, 1942, Europe*. Vol. 2. Washington, DC: US Government Printing Office, 1962. https://history.state.gov/historicaldocuments/frus1942v03.

Pawle, Gerald. *The War and Colonel Warden: Based on the Recollections of Commander C. R. Thompson C. M. G., O. B. E., R. N. (Ret.), Personal Assistant to the Prime Minister, 1940–1945*. New York: Alfred A. Knopf, 1963.

Peattie, Mark, Edward Drea, and Hans Van de Ven, eds. *The Battle for China: Essays on the Military History of the Sino-Japanese War of 1937–1945*. Stanford: Stanford University Press, 2011.

Perret, Geoffrey. *Old Soldiers Never Die: The Life of Douglas MacArthur*. New York: Random House, 1996.

Pershing, John. *My Experiences in the World War*. Charleston, SC: Arcadia Press, 2019.

Playfair, Ian Stanley. *The Mediterranean and Middle East*. Vol. 3, *British Fortunes Reach Their Lowest Ebb*. Uckfield: Naval and Military Press, 2004.

Pogue, Forrest. *George C. Marshall: Ordeal and Hope, 1939–1942*. New York: Viking, 1967.

Prados, John. *Combined Fleet Decoded: The Secret History of American Intelligence and the Japanese Navy in World War II*. New York: Random House, 1995.

Rearden, Steven. *Council of War: A History of the Joint Chiefs of Staff, 1942–1991*. Washington, DC: National Defense University Press, 2012.

Reynolds, David. *In Command of History*. New York: Random House, 2005.

Richards, Denis. *Portal of Hungerford: The Life of Marshal of the Royal Air Force Viscount Portal of Hungerford*. London: Heinemann, 1977.

Richardson, Charles. *From Churchill's Secret Circle to the BBC: The Biography of Lieutenant General Sir Ian Jacob, GBE CD DL*. London: Brassey's, 1991.

Roberts, Andrew. *Churchill: Walking with Destiny*. New York: Viking, 2018.

———. *Masters and Commanders: How Four Titans Won the War in the West, 1941–1945*. New York: Harper, 2009.

Roll, David. *George C. Marshall: Defender of the Republic*. New York: Dutton Caliber, 2019.
———. *The Hopkins Touch: Harry Hopkins and the Forging of the Alliance to Defeat Hitler*. Oxford: Oxford University Press, 2013.
Roosevelt, Elliott. *As He Saw It*. New York: Duell, Sloan and Pierce, 1946.
Sangster, Andrew. *Alan Brooke: Churchill's Right-Hand Critic*. Oxford: Casemate, 2021.
Schnabel, James. *History of the Joint Chiefs of Staff*. Vol. 1: *The Joint Chiefs of Staff and National Policy, 1945–1947*. Washington, DC: U.S. Government Printing Office, 1996.
Schofield, Victoria. *Wavell: Soldier and Statesman*. London: John Murray, 2006.
Sherwood, Robert. *Roosevelt and Hopkins: An Intimate History*. New York: Harper and Brothers, 1948.
Shortal, John. *Code Name Arcadia*. College Station: Texas A&M Press, 2021.
Slim, William. *Defeat into Victory*. London: Macmillan, 1956.
Smith, Jean. *FDR*. New York: Random House, 2007.
Smith, Michael. *The Emperor's Codes*. New York: Arcade, 2011.
Spector, Ronald. *Eagle against the Sun*. New York: Vintage, 1985.
Stimson, Henry, and McGeorge Bundy. *On Active Services in Peace and War*. New York: Harper and Brothers, 1947.
Stokesbury, James. *A Short History of World War II*. New York: William Morrow, 1980.
Stoler, Mark. *Allies and Adversaries: The Joint Chiefs of Staff, the Grand Alliance, and U.S. Strategy in World War II*. Chapel Hill: University of North Carolina Press, 2000.
———. *Allies in War: Britain and America against the Axis Powers, 1940–1945*. London: Hodder Arnold, 2005.
———. *George C. Marshall: Soldier-Statesman of the American Century*. Boston: Twayne, 1989.
———. *The Politics of the Second Front: American Military Planning and Diplomacy in Coalition Warfare, 1941–1943*. Westport, CT: Greenwood, 1977.
Strachan, Hew. *The Politics of the British Army*. Oxford: Clarendon, 1997.
Thomas, Evan. *Sea of Thunder*. New York: Simon and Schuster, 2006.
Thompson, Neville. *The Third Man: Churchill, Roosevelt, MacKenzie King, and the Untold Friendships That Won WWII*. Toronto: Sutherland House, 2021.
Thorne, Christopher. *Allies of a Kind: The United States, Britain and the War against Japan, 1941–1945*. New York: Oxford University Press, 1978.
Todman, Daniel. *Britain's War: A New World, 1942–1947*. Oxford: Oxford University Press, 2020.
———. *Britain's War: Into Battle, 1937–1941*. Oxford: Oxford University Press, 2016.
Toll, Ian. *The Conquering Tide: War in the Pacific Islands, 1942–1944*. New York: W. W. Norton, 2015.

———. *Pacific Crucible: War at Sea in the Pacific, 1941–1942*. New York: WW Norton, 2012.
Tuchman, Barbara. *Stilwell and the American Experience in China, 1941–1945*. New York: Macmillan, 1971.
Warner, Philip. *Auchinleck: The Lonely Soldier*. Barnsley: Pen and Sword Military, 2006.
Wedemeyer, Albert. *Wedemeyer Reports*. New York: Henry Holt, 1958.
Weigley, Russell. *The American Way of War: A History of United States Military Strategy and Policy*. Bloomington: Indiana University Press, 1973.
White, Theodore, ed. *The Stilwell Papers*. New York: Da Capo, 1991.
Whitman, John. *Bataan: Our Last Ditch*. New York: Hippocrene Books, 1990.
Williams, Mary. *Chronology: 1941–1945; U.S. Army in World War II*. Washington, DC: US Army Center of Military History, 1989.
Willmott, H. P. *Empires in the Balance*. Annapolis, MD: Naval Institute Press, 1982.
Woodward, Llewellyn. *British Foreign Policy in the Second World War*. Vol. 2. London: Her Majesty's Stationery Office, 1971.

INDEX

Page numbers in italics refer to images

ABC-1 (American and British Conversations), 10, 11–12
ABDA (American-British-Dutch-Australian) Command, 55–58
aircraft carriers, 198–99
aircraft production, 17, 28–29, 92
air operations, for European invasion: Bolero plan, 90–91, 116, 139; Churchill's demands for, 203; in Churchill's Jupiter plan, 134; in Churchill's Viceroy plan, 135; JUSSC plan, 83; in Marshall Memorandum, 90–91, 92, 100; redeployment to Pacific theater, 180; Roundup plan, 91, 123; Sledgehammer discussions, 100, 103–104, 174; Soviet Union pressures, 120–21
air operations, North Africa, 98, 151, 204
air operations, Pacific theater: attack on Japan, 98, 110–11, 126; for Australia, 112, 116; and Bolero cancellation possibility, 164; demands/requests for, 58, 60, 69, 74; King's request for, 114, 116; Malay Peninsula neglect, 40; in Marshall Memorandum, 90–91, 92, 93; redeployment from Britain, 180; and US army-navy tensions, 59
Aleutian Islands, 58, 69, 127, 128
Alexander, Harold, xiii, 66, 68
Algeria, in Operation Torch, 197–98, 199, 200–201, 203, 204
American and British Conversations (ABC-1), 10, 11–12
American-British-Dutch-Australian (ABDA) Command, 55–58

American Joint Planners, 79
American leaders, listed, xv–xvi
Andaman Islands, 96
Anglo-Japanese Naval Treaty, 38
Anglophobia, 10, 13
anti-colonialism vs imperialism perspectives, 11–12, 13, 49, 55, 64, 66, 87–88, 102
Antwerp, 91, 130
Arcadia Conference: overview, 33, 34, 79, 186; Britain's peripheral strategy, 21–22; British expectations, 19–20, 28; Churchill's North Africa proposal, 22–23; Churchill's portrayal of, 32–33; Germany First statement, 20–21; mutual suspicions and tensions, 19–20, 24–25; Pacific theater concerns, 30–32; private Churchill-Roosevelt meeting, 25; strategic coordination development, 27–28; and Torch planning frustrations, 194–95; unified command proposal, 26–27; unresolved issues, 33, 34
Argonaut Conference. *See* Second Washington Conference
Arizona, USS, *15*
army as scapegoat, 44–45
army leadership as scapegoat, 188
army morale, British concerns, 99, 107
army-navy tensions, US: coordination problems, 59–60; and Eisenhower's European invasion proposal, 86–87; impact on resource allocation, 75, 76; impact on strategic discussions, 62; intelligence sharing, 129; landing craft production, 131; Philippines impact, 48

Arnold, Henry "Hap": overview, xv; in European invasion planning, 69, 70, 86, 89–90, 92; Pacific theater issues, 25–26, 61; photos, *26, 207*; Portal relationship, 33; Singapore diversion controversy, 25–26
Atlantic Conference, 10–11, 12
Atlantic-European theater, Roosevelt's proposal, 74
Atlantic theater, in Roosevelt's grand strategy, 72–73
Atlee, Clement, 27
Auchinleck, Claude, xiii, 23, 30, 99, 188
Australia: in ABDA Command, 55, 57; Churchill's pressures for US resources, 30, 58, 60, 69, 71; defense expectations, 38; demands for return of troops, 56–57, 75–76; deployment of US resources, 22, 112–13; Japanese advances, 117, 126, 127; MacArthur's command change, 76; in Marshall Memorandum, 90; and resources for Philippines, 25; South Pacific communications route, *31*; troops as scapegoat, 45

Bahamas, in Roosevelt's negotiation, 7
Baldwin, Stanley, 2
bankruptcy declaration, Britain's, 8–9
basing rights, Roosevelt's negotiations, 7
Bataan Peninsula, 30, 42, 49, 53, *54*, 101
Battleship Row, Pearl Harbor, *15*
battleships, statistics, 6
Bay of Bengal, 87, 96, 129
Beaverbrook, Lord, 18, 37
Belgium, 91, 130
Benghazi, Libya, 37
Benson, William S., 5
Bermuda, in Roosevelt's negotiation, 7
Bevan, Aneurin, 155
Bismarck Archipelago, 75
blame game, British losses, 44–46, 47, 99, 155, 188
Bolero plan: codeword designations, 161; in Dill's warning to Churchill, 171; and Gymnast reconsiderations, 137–38, 139, 180–81; logistics assignments, 112; in Marshall Memorandum, 90–91, 95; mistakes in Roosevelt's communications, 122, 124; post-Torch expectations, 164; Roosevelt's priorities, 116–17, 137; in Second Washington Conference discussions, 140, 141, 142, 143, 144, 145–46, 148, 149, 152; supreme commander recommendation, 160, 161; time line discussions, 112, 116–17, 120, 123, 144; and Torch planning discussions, 194–95, 203. *See also* Roundup (US plan); Sledgehammer *entries*
Britain, capital ships statistics, 6. *See also specific topics, e.g.,* Churchill *entries;* India; Operation Gymnast
British Chiefs of Staff (and Committee): Churchill's Mediterranean campaign instructions, 203–204; Eisenhower's European invasion proposal, 86, 89–90; Indian Ocean discussions, 98, 103–104; in London Conference discussions, 173, 177; Marshall Memorandum, 94–95, 98, 99–100, 103; response to JUSSC plan, 82–83; second-front alternatives discussions, 133–36; Sledgehammer plan, 95–96. *See also* Combined Chiefs of Staff; *specific chiefs, e.g.* Brooke, Alan; Ismay, Hastings; Sledgehammer *entries*
British Defence Committee, 104–106
British Guiana, in Roosevelt's negotiation, 7
British leaders, listed, xiii–xiv
British-Soviet Treaty proposal, 119–20, 121
British War Cabinet: Churchill's Middle East trip, 189; Churchill's post-Arcadia presentation, 32–33; in London Conference discussions, 176; post-Argonaut strategy review, 156–57; and post-London Gymnast decision, 180–81; Roundup planning, 160. *See also* British Chiefs of Staff; Combined Chiefs of Staff

INDEX

Brooke, Alan: overview, xiii; during Arcadia Conference, 18; blame explanation for British losses, 44–45; opinions of Marshall and King, 100–101; photos, *18, 73, 207*; at US troop review, 149–50

Brooke, Alan (European invasion planning): air support resources, 104; Bolero discussions, 140, 143, 180–81; Churchill's proposed Roosevelt meeting, 125, 133, 136, 139–40; Marshall Memorandum discussions, 86, 93, 99–100, 107; response to JUSSC plan, 82–83; Sledgehammer discussions, 96, 100, 104, 141, 156, 173, 175, 176

Brooke, Alan (North Africa planning): Crusader aftermath, 30; Gymnast operation, 140, 143, 173, 175, 180–81; Tobruk surrender aftermath, 144; Torch command discussions, 183

Brooke, Alan (Pacific theater issues): blame for Singapore loss, 44; Indian Ocean threats, 97, 105; opinion of Marshall, 100–101; Roosevelt's proposed grand strategy, 72–73; unified command opposition, 58

Burma, 36, 42, 56, 57, 62–63, 129

Cadogan, Alexander, 44, 154–55
Canada, 38, 108–109. *See also* King, Mackenzie
capital ships, statistics, 6
Carawy, Paul, 94
Casablanca, in Operation Torch, 197, 199, 200–201, 203
CCS 94, mutual misunderstandings, 181–83, 194–95
Ceylon, 96–97, 101, 129
Chamberlain, Neville, 39
Channel Dash, Germany's, 46–47
Cherbourg, in Sledgehammer planning, 174, 176, 177
Chiang Kai-shek, 65
Chiefs of Staff. *See* British Chiefs of Staff; Combined Chiefs of Staff; US Joint Chiefs of Staff

China, 42, 58, 62, 64–65, 90
Churchill, Winston: conflicts with Parliament, 36, 37, 151, 154–55; as historian, 1–3, 11, 24; interwar period, 6–7, 38–39; perspective of Marshall, 159–60; photos, *18, 150, 207*; post-Arcadia public criticisms, 35–36; pre-Pearl Harbor discussions with US, 7–12; and Roosevelt's global grand strategy, 72. *See also specific topics, e.g.,* India; Operation Gymnast

Churchill, Winston (Arcadia Conference): expectations for, 19; in his memoirs, 28, 32; North Africa proposal, 22–23, 29–30, 32; private meeting with Roosevelt, 25–26; unified command idea, 27, 55

Churchill, Winston (European invasion planning): Dieppe raid expectations, 189–90; Eisenhower's proposal, 86, 89–90; in his memoirs, 107–108, 205; in London Conference discussions, 171–73, 175–78; Marshall Memorandum discussions, 93, 98–99, 104–105, 106, 107–108; post-Torch expectations, 203–204; Roosevelt's new front proposal, 73–74; Soviet Union pressures, 119–22, 123–25, 188–89, 204–205. *See also* Bolero plan; Roundup (US plan); Sledgehammer *entries*

Churchill, Winston (Pacific theater actions): Australian defense discord, 56–57; expectations from Midway success, 129; and Gymnast postponement, 60, 72; in his memoirs, 44; India's importance, 68–69, 87–88; initial downplaying of Japanese threat, 38–39, 40; instructions to Dill, 74–75; intelligence sharing frustrations, 129–30; opposition to Stilwell command, 65; Philippines directive, 12; pressures for US resources, 58, 68, 71–72, 97, 109; response to Indian Ocean losses, 97, 102–103; response to Pearl Harbor news, 15–18; response to Singapore loss, 40, 42, 44,

68; Singapore diversion controversy, 25–26; in speech to Britons, 47. *See also* India; Indian Ocean
Churchill, Winston (Second Washington Conference): conflict with Combined Chiefs of Staff, 142–43; frustrations with, 155–56; impact of Tobruk surrender, 144, 148, 151; Marshall's perspective summarized, 152; meeting with Dominion representatives, 151; meeting with Marshall, 138–39; preparations for, 136–37; private meeting with Roosevelt, 139, 141–42; request for, 136; smaller group discussions, 143–45, 148–49; troop review, 149
cipher systems, 78–79, 128, 130
Clark, Mark, xv, 148–49
Cocanada bombing, 96
code systems, 78–79, 128, 130
Coleridge, Richard D., 78
Colombo, Ceylon, 96–97
Combined Allocation and Priorities Committee, 28
Combined Chiefs of Staff: Dill's assignment from Churchill, 74–75; establishment of, 27–28, 34; European invasion planning, 85–86, 112; in London Conference discussions, 176; Mountbatten's assignment from Churchill, 130; North Africa agreement, 72; Pacific theater issues, 32, 57, 60; photo of, 78; and Roosevelt's post-London Conference recommendations, 179–80; at Second Washington Conference, 139, 140–41, 142–43, 145, 151; shipping shortage discussion, 78; strategy debates summarized, 205–207; Torch operation discussions, 183–84, 194, 199. *See also* British Chiefs of Staff; US Joint Chiefs of Staff
Combined Intelligence Committee, creation, 28
Combined Movements Committee, creation, 28

Combined Staff Planners, Europe invasion discussions, 83
"common law marriage" comparison, 10
Coral Sea, Japanese advances, 117
Corregidor, 48, 49, 53, 114
"Critical Points... of Coordinated Viewpoint" (Eisenhower's proposal), 85
cross-channel invasion planning. *See specific topics, e.g.*, Bolero plan; Marshall, George (Marshall Memorandum discussions); Sledgehammer *entries*
cruisers, statistics, 6
Crusader, Operation, 22–23, 30, 35, 36–37
Curtin, John, 25, 56, 75–76

Daily Mail, 151
Darwin, Japanese bombing, 56
"Day of the Dupes," 142
Deane, John R., 78
Defence Committee, British, 104–106
Denmark, in second-front planning, 135
destroyers, statistics, 7
Detroit, USS, 16
Diego-Suarez, 75
Dieppe raid, 189–90
Dill, John: overview, xiii; at Arcadia Conference, 18, 33; in European invasion planning, 83–84, 94, 163, 166; opinion of direct approach, 24; Pacific theater issues, 66, 74–75; photos, 78, 119, 207; at US military review, 149
Dill, John (North Africa planning): Gymnast operation, 160–61, 163, 166, 171; Torch operation discussions, 184, 194, 198
direct vs. peripheral strategy, overview, 24, 34
Duke of York, 18
Dunkirk evacuation, 7
Dutch East Indies, 30, 42, 60, 62
Dutch Harbor, Aleutian Islands, 128
Dykes, Vivian: overview, xiii; on coalition strategy problem cause, 206; with Combined Chiefs of Staff, 78; European invasion planning, 94, 145,

163, 166; North Africa planning, 145, 194, 198, 199; opinion of American Navy planner, 25; Pacific theater issues, 74–75

Eden, Anthony, 176
Egypt: and Bolero resources, 149; in British command reorganization, 188, 189; Churchill's expectations, 151; German advances, 147, 148, 149, 154; in London Conference discussions, 170, 175; in Torch Operation, 198, 200
Eighth Army, 140, 148, 179, 188, 198
Eisenhower, Dwight D.: overview, xv; criticism of Churchill, 2; criticism of King, 59; Pacific theater issues, 59, 70, 76, 87; photo, *182*; on resource shortages, 30
Eisenhower, Dwight D. (European invasion planning): Bolero discussions, 140; Churchill's Roundup alternative, 148–49; "Critical Points" document, 85–86, 89; instructions from Marshall, 61, 84–85; and resource dispersal problem, 70–71, 76, 87; Roundup assignments, 158, 183, 184; Sledgehammer discussions, 141, 158, 166–68, 171; Sledgehammer revision option, 174, 177, 178
Eisenhower, Dwight D. (North Africa planning): Gymnast Operation, 179; Torch Operation, 183, 184, 199, 200, 201, 203
El Alamein, British success, 202
English Channel, German transit, 46–47
Enigma machines, 79
European invasion planning. *See specific topics, e.g.,* Bolero plan; Marshall, George (Marshall Memorandum discussions); Sledgehammer *entries*
Evill, Douglas, 78

Fiji, 60
Filipino soldiers, 49, 51–53, 55
Finland, 134, 135
Foch, Ferdinand, 4

Ford Island, *16*
France: German invasion, 7; and North Africa operations, 23, 29, 201, 203; Pacific theater issue, 75; tensions with British, 29; World War I, 3–4
France, and Allies' second-front planning: alternatives to Sledgehammer, 139–40; British raid on Dieppe, 189–90; Churchill's Round-Up memorandum, 135–36; in Marshall Memorandum, 90–91, 92, 99–100; Mountbatten's discussions in Washington, 130–32; in Sledgehammer plan, 92, 96, 118, 133
Frankfurter, Felix, 13
French Algeria, in Operation Torch, 197–98, 199, 200–201, 203, 204

Gandhi, Mahatma, 87
George VI, 33
Germany First strategy: at Arcadia Conference, 20–21, 28, 34, 186; and Churchill's Indian Ocean recommendation, 98; and Churchill's pressures for resources, 69–71; in Eisenhower's proposal, 85; initial agreement, 11; and Pacific theater needs, 60–62, 79–80. *See also specific topics, e.g.,* Bolero plan; Marshall, George (European invasion planning); Sledgehammer *entries*
Gibraltar, 32, 75, 197, 198, 199, 200, 203
global grand strategy recommendation, Roosevelt's, 72–73
Gneisenau, 46
Goebbels, Joseph, 29
Grand Strategy paper, Britain's, 94
Guadalcanal, 162, 190–92, 198
Guam, 35
Gymnast. *See* Operation Gymnast

Haig, Douglas, 4
Halifax, Lord, 12–13, 171
Hammond, T. H., 78
Handy, Thomas, xv, 20, 167, 194
Harriman, Averell, 106–107, 188–89

Harris, Arthur, 16
Hart, Basil Liddell, 151
Herridge, William Duncan, 93–94
Hewitt, H. Kent, 131
Hiryu, 128
Hitler, Adolf, 29
Hong Kong, 35
Hopkins, Harry: overview, xv; on Britain-American coordination at WWII's beginnings, 10; and Churchill's vote of confidence, 37; in North Africa planning, 143, 144, 148, 181; Pacific theater issues, 26, 69, 101, 102; photos, *105, 169*
Hopkins, Harry (in European invasion planning): frustration with uncoordinated deployments, 80–81; at London Conference discussions, 171–73, 176–78; at Marshall's briefings, 86, 89–90, 91–93; at meetings with Churchill, 98–99, 101, 104, 105, 106; meeting with Soviet prime minister, 122–23; Sledgehammer option, 141, 143
Horne, Frederick J., *78*
Hornet, 110
House of Commons, 36–37
Hull, Cordell, *121*, 193–94

Iceland, 22, 30
Imperator Operation, 134
imperialism vs.anti-colonialism perspectives, 11–12, 13, 55, 64, 66, 87–88, 102. *See also* independence activity; India; Indian *entries*
imperial preference system, 9
independence activity, 49, 55, 87–88, 101
India: as Britain's priority, 62, 64; Burma's role, 57, 64, 66; Churchill's pressures for US resources, 58, 68–69, 74–75, 105, 109; Churchill's resentment about American participation, 101, 102–103; Japanese advances, 87, 96–97; King's aircraft transfer, 151; in Marshall Memorandum discussions, 104, 105; pro-independence tensions, 55, 87–88; significance of Midway success, 129. *See also* Indian Ocean
Indian National Congress, 87–88, 101–102
Indian Ocean: Churchill's discussion with Hopkins and Marshall, 99; in global grand strategy, 72–73; impact of Tokyo bombing, 110–11; Japanese advances, 87, 96–97; Japanese withdrawal, 110–11; significance of Midway success, 129; and Singapore's surrender, 42
Indian troops, as scapegoat, 45–46
Ingersoll, Ralph, 2
"Instructions for London Conference," 170
intelligence sharing, 94, 101, 129–30, 201–202
Iran (Persia), 188, 189
Iraq, 188
"iron curtain" phrase, 1
Ismay, Hastings: overview, xiv; Churchill's Singapore order, 40; on Operation Torch, 201; on Roundup/Sledgehammer discussions, 107; at Second Washington Conference, 143, 144, 145–46, 149–50
isolationist sentiment, US, 7, 10
Italy, 163, 176, 204

Jackpot Operation, 134–35
Jacob, Edward Ian Claude, xiv, 19, 20, 25
Jamaica, in Roosevelt's negotiations, 7
Japan, capital ships statistics, 6. *See also* India; Indian Ocean; Pacific theater area
Japanese Naval General Staff, 127
Java, 56, 57
JCS. *See* US Joint Chiefs of Staff (JCS)
JIC (Joint Intelligence Committee), 129, 173
Johnson, Louis, 101
Johore, Australian troops, 45
Joint Chiefs of Staff (JCS). *See* US Joint Chiefs of Staff (JCS)
Joint Intelligence Committee (JIC), 129, 173

INDEX

Joint US Strategic Committee (JUSSC), 80, 84
Jupiter. *See* Operation Jupiter
JUSSC (Joint US Strategic Committee), 80, 84

Kennedy, John, 45, 46, 82
Keynes, John Maynard, 9
Kharkov, Ukraine, 118
Kilindi, East Africa, 97
King, Ernest J.: overview, xv; Eisenhower's opinion of, 59; opinion of British, 5, 12, 75; photos, *59, 78, 119, 121, 169, 207*
King, Ernest J. (in European invasion planning): Bolero discussions, 114, 116, 162, 164; in discussions with Mountbatten, 130–31; landing craft program, 131; London Conference discussions, 170, 171–74, 177–78; Marshall Memorandum briefings, 86, 90, 92–93; at meeting with Soviet prime minister, 122–23; priority conflicts, 86–87, 90; Sledgehammer option, 141, 142, 162, 166, 177; and Stimson's proposal, 69, 70
King, Ernest J. (in North Africa planning): Churchill's post-Torch complaint, 204; Gymnast operation, 132, 141, 164–65, 180; resource shifting, 151; Roosevelt's invasion decision, 181–83; Torch operation discussions, 183–84, 194, 195, 199, 201
King, Ernest J. (Pacific theater actions): Guadalcanal plan, 162, 190–92; Indian Ocean resources, 75, 109–10; long-term plan, 71, 75; requests for resources, 57, 114, 116, 152
King, Mackenzie, 108–109, 138, 151–52, *207*
Kirkines, in Operation Viceroy, 135
Kiska, Aleutian Islands, 126
Knox, Henry, xv, 86–87, 91, 148, 194

Labour Party, 155
Lae, Japanese landing, 75
landing craft, 91, 95, 100, 120, 130–31, 132, 174

Leahy, William D., xv, *183*, 194, *207*
Lend-Lease activity, 8–9, 16–17, 28, 123, 124, 134–35, 189
Libya, 22–23, 30, 35, 36–37, 99. *See also* Rommel, Erwin; Tobruk, Libya
Little, Charles, 141
Litvinov, Maxim, *121*
Lloyd George, David, 4
London Conference, 171–80
Louis XIII, 142

MacArthur, Douglas: command change, 76; Philippines defense, 25–26, 48–49, 52; photos, *51, 53*; Rabaul offensive plan, 190
MacDonald, Malcolm, 138
MacReady, Gordon, *78*
Madagascar, 75
Malay Peninsula, 39–40, *41*
Malta, 32, 200
Manchester Guardian, 151
Manila, 30, 35, 48. *See also* Philippines
Manila Bay, defense planning, 48–49
maps: Bataan Peninsula, *54*; Burma, *63, 67*; Malay Peninsula, *41*; Pacific theater area, *115*; Philippines, *50*; Solomons-New Guinea area, *77*; South Pacific communications route, *31*
Marshall, George: overview, xvi; at Arcadia Conference, 22, 25, 26–27, 33, 55; Churchill's perspective of, 159–60; direct approach perspective, 22; Pacific theater issues, 53, 58, 65, 66, 129; photos, *23, 78, 105, 119, 121, 169, 207*; at Second Washington Conference troop review, 149–50
Marshall, George (European invasion planning): Churchill's post-Torch complaint, 204; and Churchill's Sledgehammer cancellation, 161–66, 167; communications to Eisenhower, 167–68, 171; Eisenhower's proposal, 85–87, 89–90; London Conference discussions, 170, 171–74, 176–77; meeting with Canadian ambassador, 93–94; Mountbatten meeting, 130–31;

Pacific theater pivot argument, 163–64; Roundup operation, 179–80; at Second Washington Conference, 140, 141, 142, 143, 145–46; selection of Eisenhower, 148–49; Soviet Union pressures, 73, 122–23; Stimson's proposal, 69. *See also* Bolero plan; Sledgehammer *entries*
Marshall, George (Marshall Memorandum discussions): briefing to Roosevelt, 89–93; discussions with British, 98–103, 104–106; Eisenhower's preliminary planning, 84–86, 89; secrecy problem, 94, 106–108
Marshall, George (North Africa planning): and Churchill's pressures for resources, 71; Gymnast objections, 29, 138, 168, 180; Roosevelt's reconsiderations, 81, 132, 137; at Second Washington Conference, 137–38, 143–44, 145–46; Stimson's dispute with Roosevelt, 193–94; Tobruk surrender response, 144, 147–48; Torch operation, 181–83, 184, 194, 195, 199, 200–201
Massey, William F., 38
McCrea, John, xvi, 20, *119,* 142
McNarney, Joseph, xvi, *78,* 104, 185
Mediterranean, Churchill's pressures for resources, 75, 203–204. *See also* Middle East; North Africa
merchant shipping, 5, 7, 79, 96, 97
Middle East: Churchill's Indian Ocean recommendation, 98; Churchill's trip to, 188–89; and Eisenhower's European invasion proposal, 86; in Marshall Memorandum discussions, 99, 104; and Pacific pivot argument, 164, 165; Roosevelt's London Conference instructions, 170; in Second Washington Conference discussions, 147–48, 151; and shipping shortages, 70–71. *See also* North Africa
Middle East Command, 188, 189
Midway, 111, 126–29, 130, 151
Molotov, Vyacheslav, 119–23, 124–25
Montgomery, Bernard, xiv, 188, 189, 202

Moran, Lord (Charles Wilson), 40, 106, 149
Morocco, 170, 179, 197, 198, 201
Mountbatten, Louis, xiv, *18,* 100, 130–32, 136, 176

natural resources, Pacific theater, 42, 64
naval arms limitations, post-WWI, 6
Near East Command, 188, 189
Netherlands, 55–56, 57
Netherlands East Indies, 30, 42, 60, 62
New Caledonia, 127
Newfoundland, 7
New Guinea, 60, 75
New Hebrides, 75
New Zealand, 38, 58, 60, 69, 71, 90
Nicolson, Harold, 155
Nimitz, Chester, 128
North Africa: in Arcadia Conference discussions, 23–24, 29–30, 32, 33; Britain's Operation Crusader, 22–23, 30, 35, 36–37; map, *178–79, 196–97.* See also Egypt; Libya; Middle East; Operation Gymnast; Operation Torch
North Borneo, 30
Northern Ireland, 22, 30, 36, 61
Norway, 120, 122, 134–35, 140, 158

Operation Crusader, 22–23, 30, 35, 36–37
Operation Gymnast: Churchill's persistent advocacy, 29–30, 156, 158, 159, 160, 166; impact of shipping shortages, 60; Joint Chiefs of Staff recommendation, 162; King's objections, 161, 162; in London Conference discussions, 173, 174, 175, 176, 177; Marshall's objections, 138, 161, 163, 168; postponement, 35, 60, 71–72, 73; reconsiderations, 81, 132–33, 137–38, 170, 179; and Roosevelt's political pressures, 165, 166; in Second Washington Conference discussions, 138–39, 140, 141, 142, 143–47, 152; Stimson's objections, 139, 164, 192; War Cabinet's agreement, 160. *See also* Operation Torch
Operation Jupiter: Churchill's advocacy, 134, 137, 143, 157; in Churchill's cable

INDEX

to Roosevelt, 168; Joint Chiefs of Staff evaluation, 162, 174; Roosevelt's recommendation, 179; War Cabinet opposition, 140, 143, 158
Operation Round-Up (British plan), 82, 135–36. *See also* Roundup (US plan)
Operation Torch: agreement finalizing, 180–85; Churchill-Montgomery discussions, 189; Churchill's re-involvement, 200–201; Eisenhower's planning assessment, 199; frustrations and resentments about, 194–96; intelligence findings, 201–202; invasion success, 202–203; Knox's support, 194; map, *196–97*; Marshall's opposition, 193; Pacific theater pressures, 195, 198–99; presentation to Stalin, 188–89; Roosevelt's decision, 192; Stimson's opposition, 192–94; strategy conflicts summarized, 195–98, 199–200. *See also* Operation Gymnast
Oran, in Operation Torch, 197, 200–201, 203

Pacific Council, 108
Pacific strategy talks, before Pearl Harbor, 11–12
Pacific theater area: in Arcadia Conference discussions, 30–32, 33; and Bolero planning, 112–13, 117; and Churchill's Sledgehammer cancellation, 161–66; in Dill's warning to Churchill, 171; and Eisenhower's European invasion proposal, 86–87, 90; and Germany First strategy, 60–62, 79–80; in global grand strategy, 72–73; Guadalcanal plan, 190–91; in JUSSC cross-channel invasion planning, 80; in London Conference discussions, 176; maps, *31, 41, 50, 54, 63, 67, 77, 115*; and Marshall Memorandum, 90, 101, 102–104; Midway plan, 111, 126–29, 130, 151; and Operation Crusader, 30–31; Pearl Harbor attack, 15–17, 47; pivot arguments, 163–65, 168–69; and post-London Gymnast decision, 180, 181; resource limit problem, 60–61; Stilwell command, 65–66; and Torch planning, 195, 198–99. *See also* Australia; India; Indian Ocean; King *entries*; Philippines; Singapore
Pacific War Council, 151–52
Paget, Bernard, 82
Palestine, 188
Papua New Guinea, 117, 190
Parliament, Churchill's conflicts, 36, 37, 151, 154–55
Patterson, Wilfrid R., 78
Pearl Harbor attack, 15–17, 47
Percival, Arthur, 42, *43*
peripheral vs. direct strategy, overview, 24, 34
Pershing, John J., 4
Persia (Iran), 188, 189
Petsamo, in Operation Viceroy, 135
Philippines: defense planning, 48–49; Japanese invasion expectations, 49; map, *50*; Quezon's independence proposal, 51–52; Roosevelt's statement, 52–53; surrender to Japanese, 113–14; troop diversion to Singapore, 25–26; as US priority, 12, 22, 47–48, 57
Plumb, John Harold, 2
Poland, 119–20
Portal, Charles: overview, xiv; at Arcadia Conference, 18, 33; on eastern front problems, 124; European invasion planning, 86, 100; and Gymnast decision, 180; photo, *207*; at Second Washington Conference, 150
Port Moresby, 117, 190
Portugal, in Marshall Memorandum, 90
Pound, Arthur Dudley: overview, xiv; at Arcadia Conference, 18, 33; European invasion proposal, 86, 109; Operation Torch planning, 200; Pacific theater issues, 97, 129; photo, *207*; at Second Washington Conference, 141; significance of Midway success, 129
Pownall, Henry, 25, 46
Prince of Wales, 37
Prinz Eugen, 46
public opinion factor, 116, 165, 166

Quezon, Manuel, 51–53

railways, 189
Raleigh, USS, *16*
Rangoon, Burma, 42, 64, 65
Repin, Alexander, 81
Repulse, 37
Reynolds, David, 2
Richelieu, Cardinal, 142
Rommel, Erwin, 32, 126, 148, 149, 154, 188, 202
Roosevelt, Elliott, 2
Roosevelt, Franklin D.: anti-imperialism perspective, 87–88; Arcadia Conference, 17–18, 22, 23, 27, 32; leadership style, 2, 132–33, 146, 165, 170, 176–77, 178; photos, *119, 207*; Second Washington Conference, 142–45, 147, 148; supportive cables to Churchill, 37–38, 47
Roosevelt, Franklin D. (European invasion planning): Bolero priority, 116–17; Canadian prime minister meetings, 108, 109; Eisenhower's proposal, 84, 86, 90, 91–92; frustration with uncoordinated deployments, 80–81; global grand strategy recommendation, 72–73; London Conference instructions, 169–70, 172; Marshall Memorandum, 90, 91–93, 99, 102–103, 106; meeting with Churchill, 136–37; Mountbatten meeting, 131–32; new front proposal to Churchill, 73–74; Pacific pivot arguments, 163–65, 168–69; Soviet pressures, 73, 121–23; Stimson's proposal, 69, 72. *See also* Roundup (US plan); Sledgehammer *entries*
Roosevelt, Franklin D. (North Africa planning): Churchill's proposal at Arcadia, 23, 29–30, 32; dispute about military advice, 192–93; invasion decisions, 181–82, 192; London Conference instructions, 170, 172; Mid East rail system agreement, 189; reconsideration of Gymnast, 137–38; Stimson's frustrations with, 192–94; Torch operation, 200–201
Roosevelt, Franklin D. (Pacific theater actions): Australia defense support, 57; Burma's importance, 64; on Churchill's blame game, 47; Churchill's pressures, 25, 26, 68, 69–70, 71–72, 75, 109–10; defense reallocation after Pearl Harbor, 17; India's independence negotiations, 101–102; MacArthur's command change, 76; Midway success, 129; Philippines defense, 49, 51–53, 76; resource assignments, 112–14, 116; response to Indian Ocean losses, 97–98; shipping shortage communication, 76; Stilwell command, 65–66
Roundup (US plan): British agreement, 103, 104, 107; British reconsideration, 137–38; Churchill's ambivalence, 133; Churchill's arguments, 156–57, 159, 163, 166–67, 168; codeword designations, 161; Hopkins' instructions from Roosevelt, 169–70; Joint Chiefs of Staff recommendation, 162; in London Conference discussions, 173, 176, 177–78; in Marshall Memorandum, 91, 95, 96, 99–100; and North Africa planning, 137–38, 179–85, 203, 204; in Second Washington Conference discussions, 143, 144, 146, 149; and Sledgehammer operation, 103, 104, 107, 118, 133; supreme commander recommendation, 160, 161, 167, 183
Royal Navy-American Navy, tensions: before Pearl Harbor, 5–7
Rumania, 119–20
Russia. *See* Soviet Union

Salamaua, Japanese landing, 75
Santa Lucia, 7
scapegoats, British losses, 44–46, 47, 99, 155, 188
Scharnhorst, 46
Second Washington Conference: Combined Chiefs recommendations,

INDEX

145–47; Pacific War Council session, 151–52; perspectives summarized, 152–53; preparations for, 137–38; Sledgehammer discussions, 138, 139–40, 141–42, 143, 145, 146–47, 152; smaller group discussions, 143–45, 148–49; US troop review, 149–50. *See also* Churchill, Winston (Second Conference)

Sherwood, Robert, 2

shipping shortages, impacts: European invasion, 91, 105, 113, 123; North Africa operations, 30, 60, 70–72; Pacific theater, 57, 60; troop transport, 76, 78

Sims, William, 5

Singapore: Britain's promises, 11–12, 38–39; British naval losses, 37; Japanese advances, 30, 35, 40–42; loss consequences, 42–44, 56, 68, 99; Pownell's troop request, 25; resource problems, 39–40; surrender to Japan, 42, *43*

Sledgehammer plan: British initial response to, 95–96, 100–108, 117–19; Canadian response to, 108–109; Churchill's post-Argonaut arguments, 156–60; conflicts with Pacific needs, 113; designation as deception, 180; Marshall's introduction of, 92, 94; Mountbatten-Roosevelt discussions, 122, 130, 131–32; Roosevelt's mistakes in communications, 122, 124; second front alternatives, 133–37, 136, 139–40, 178–79; in Second Washington Conference discussions, 138–47, 152–53

Sledgehammer plan, British cancellation: British communications of, 133, 160–61; Churchill's cables to Roosevelt, 158, 159, 161, 168; Churchill's meeting with Eisenhower, 166–67; Joint Chiefs of Staff responses, 160, 161–66; in London Conference discussions, 168, 171–75, 176–77, 178; Roosevelt's actions, 163–65, 168–70, 178–79. *See also* Operation Gymnast

Slim, William, 3, 19

Smith, Walter Bedell, xvi, 94–95, 145, 199

Solomon Islands, 75, 117, 162, 174, 190–91, 194, 198

Somervell, Brehon, 60

Somerville, James, 129

South Pacific communications route, *31*

Soviet Union: Churchill's trip, 188–89; in Eisenhower's proposal, 85; German advances, 118–19, 154, 172–73; in Germany First strategy, 70; in JUSSC European invasion plan, 80, 84; Lend-Lease program, 123, 124, 134–35, 189; and Marshall Memorandum, 90, 91, 107–108; in North African planning, 159, 201–202, 204; pressures for Allied "second front," 73, 81, 93, 119–21, 122–25, 188–89, 204; Roosevelt's priority, 114, 116, 132–33; in Second Washington Conference discussions, 140, 141, 142, 143, 151; and Sledgehammer cancellation, 162, 164; in Sledgehammer planning, 92, 99–100, 118, 137, 156, 174; Stimson's perspective, 84

SPAB (Supply Priorities and Allocation Board), 16–17

Spain, 196–98, 201, 203

special relationship belief: overview, 13–14; about Lend-Lease provisions, 8–9; Churchill's portrayals, 1–3, 8, 9, 20, 32–33, 36; "common law marriage" comparison, 10; before Pearl Harbor, 3–4, 10–11. *See also* Churchill *entries;* Roosevelt *entries*

Stalin, Joseph, 2, 188. *See also* Soviet Union

Stark, Harold: overview, xvi; at Arcadia Conference, 33; at Atlantic Conference, 12, 20, *21*; on Britain's peripheral strategy, 22; Jacob's opinion of, 20; Sledgehammer planning, 177

Stilwell, Joseph, xvi, 19, 65–66, 68

Stimson, Henry: overview, xvi; Arcadia Conference role, 19; and Roosevelt's global grand strategy, 72; at Second Washington Conference, 139, 144, 148, 149–50

Stimson, Henry (European invasion planning): Churchill's Sledgehammer cancellation, 163, 164–66; Eisenhower's proposal, 86, 89–90; France offensive proposal, 69–70; Marshall Memorandum discussions, 91–94, 104, 106; Pacific theater pivot arguments, 164, 168; private meeting with Dill, 83–84; resource limit problem, 60–61

Stimson, Henry (North Africa planning): frustrations with Roosevelt, 192–94; Gymnast objections, 173, 192; Roosevelt's invasion decision, 182; Roosevelt's reconsiderations, 137–38; Torch objections, 193

Stimson, Henry (Pacific theater issues): and Churchill's pressures for resources, 69; defense allocations after Pearl Harbor, 16–17; MacArthur's command change, 76; Philippines defense support, 52–53; pivot arguments, 164, 168; resource limit problem, 60–61; Singapore troop diversion controversy, 25–26; Stilwell command, 65, 66

strategic planning. *See specific topics, e.g.,* Bolero plan; Marshall, George (Marshall Memorandum discussions); North Africa

strategic talks, before Pearl Harbor, 10–11
submarine activity, 5, 7, 78–79
Supply Priorities and Allocation Board (SPAB), 16–17
Sydney Harbor, Japanese attack, 56
Syria, 188

Tangier, USS, *16*
tanks, 17, 28–29, 144, 147, 204
Tennessee, USS, *15*
"ten-year-rule," 38
Their Finest Hour (Churchill), 8
Thompson, Charles, xiv
Times, 151
Tobruk, Libya, 144, 147–48, 151, 154–55, 158, 160, 188

Tokyo, US bombing, 110
Torch. *See* Operation Torch
Trans-Iranian Railway, 189
Trans-Siberian Railway, 189
Treaty of Paris, 47–48
Trincomalee, Ceylon, 97
Trinidad, in Roosevelt's negotiation, 7
troop statistics, 22, 90–91
Tulagi, in Solomons campaign, 190
Tunisia, 198, 199–200, 204, 205
Turkey, in Marshall Memorandum, 90
Turner, Richmond Kelly, 25
Tydings-McDuffie Law, 49

U-boat activity, 5, 7, 78–79
Ukraine, German success, 118
Ultra intercepts, 201–202
unified command proposal, 26–27, 34, 56–58
United States, capital ships statistics. *See also specific topics, e.g.,* Marshall *entries*; Pacific theater area; Roosevelt *entries*
US Joint Chiefs of Staff (JCS): Bolero plan, 112, 114, 117; and Churchill's pressures for resources, 69, 71; Churchill's Sledgehammer cancellation, 160, 161–66; establishment of, 28, 34; JUSSC's Europe invasion plan, 80, 81; priorities problem, 79–80, 205, 207; Roosevelt's Torch instructions, 182, 184; Solomons offensive plan, 190; Soviet negotiations, 123. *See also specific chiefs, e.g.,* King *entries*; Marshall *entries*
US leaders, listed, xv–xvi
US Navy: Pearl Harbor attack, 15–17, 47; Roosevelt's irritation with, 116–17. *See also* army-navy tensions, US; King *entries*; Pacific theater area
Utah, USS, *16*

Viceroy Operation, 135
Vichy regime. *See* France *entries*
Vizagapatam bombing, 96

INDEX

Wainwright, Jonathan, *53,* 113–14
Wake Island, 35
Wallace, Henry, 13, 16
War Cabinet: Operation Jupiter opposition, 140, 143, 158. *See* British Chiefs of Staff; British War Cabinet
Wardlaw-Milne, John, 155
War Plan Orange, 48
wartime production: Churchill's post-Torch complaint, 204; in Churchill's speech, 36; European invasion planning, 91–92; German dismissal, 29, 36; statistics, 28–29, 32
Washington Naval Conference, 6
Washington Naval Treaty, 48
Wavell, Archibald: overview, xiv; Burma defense, 64; Churchill's Singapore orders, 40, 42; command responsibilities, 55–56, 57; opposition to Stilwell command, 65; significance of Midway success, 129; on troop failures, 45
weather, in operational planning, 95, 135, 177
Wedemeyer, Albert, xvi, *146*
West Virginia, USS, *15*
Wilhelmshaven, 46
Wilson, Charles (Moran, Lord), 40, 106, 149
Wilson, Woodrow, 4, 6
Winant, John G., 47, *105,* 172
World War I, 3–5, 38, 45

Yamamoto, Isoroku, 111, 126–27
Yamashita, Tomoyuki, *43*

www.ingramcontent.com/pod-product-compliance
Lightning Source LLC
LaVergne TN
LVHW020755150425
808483LV00004B/14